Rhetorical Realism

> In the same vein as Thomas Rickert's *Ambient Rhetoric*, Barnett offers some of the most original and compelling research to date with respect to rhetoric's growing interest in nonhuman agency, posthumanism, and material rhetorics. I can see many audiences in rhetorical studies being intrigued with his creative idea to revisit and recast entirely a debate (realism/anti-realism) that our field (falsely) believed to be settled decades ago. In turn, Barnett's realist approach to rhetorical historiography promises to call into question some of the most well entrenched epistemic and human centered foundations that continue to undergird a great deal of twentieth- and twenty-first century rhetorical theory. For this reason, his research will foster some much needed engagement by rhetoricians regarding Bruno Latour's basic question to many of our field's prevailing theoretical interests in postmodernism and poststructuralism: 'Do you believe in reality?'
> —*Steve Holmes, George Mason University, USA*

Rhetorical Realism responds to the surging interest in nonhumans across the humanities by exploring how realist commitments have historically accompanied understandings of rhetoric from antiquity to the present. For a discipline that often defines itself according to human speech and writing, the nonhuman turn poses a number of challenges and opportunities for rhetoric. To date, many of the responses to the nonhuman turn in rhetoric have sought to address rhetoric's compatibility with new conceptions of materiality. In *Rhetorical Realism*, Scot Barnett extends this work by transforming it into a new historiographic methodology attuned to the presence and occlusion of things in rhetorical history. Through investigations of rhetoric's place in Aristotelian metaphysics, the language invention movement of the seventeenth century, and postmodern conceptions of rhetoric as an epistemic art, Barnett's study expands the scope of rhetorical inquiry by showing how realist ideas have worked to frame rhetoric's scope and meanings during key moments in its history. Ultimately, Barnett argues that all versions of rhetoric depend upon some realist assumptions about the world. Rather than conceive of the nonhuman as a dramatic turning point in rhetorical theory, *Rhetorical Realism* encourages rhetorical theorists to turn another eye toward what rhetoricians have always done—defining and configuring rhetoric within a broader ontology of things.

Scot Barnett is Assistant Professor of English at Indiana University-Bloomington, USA where he teaches courses in rhetorical theory and digital rhetoric. With Casey Boyle, he is the editor of *Rhetoric, Through Everyday Things* (2016). His work has also appeared in the journals *Enculturation*, *Kairos*, and *Itineration* as well as in several edited collections.

Routledge Studies in Rhetoric and Communication

For a full list of titles in this series, please visit www.routledge.com.

22 **Identity and Power in Narratives of Displacement**
   Katrina M. Powell

23 **Pedagogies of Public Memory**
   Teaching Writing and Rhetoric at Museums, Archives, and Memorials
   Edited by Jane Greer and Laurie Grobman

24 **Authorship Contested**
   Cultural Challenges to the Authentic, Autonomous Author
   Edited by Amy E. Robillard and Ron Fortune

25 **Software Evangelism and the Rhetoric of Morality**
   Coding Justice in a Digital Democracy
   Jennifer Helene Maher

26 **Sexual Rhetorics**
   Methods, Identities, Publics
   Edited by Jonathan Alexander and Jacqueline Rhodes

27 **Rhetorical Delivery and Digital Technologies**
   Networks, Affect, Electracy
   Sean Morey

28 **Rhetorics of Names and Naming**
   Edited by Star Medzerian Vanguri

29 **Vernacular Christian Rhetoric and Civil Discourse**
   The Religious Creativity of Evangelical Student Writers
   Jeffrey M. Ringer

30 **The Aboutness of Writing Center Talk**
   A Corpus-Driven and Discourse Analysis
   Jo Mackiewicz

31 **Rhetorical Realism**
   Rhetoric, Ethics, and the Ontology of Things
   Scot Barnett

Rhetorical Realism
Rhetoric, Ethics, and the Ontology of Things

Scot Barnett

NEW YORK AND LONDON

First published 2017
by Routledge
711 Third Avenue, New York, NY 10017

and by Routledge
2 Park Square, Milton Park, Abingdon, Oxon OX14 4RN

Routledge is an imprint of the Taylor & Francis Group, an informa business

© 2017 Taylor & Francis

The right of Scot Barnett to be identified as author of this work has been asserted by him in accordance with sections 77 and 78 of the Copyright, Designs and Patents Act 1988.

All rights reserved. No part of this book may be reprinted or reproduced or utilised in any form or by any electronic, mechanical, or other means, now known or hereafter invented, including photocopying and recording, or in any information storage or retrieval system, without permission in writing from the publishers.

Trademark notice: Product or corporate names may be trademarks or registered trademarks, and are used only for identification and explanation without intent to infringe.

Library of Congress Cataloging-in-Publication Data
CIP data has been applied for.

ISBN: 978-1-138-64821-0 (hbk)
ISBN: 978-1-315-62655-0 (ebk)

Typeset in Sabon
by codeMantra

For Jhondra, Pierce, and Sam

Contents

List of Figures   xi
Acknowledgements   xiii

   Introduction: Into the Well   1

1   Reclaiming Rhetorical Realism   26

2   Aristotle's Rhetorical Realism: *Technē, Phusis,* and *Logos*   66

3   Speaking with Things: Early Modern Rhetoric and the Dream of a Common Language   102

4   The Question Concerning Reality: Post-Kantian Rhetorical Realism   142

5   Care for Things: Ethics and Responsibility in the World of Things   186

   Index   223

List of Figures

1.1	*The School of Athens* by Raphael, public domain.	28
3.1	General Scheme, *An Essay Toward a Real Character and a Philosophical Language* by John Wilkins, public domain.	122
3.2	Of the Varieties of the Marks for Real Characters, *An Essay Toward a Real Character and a Philosophical Language* by John Wilkins, public domain.	124
3.3	The Lord's Prayer and the Creed, *An Essay Toward a Real Character and a Philosophical Language* by John Wilkins, public domain.	126
5.1	Coast Guard Responds to the Fire on the Deepwater Horizon, National Oceanic and Atmospheric Administration, public domain.	202

Acknowledgements

In the wake of the postmodern turn, it has become something of a commonplace to say that one's work is not wholly his or her own. That the work is, and always has been, informed and inflected by past (and present) others. If this is true, then much (if not all) of what a writer is doing is adapting, building upon, and transforming that which has already been said. While this book questions some of the major tenets of postmodernism, there is one postmodern "truth" from which it cannot escape. In the end, this book is not—indeed, never was—my own. At best, it is a collage or assemblage of ideas, conversations, and debates I have shared with others and that have in turn influenced my thinking on these subjects over the past several years. It is to these many friends and colleagues that I am most indebted and to whom I owe the most heartfelt thanks.

I am grateful in particular to many current and former colleagues at Indiana University and Clemson University. Since joining the faculty in 2012, the Indiana English Department has been enormously supportive of my research and teaching. In particular, I thank my past department chair, Paul Gutjahr, my current chair, Patty Ingham, and numerous friends and colleagues in the department: Michael Adams, Dana Anderson, John Arthos, Christine Farris, Justin Hodgson, John Lucaites, Ellen MacKay, Jesse Molesworth, Monique Morgan, John Schilb, Rebekah Sheldon, Katie Silvester, Kathy Smith, Robert Terrill, Freya Thimsen, and Kurt Zemlicka. I began writing this book when I was a new Assistant Professor at Clemson University. While at Clemson, I received tremendous support from my department chair, Lee Morrissey, as well as my colleagues and friends in the Department of English: David Blakesley, Erin Goss, Cynthia Haynes, Jan Holmevik, Steve Katz, Michael LeMahieu, Brian McGrath, Sean Morey, and Victor Vitanza. I have benefited as well from classes and conversations held with excellent graduate students over the years, including Caddie Alford, Jake Greene, Jennifer Warfel Juszkiewicz, Saul Kutnicki, Martin Law, Dan Liddle, Drew Stowe, Glen Southergill, Mike Utley, and Tsaiyi Wu.

I would like to thank the Routledge Press reviewers who offered valuable and encouraging feedback on the manuscript for this book. In addition, I would like to thank the fantastic editorial staff at Routledge, in particular Felisa Salvago-Keyes, for their support and interest in the project.

xiv *Acknowledgements*

I am grateful to Parlor Press and Southern Illinois University Press for granting permission to use excerpts from previous publications in this book. Passages from Chapter 3 are reprinted from *Augmented Reality: Perspectives Across Art, Industry, and the Humanities*. Edited by Sean Morey and John Tinnell. Anderson, SC: Parlor Press, 2016. Used by permission. Passages from Chapter 2 are reprinted from "Chapter 5: Rhetoric's Nonmodern Constitution: *Techne, Phusis*, and the Production of Hybrids," pp. 85–96 as they appear in *Thinking with Bruno Latour in Rhetoric and Composition* edited by Paul Lynch and Nathaniel Rivers. Copyright © 2015 by the Board of Trustees, Southern Illinois University; reprinted by permission of Southern Illinois University Press.

Many of the seeds for this book were sown while I was a doctoral student at the University of Wisconsin-Madison. Above all, I thank Michael Bernard-Donals whose generosity, encouragement, and friendship continues to be an inspiration and a model for what it means to be a scholar, teacher, and mentor in this profession. I benefited as well from classes and conversations with faculty in Composition and Rhetoric and Communication Arts at Wisconsin: Jon McKenzie, Rob Asen, Erik Doxtader, Brad Hughes, Melissa Tedrowe, Deb Brandt, Morris Young, Marty Nystrand, and David Fleming. A special word of thanks to Carolyn Miller, who first introduced me to rhetoric as a master's student and remains one of my dearest friends in the field and whose question in passing ("isn't this something we've been thinking about forever?") led to one of the central claims of this book.

Over the years, I have had the opportunity to discuss pieces of this book with several amazing friends and colleagues. In particular, I wish to thank Steve Holmes, who read and commented on a number of drafts of this work. I have also benefited from conversations and friendships with Marilyn Cooper, Thomas Rickert, Byron Hawk, Casey Boyle, Nathaniel Rivers, Collin Brooke, John Muckelbauer, David Rieder, and Josh Shepperd.

Finally, my heartfelt thanks to Jhondra, whose love, friendship, and understanding has helped guide me through the years it took to write this book. I could not have hoped for a better friend and partner in this life. And to Pierce and Sam: I have been writing this book since before either of you were born, but in many ways its argument only came into focus when I met the two of you. Both of you have taught me the importance of care and responsibility in their various forms, and for that I am forever grateful.

Introduction
Into the Well

One of the founding myths of philosophy says that philosophy began when Thales of Miletus, one of Seven Sages of Greece, fell into a well. In the *Theaetetus*, Plato's Socrates recounts how Thales fell into the well while in deep contemplation of the stars above. According to Socrates, Thales was "wild to know what was up in the sky but failed to see what was in front of him and under his feet."[1] In wanting to know more about the world above, Thales failed to appreciate how his own being—his existence as a thinking being—is necessarily bound to the earth under his feet. To add insult to injury, in Plato's version of the story Thales's fall is witnessed by a Tracian servant-girl who goes on the ridicule antiquity's great materialist for focusing too much on what is above at the expense of the world below. "The same joke applies to all who spend their lives in philosophy," Socrates explains: "It is really true the philosopher fails to see his next-door neighbor; he not only doesn't notice what he is doing; he scarcely knows whether he is a man or some other kind of creature."[2] Several centuries later, the Roman poet Ennius would help make the Thales fable proverbial in a line that is quoted twice by Cicero in *De Re Publica* and *De Divinatione*: *Quod est ante pedes nemo spectat, caeli scrutantur plagas*, "No one regards what is before his feet when searching out the regions of the sky."[3] And in the seventeenth century, the fabulist Jean de La Fontaine would offer an even more pointed critique of Thales in the final lines of his poem "The Astrologer Who Stumbled into a Well":

> Besides the folly of his lying trade,
> This man the type may well be made
> Of those who at chimeras stare
> When they should mind the things that are.[4]

It would appear that for Socrates, Ennius, and La Fontaine there is no more arrogant class than the philosopher who preoccupies himself with the world above at the expense of things of the world.[5]

Given the ironic nature of his fall, it is perhaps surprising that Thales has managed to retain his status as one of the founders of natural philosophy. No doubt, Thales's status within the discipline of philosophy is owed in part to the radical shift in thinking he and his fellow pre-Socratics signaled when they rejected mythology in favor of more rational ways of understanding reality. Although none of his writings exist today, we know from multiple accounts that Thales had keen interests in astronomy and mathematics. As chronicled in Herodotus, Thales became famous in Miletus for predicting an eclipse of the sun that occurred on May 8, 585 BCE.[6] While in Egypt, he also correctly calculated the height of a pyramid by measuring the length of its shadow, "having observed the time when our own shadow is equal to our height"[7] Through experiments such as these, Thales and his fellow pre-Socratics helped invent a new materialist approach for philosophy, one deeply attuned to issues of reality and material reality in particular. As Craig R. Smith explains, "In short, they [Thales and the pre-Socratics] changed the focus of human attention from the gods to matter—and hence to earthly externalities."[8] That Thales himself would end up dying from his fall into the well makes his contributions to materialist philosophy all the more ironic, of course—a point not lost on Plato who relishes yet another opportunity to poke fun at the pre-Socratics in the *Theaetetus*. But the irony of the fall is just one of the reasons why Thales's status as one of the founders of philosophy continues to hold sway in many quarters today. In addition to his comical demise, what makes the Thales story such a foundational one for philosophy is how it manages to capture a longstanding tension within the history of philosophy itself, one that sees philosophers, on the one hand, as concerned with (divine, fixed, or eternal) truth and, on the other, with the realities of worldly existence—the "things that lie at his feet and before his eyes," as Socrates puts it.[9] The real irony in the Thales story, perhaps even its tragedy, is not that Thales forgets to practice what he preaches, but that he cannot find a way to do both at the same time. This is the tension that more or less defined philosophical thought during the classical period and it is one that continues to haunt philosophy to this day: how to strike the appropriate balance between the abstract and the worldly, the celestial and the things that are.

As the Thales story indicates, questions about the nature and knowability of reality are nothing new for philosophy. But what about rhetoric, philosophy's elder if sometimes least admired sibling?[10] To what extent have questions about reality and earthly externalities informed understandings of rhetoric and rhetorical approaches to producing, theorizing, and teaching discourse? Have efforts to negotiate a balance between the abstract and the worldly played as much of role in the formation of rhetorical theory as they have in the history of philosophy? Have rhetoricians ever noticed or, God forbid, fallen into the well themselves? These are a few of the questions that initially inspired me to write this book. Over the past decade, scholars in rhetoric have increasing turned their attentions to less traditional objects of inquiry, including animals, things, spaces, and technologies in an effort to explore—and ultimately expand—rhetoric's scope beyond just that of persuasion and human symbolic action. In many of these cases, rhetoricians' engagements with nonhuman animals and material realities have paralleled broader theoretical trends in humanities research that have sought new perspectives on the "productivity and resiliency of matter" as a way to finally "give materiality its due."[11] Borrowing the title from a collection edited by literary theorist Richard Grusin, we might describe these recent transformations in thought as representing a *nonhuman turn* for the humanities, a turn that has sought to decenter the human "in favor of a turn toward and concern for the nonhuman, understood variously in terms of animals, affectivity, bodies, organic and geophysical systems, materiality, or technologies."[12]

At the present moment, these emerging theoretical trends have tended to coalesce around a handful of new schools of thought that, while different in significant ways, share in the desire to incorporate nonhuman actors into humanities research. Among the most prominent of these schools of thought are object-oriented ontology (OOO), speculative realism, thing theory, new materialism, actor-network theory (ANT), and the posthumanities. I will have more to say about some of these theoretical perspectives in the pages ahead. Generally speaking, however, each of these perspectives sees itself as correcting some of the excesses of the past century's linguistic turn and its emphasis on language as a constitutive—at times even determinative—force in the production of social realities. In the latter decades of the twentieth century, it became orthodoxy to assume that what we call "reality" is a social construction that can only be understood from within the so-called prisonhouse of language. The waning decades of the last century found scholars eagerly willing to extend this idea to anything and everything under the sun, thus establishing a nearly inexhaustible list of things that could be understood as social constructions, including: authorship, gender, race, identity, sexuality, nature, ideology, geography, history, science, facts, truth, knowledge, money, citizenship, and many, many more.[13] As Karen Barad pointedly observes in her foundational article on new materialism:

> Language has been granted too much power. The linguistic turn, the semiotic turn, the interpretative turn, the cultural turn: it seems that at every turn lately every "thing"—even materiality—is turned into a matter of language or some other form of cultural representation. The ubiquitous puns on "matter" do not, alas, mark a rethinking of the key concepts (materiality and signification) and the relationship between them. Rather, it seems to be symptomatic of the extent to which matters of "fact" (so to speak) have been replaced with matters of signification (no scare quotes here). Language matters. Discourse matters. Culture matters. There is an important sense in which the only thing that does not seem to matter anymore is matter.[14]

While not dismissive of language's importance or power, Barad nonetheless wonders how, in the wake of so many "turns," one could even go about "inquiring after the material conditions that have led us to such a brute reversal of naturalist beliefs."[15] In Barad's view, humanists' inability to see matter as anything more than discourse or the effects of signification reduces their ability to engage some of the most serious crises facing the world today. As Diana Coole and Samantha Frost suggest in their indispensable introduction to new materialism, by the beginning of the twenty-first century traditional humanistic methods for reading and understanding society had become unsuitable to the task of explaining "some of [society's] most urgent challenges regarding environmental, demographic, geopolitical, and economic change."[16] Fully understanding the scale and stakes of these challenges requires more than just another theory of language, consciousness, subjectivity, or mind, they argue.[17] In addition, it requires a revised conception of matter that understands materiality as "something more than 'mere' matter: an excess, force, vitality, relationality, or difference that renders matter active, self-creative, productive, unpredictable."[18] In tune with these and other ideas, scholars in rhetoric have begun to press the question of who and what should be counted within the realm of rhetoric, in the process developing the initial frameworks for what I have elsewhere called an "object-oriented rhetoric."[19]

As one might expect, the pivot away from language and anthropomorphic conceptions of reality we find in the theoretical perspectives mentioned above poses particular challenges for rhetoric given its long-standing investment in understanding the power language holds in shaping public opinion and changing minds. While rhetoricians, more so than philosophers, have tended to embrace rhetoric's role in guiding the practical affairs of everyday life, this concern has not always resulted in more robust understandings of material realities and the effects nonhuman forces have on rhetoric. For the most part, rhetorical theory from antiquity through the twentieth century set for itself a more modest goal: to understand how human speakers and writers interact with one another through language or other symbol systems. Where philosophy's history of exploring and debating realist ideas has enabled contemporary philosophers to more easily propose *new* realisms and *new* materialisms, in rhetoric it has been much harder (although not impossible) to find comparable historical antecedents that might prepare the way for something like an object-oriented rhetoric attuned to the suasive natures of nonhuman beings and materialities. This is so, I believe, because so much of rhetoric's history in the West has been explicitly concerned with understanding the contours and possibilities of human communication. The apparent lack of historical precedence is perhaps one reason why many of the efforts to articulate an object-oriented rhetoric (including my own) thus far have begun with the assumption that rhetoric as it has traditionally been understood must be rethought if nonhuman and extrahuman realities are to have any place in rhetorical theory. Writing about rhetoric's historical uneasiness with nonhuman animals, Debra Hawhee captures well the challenges contemporary rhetoricians face in trying to broaden the realm of rhetoric beyond just language and symbolic action: "nonhuman animals invite those of us (human ones) interested in questions of rhetoric and communication to suspend the habituated emphasis on verbal language and consciousness. Animals instead offer models of rhetorical behavior and interaction that are physical, even instinctual, but perhaps no less artful."[20] Suspending emphasis on verbal language and consciousness is no easy task, of course, especially for a discipline that has for centuries positioned these ideas—what Kenneth Burke has called "the Human Barnyard"[21]—at the center of its identity and its disciplinary mission.

Having participated in a number of these conversations about the applicability of object-oriented ideas for rhetorical theory, I became increasingly curious whether some of the questions we were asking (for example, can contemporary rhetorical theory find ways to accommodate nonhuman agents such as animals, technologies, spaces, and everyday things?) were really as novel or radical as some of us may have thought. Simply put, I began to wonder whether the questions we were asking were truly original or whether they had been creeping around in the dustbins of rhetorical history for much longer than we realized. My wager as I began to research these questions was this: If we could find historical evidence of rhetoric's affinities with material realities—and, specifically, with questions about the ontological and epistemological natures of things—such evidence might allow rhetorical theorists interested in object-oriented rhetoric to make an even bolder claim: that attunements to nonhuman beings and extrahuman realities are nothing new for rhetoric, and that such attunements are in fact woven into the fabric of rhetorical theory itself. As I would come to learn, this claim, while ultimately true in my view, is not always as self-evidently true as it is in philosophy. Like rhetoric itself, extrahuman realities have been theorized in many different ways throughout rhetoric's long history. For every explicit mention of nonhumans in the history of Western rhetoric, there are countless more examples where their existence has been marginalized or occluded in favor of other topics and concerns, most prominently language, speech, and being-with human others. At first glance, the primacy of human communication in rhetoric would appear to confirm the suspicions mentioned above that the inclusion of nonhumans into rhetorical theory requires radically new frameworks for understanding rhetoric. As I would come to learn, however, even instances where rhetoricians have marginalized or dismissed nonhumans in favor of more human-centric concerns have the potential to teach us a great deal about the roles these beings have played in the history of rhetorical theory. Revisiting several key episodes in the history of rhetoric with an eye toward both discussions and omissions of nonhuman beings ultimately led me to what would become the central thesis of this book: Even when they are not the direct objects of rhetorical inquiry, material and extrahuman realities have served as conditions of possibility for numerous accounts of rhetoric from Aristotle to twentieth-century conceptions of rhetoric as epistemic or as a knowledge-making art. As it turns out, the existence and knowability of such realities are indeed nothing new to rhetoric. However, unlike in philosophy, recovering rhetoric's engagements with these realities requires different historiographic methods and reading styles capable of bringing to the fore things that have sometimes been ignored or intentionally written around. Defining and performing such methods is one of the primary goals of this book. By the end of this book, I hope to have convinced you that it is worthwhile to continue asking the questions I asked myself several years ago: Hasn't rhetoric always been concerned with the realities of worldly existence? Haven't we always been trying to see the well? And, at the end of the day, isn't this what it means to study rhetoric?

* * *

Another origin story. As rhetoricians, we are told that rhetoric in the Western tradition began when Corax first defined rhetoric as "the art of persuasion" in Syracuse in the fifth century BCE. This well-known fable tells that Corax's student, Tisias, failed to pay tuition for learning the art of rhetoric from his teacher. When Corax eventually brings suit against his student, Tisias attempts to put what he has learned about rhetoric to use. He proposes that if he fails to successfully defend himself in the case he should not be obligated to pay Corax because "clearly his training had not been adequate."[22] Corax counters that "if Tisias did define himself successfully in the case, payment should be made since clearly the student had learned his lessons well."[23] The jury eventually decides to throw out the case, shouting out "bad crow [Greek *corax*], bad egg" to the two rhetors as they left.[24] Like the story of Thales's fall into the well, the fable of Corax and Tisias is most likely the stuff of fiction. But as a founding myth for the creation of rhetorical studies in fifth-century Greece, it has persisted over time in large part because, much like the Thales myth, it seems to capture something essential about rhetoric as both a practical art and a course of study intended to train students to understand and use the arts of persuasive discourse.

Taken at face value, the origins of philosophy and rhetoric could not be farther apart. Whereas Thales's fall dramatizes tensions between epistemology and metaphysis, the Corax fable accentuates the power language wields to shape opinion and influence the minds of others. Based on their respective origin stories, one could reasonably conclude that for philosophy the most prominent questions center on the nature of reality: What is real and how should reality (however we understand "reality") factor into philosophical inquiry? In contrast, the Corax and Tisias fable suggests a different focus and set of concerns for rhetoric, specifically, power and responsibility: What is the nature of persuasive speech and what responsibility does the rhetor have to use such speech in public settings? On the basis of these two stories, then, one could conclude that philosophy is the discipline most suited to exploring questions about reality, including the role everyday things play in shaping understandings of knowledge and existence. This is certainly one way to read the history of philosophy—as an ongoing and irresolvable debate about the nature of reality and the best way to balance philosophy's love of wisdom with the recognition that such love must always take place in the world and among other beings (and things) in the world. But what about rhetoric? Are questions about reality, existence, and things only the concern of philosophers, or are they also woven into the fabric of rhetorical theory as well?

One possible answer to this question can be found in the margins of the Corax fable itself. While the most obvious subject of the fable is persuasive language and the ethics of teaching such language (for a fee or pro bono), the setting of the fable (a courtroom) and its implication that rhetorical education constitutes pupils as persuasive speakers prepared to speak in particular situations (and in relation to specific institutions such as the law) gives the fable a strong grounding in worldly affairs. Furthermore, Tisias's claim that he should not be held responsible for his tuition if he is unable to successfully defend himself in court suggests that persuasion is not simply a thing that happens on its own or that is inextricably linked to the identity of the rhetor himself or herself. Tisias's admission is more radical than this: Rhetorical ability is not something a person is born with, but is instead a skill—a way of knowing and being—that one learns to cultivate under the tutelage of a master rhetor. At the heart of rhetoric's origin story, in other words, lies the recognition that rhetoric comes into being not from *within* but from the *outside*, from a place external to and independent of our individual being or ways of knowing and understanding the world. Perhaps Tisias, like all great students, possessed some innate talent for rhetoric. Perhaps he was already well-poised to become an effective and successful orator (indeed, one of the founders of Western rhetoric!). But, as Isocrates, Quintilian, and numerous other ancient and modern rhetoricians have suggested, talent or aptitude alone do not an effective rhetorical education make. Even the most talented student must allow herself to be transformed through education, through ideas that are not (yet) her own. Tisias appears to have learned this lesson quite well as evinced by his confidence in allowing his rhetorical abilities to be put on trial in the first place. When we read the Corax fable as a literal origin story—as a story about where rhetoric comes from—we thus find a different sense of what rhetoric might have meant in antiquity and what it could (again) mean for us today. Not only a form of persuasive speech, force, or power, the Corax fable suggests that rhetoric comes into being, into existence, at precisely the moment when the issue of its externality—its being other than ourselves as rhetors and audiences—comes into question. Rhetoric originates not in the mind or immediate desires of the rhetor but *somewhere else*, some place outside of and on the hither side of being and ability.

While origin myths are probably not the best grounds on which to assess scholarly agendas for either rhetoric or philosophy today, as metaphors they offer some insight into why these two disciplines over the centuries have taken such different paths when it comes to exploring relationships between language, knowledge, existence, and reality. As mentioned already, it is possible to tell the history of philosophy as a story of repeated attempts to negotiate tensions between things and the idea of things themselves. This, of course, was Plato's great question and his endless source of frustration, and as a provocation for thought it has persisted in various guises ever since, from the British empiricists and neo-Kantians to the Hegelians and twentieth-century phenomenologists. Suffice it to say, philosophy has a long history of taking questions about reality seriously, asking in a thousand different ways and voices: What is real? How do we know? Such preoccupations were anticipated centuries ago in the Thales story. In a reading of the myth that opens her book *The Face of Things: Another Side of Ethics*, Silvia Benso suggests that, "What Thales does not notice, that to which he pays no attention, is precisely what is nearest to him: not simply the things, but the abysmal depths of things, exemplified by the well into which he fell, by which he is, in the story, captured."[25] By directing his attention to the realm of divine truth, Benso suggests, Thales fails to take into account the everyday things of the world, the stuff literally under his feet, whose depths and mysteries are just as real and consequential as those of the Forms above. More than a fable about pre-Socratic arrogance or philosophical idealism, Thales's story captures something important about the real and the fulsomeness of things in the world. Things are not only what we see or think them to be, the story suggests; they are also deeper and more complicated—more *other*, Benso will argue—than we sometimes think.

While it may have its roots in philosophy, the notion that things exceed and possibly precede our comprehension of them can also be found in rhetoric's various engagements with things and other extrahuman realities. As we will see in the chapters ahead, for rhetoric things are not always what we perceive or understand them to be. Sometimes, in fact, our only way to see things is to follow the traces of their probable existence. For all of its commitments to human forms of communication, rhetoric for centuries has inspired theorists and practitioners to cultivate attunements to the reality and alterity of things, if for no other reason than to enable rhetors to "see the available means of persuasion in each particular case," as Aristotle's famous definition of rhetoric puts it.[26]

* * *

As suggested above, while nonhuman animals and material realities are nothing new for rhetoric, recent years have witnessed a surge of interest in these areas in rhetorical theory and history. For the most part, this growing body of research agrees that nonhumans pose unique challenges for rhetoric. However, by engaging these challenges rather than avoiding them, this work demonstrates as well how nonhuman rhetorics can be leveraged to productively complicate current understandings of rhetoric and rhetorical history. As mentioned above, Debra Hawhee has been at the forefront of the field's emerging interest in animality, in particular, how animals and assumptions about human-animal distinctions factored into classical understandings of rhetoric. Taking inspiration from George A. Kennedy's account of rhetoric as a "type of energy inherent in communication,"[27] one that exists prior to speech, interpretation, and intentionality, Hawhee argues for expanding rhetoric's scope so that it includes more than just human speakers and writers. Nonhuman animals in particular offer particularly rich possibilities for rhetorical inquiry, Hawhee suggests, insofar as animals—much like things, I would add—have a long if sometimes hidden history within rhetorical theory. For Hawhee, conceiving of rhetoric as a form of energy has the effect of expanding the realm of rhetoric to include those "places where human animals may not even tread."[28] This insight, Hawhee goes on to suggest, has broader implications for historians of rhetoric in particular who "can now devote energy to rhetoric's nonhuman forebears,"[29] a charge Hawhee herself takes up in her recent study *Rhetoric in Tooth and Claw: Animals, Language, Sensation*. In *Inessential Solidarity: Rhetoric and Foreigner Relations*, Diane Davis offers a similar rationale for including nonhuman animals in rhetorical theory. Building on the ethical writings of Emmanuel Levinas and Jacques Derrida, Davis argues for an other-oriented conception of rhetoric in which response-ability (that is, one's capacity to respond to the Other) precedes and exceeds intentional acts of persuasion. Refiguring rhetoric in this way enables Davis to make a compelling case for animal rhetorics rooted in a strong ethical sense of responsibility, a prospect I take up at more length in Chapter 5. While Davis herself does not explore the implications of a preoriginary rhetoricity for things or other material realities, her account of rhetoric leaves open the possibility that things, too, have a role to play in constituting the environs in which rhetoric circulates and comes into meaning. Thomas Rickert explores this prospect at length in *Ambient Rhetoric: The Attunements of Rhetorical Being* where he argues for more holistic, worldly, and emplaced understandings of rhetoric. In Heidegger's idiom, rhetoric constitutes a form of dwelling, Rickert argues, "a way of being conditioned and permeated by things so that they are inseparable from what it means to live in the world."[30] As for Davis, for Rickert rhetoric in an ambient key suggests strong ethical implications. From the perspectives of ambience and dwelling, ethics is not something we possess in advance—that is to say, ethics is not reducible to abstract and universal principles removed from the contingencies of worldliness that we subsequently *apply* to our lives. "Our ethics are not something exterior we bring in and deploy," Rickert writes, "but rather a set of comportments that emerge from life as it is lived, from what we do, say, and make."[31] The turns to history and ethics we find in Hawhee, Davis, and Rickert are important for how they push the question of object-oriented rhetoric beyond viability and applicability toward consideration of a more fundamental (and thus far more beguiling) question: not just, *what is object-oriented rhetoric?* but, also, and more pointedly, *why should we care*? Understanding nonhumans as unheralded agents in rhetoric's history is one way to begin answering the latter question. As I argue in the final chapter of this book, taking the question of "care" seriously can go a long way toward further legitimating object-oriented rhetoric's place within the field of rhetoric writ large. As an ethical disposition, care for things suggests a form of attention, an *ad-tending* toward things, in which we become attuned to how things participate in being and yet are never fully exhausted by it.

With Hawhee, Davis, and Rickert, I am most interested in the historiographic and ethical implications of the nonhuman turn for rhetoric. While it may not always foreground these implications, additional work on nonhuman and object-oriented rhetorics provides a wider context for this book and for its turn (back) to the rhetorical tradition. In an essay on dwelling and new media, Jennifer Bay and Thomas Rickert argue that "learning to dwell with new media and its technologies entails a harkening to their ontological weight and rhetorical agency."[32] Many understandings of culture, technology, and new media tend to adopt a humanist paradigm in which a will to mastery and instrumentalism governs our attitudes towards and assumptions about technology. Bay and Rickert argue, however, that "new media technologies do in fact have their own unique trajectories sundered from direct human control,"[33] thus suggesting a strong, if revamped, form of agency circulating within and between human and nonhuman beings. Bay and Rickert are not alone in inquiring about the agential status of nonhumans. Indeed, the question of agency and whether or not agency can be possessed or enacted by nonhuman actors is a recurrent one in object-oriented rhetoric. Writing about Detroit's "Monument to Joe Lewis" (a bronze forearm and fist suspended in midair by steel cables), which he reads as an embodiment of rhetorical agency, Richard Marback concludes that a material theory of rhetoric must be able to account for both the agencies of human interpreters and the agencies of matter itself. Such a theory, he explains, "maintains the dynamics of corporeality and spatiality and textuality not out of reverence for reality but out of recognition that the significance of spaces grounds the uses of texts at the same time that the meanings of texts ground the uses of spaces."[34] More recently, rhetoricians such as Nathaniel Rivers, Paul Lynch, Laurie Gries, Steve Holmes, and Alex Reid have extended object-oriented and new materialist insights to more traditional topics of rhetorical inquiry, including public rhetorics,[35] environmental rhetorics,[36] visual rhetorics,[37] and digital rhetorics.[38] In many of these cases, the problem of agency continues to loom large. As Rivers suggests in terms of environmental rhetoric, "By giving ourselves the responsibility to save or fix the planet, we have over-invested in our own agency, enacting the same hubris that results in dispositions toward nonhuman nature that environmentalists themselves might very well (and rightly) condemn."[39] As a result of presuming distinct ontological differences between humans and nature, where "nature" is thought to exist someplace apart from human beings and cultures, many modern environmental movements fail "to acknowledge not simply the limits of human agency, but that human agency emerges with, alongside, and sometimes against the agency of others"[40]—thus further complicating our reactions to major environmental crises such as global warming. I explore some of the connections and tensions between nature and culture in this book's second chapter in the context of Aristotle's intertwined understandings of *technē* (art) and *phusis* (nature) in works such as the *Physics* and *Metaphysics*.

Much of the work in object-oriented rhetoric draws on a range of theorists and theoretical frameworks. In particular, Bruno Latour's work has attracted considerable attention in rhetorical studies. A sociologist of science and one of the figures most associated with actor-network theory (ANT), Latour has been at the leading edge of efforts to incorporate nonhuman actors and agencies into understandings of society, politics, and knowledge production generally. "To balance our accounts of society," Latour says, "we simply have to turn our exclusive attention away from humans and look also at nonhumans."[41] For Latour, nonhumans are the "hidden and despised" masses knocking "at the door of sociology, requesting a place in the accounts of society as stubbornly as the human masses did in the nineteenth century."[42] As passages like this indicate, at times Latour's work can feel more rhetorical than sociological. For his part, however, Latour has been frustratingly inconsistent in his attitudes toward rhetoric. In several of his earlier works, most notably *Irreductions* and *We Have Never Been Modern*, Latour invokes rhetoric in its largely pejorative sense. At its worst, he says, rhetoric is a kind of "magic of those who have lost the world."[43] At its best, rhetoric is helpful in helping trace networks but only if it can be purged from constructionist theories of language.[44] In his more recent work, Latour finally seems to have adopted a more nuanced understanding of rhetoric, at times going so far as to suggest that rhetoric holds the key to assembling what he calls an "object-oriented democracy" by providing a set of procedures for bringing into the collective "objects of worry" or "matters of concern."[45] Notwithstanding his ambivalence, many contemporary rhetorical theorists have found strong rhetorical inflections in Latour's work, most notably in his sense that reality is constructed or assembled from relations between human and nonhuman actants.[46] As I suggest in the next chapter, one additional contribution Latour has made is in developing a new historiographic methodology for recovering nonhuman actants from the dustbins of history. This methodology, largely implicit in his writings, has guided Latour in developing novel perspectives on important thinkers in the history of science such as Pasteur and Boyle. Similar gains can be made for rhetoric, I argue, by bringing to its history a counter-revolutionary conception of time in which historical epochs are understood as ways of mixing humans and nonhumans rather than as serial episodes in an otherwise temporal progression from immaturity toward more enlightened understandings of the world.

At its heart, then, this book seeks to dig deeper roots for object-oriented rhetoric within the histories of Western rhetorical theory. Modern rhetoricians from Kenneth Burke to James Berlin have argued that rhetoric at its simplest is the advocacy of one version of reality over another.[47] This way of thinking about rhetoric became dominant in the latter half of the twentieth century when rhetoricians' attentions, like many in the academy, shifted to language and social constructionist theories of truth and knowledge. Across many fields during this time, including rhetoric, debates raged between social constructionists and realists who remained skeptical of epistemologies that reduce knowledge to one's individual perspective or to social consensus. It is safe to say, however, that constructionists succeeded for the most part in shifting understandings of reality away from traditional realist frameworks toward more linguistic and ultimately rhetorical orientations. In the wake of the linguistic and social turns, realism and realist ideas came increasingly under scrutiny—so much so, in fact, that by the turn of the century the word "realism" (much like the word "rhetoric," ironically) carried so many negative connotations that its mere mention often called to mind the specter of "naïve realism" in which we perceive the world as it actually is and thus have direct knowledge of it. For many in rhetoric, "naïve realism" became synonymous with realism as a whole. The emergence of object-oriented ontology and speculative realism over the last decade and a half has helped complicate this understanding of realism, reminding us that realism has taken many forms over the centuries and, as such, offers a much more nuanced approach to reality than its pejorative renderings as "naïve realism" indicate at first glance. As rhetoricians have begun to follow suit with the nonhuman turn to investigate the prospects of object-oriented rhetorics, the time is right to revisit the legacy of realism in rhetorical theory in order to consider what a more robust conception of realism might offer the field going forward.

With this in mind, *Rhetorical Realism* takes as its primary subject realism and realist ideas' place in the Western rhetorical tradition. In so doing, it seeks to develop another approach to the history of rhetoric in which things and extrahuman realities have held more pivotal roles in influencing various (and sometimes competing) understandings of rhetoric. While rhetorical theory over the past several decades has tended to focus on language and discourse, and thus primarily on the human rhetors and audiences, I aim to show how rhetoricians—even the postmodern ones—have always been attuned to the material realities of everyday life. By recovering these attunements to things (which for this book include natural, artificial, and, at times, extra-sensory actors and forces such as Kant's noumenon or "thing-in-itself"), I hope to continue expanding the scope of historiography to include less traditional objects of inquiry. Rather than accept the notion that rhetoric is at root anti-realist and thus at odds with the nonhuman turn, I use the occasion of the nonhuman turn as an exigency for revisiting key moments in the rhetorical tradition when debates about knowledge, existence, and reality have played significant roles in shaping attitudes toward rhetoric. My argument in a nutshell is that, in spite of their historical differences, all versions of rhetoric depend upon some realist assumptions about the world. These include, for example, the existence of audiences capable of being persuaded (or resisting a rhetor's attempts to persuade) and the facticity of the events under consideration in a rhetor's speech or writing. Although each period I examine developed its own particular ways of accommodating rhetoric with non- or extrahuman realities, and thus its own unique version of rhetorical realism, in general we can define *rhetorical realism* as a set of existential commitments, whether stated or unstated, that situate understandings of rhetoric in relation to mind-independent realities and the limits of our abilities to know that reality.

From its beginnings rhetoric has been defined and understood in conjunction with the practical affairs of everyday human (and nonhuman) life. From issues of war and peace to arguments about global warming, rhetors routinely invoke the existence of things in order to make their cases and imbue their arguments with a strong sense of worldly relevance. Such invocations do not necessarily make rhetors naïve realists who believe in the objectivity of facts or events. As I demonstrate in the chapters ahead, rhetorical realism is a complicated orientation that blends epistemology and ontology into differing configurations depending on the needs and mentalities of a given historical epoch. Alongside questions about the limits of representation and human cognition, we find throughout the rhetorical tradition speculations about the ontology of things and other beings in the world. The history of rhetoric, I therefore want to argue, has never been about discourse alone. Nor can it easily be placed within a modernist understanding of history that treats time as a steady and progressive movement, with intellectual crises and revolutions constituting ruptures in time's otherwise linear trajectory. From the perspective of rhetorical realism, the primary task of rhetorical theory and historiography shifts to recovering how rhetorical theorists over time have constituted, managed, and negotiated distinctions between humans and nonhumans, rhetorics and realities.

Ultimately, the readings I offer suggest that contemporary interest in nonhuman rhetorics can be fruitfully leveraged to inform new work and new methods in rhetorical historiography. Rather than conceive of the nonhuman as a thematic rupture within rhetoric's long-standing investments in language and symbolic expression, the realist approach I develop encourages rhetoricians to bring rhetoric's nonhumans to light while at the same time making visible *what it is rhetors and rhetoricians have always done*, that is, sorting and producing hybrids that are both natural and cultural, human and nonhuman, political and scientific, and so on. As John Muckelbauer suggests in terms of animal rhetorics, such an approach "involve[s] nothing short of a fundamental reorientation of the intellectual lineage associated with rhetoric—not an abdication of this lineage but a reorientation."[48] Not another revolution in the history of rhetoric, in other words—just another way of understanding what it is we have always been.

* * *

In a recent essay, the historian of rhetoric Richard Leo Enos calls on rhetoricians to develop what he calls an "archaeological rhetoric" that would expand "*the domain of empirical evidence*" in historical research "*to include archaeological artifacts beyond the printed page.*"[49] "If a theory of rhetoric is to capture historical mentalities," Enos writes, "then a theory of rhetoric ought to account for all relevant, contextual phenomena—*even those that can be classified as 'unobservable' notions outside of the parameters of content-analysis methodologies but instrumental in the process of language development.*"[50] According to Enos, the primary task of the historian is to reconstruct the mentalities of the past in order to better understand the social and cultural contexts of rhetoric. This is best accomplished, he argues, by "recognizing that the epistemic nature of thought and its contextual grounding shapes (and is in turn shaped by) a view of reality by the rhetor or by the rhetorician."[51] While my goal here is not to recover or interpret archaeological evidence from rhetoric's past, I share Enos's belief that historical research ought to be able to account for "unobservable" phenomena and the role these have played in shaping past perceptions of rhetoric. Like Enos's archaeological rhetoric, rhetorical realism "expands our range of evidence both by assimilating physical artifacts [and extrahuman realities] into our analysis of the context of ancient [and modern] rhetoric, and also by providing theories that account for the mentalities that produce rhetoric."[52]

At the same time, the impetus for defining rhetorical realism and establishing it as a historiographic methodology belongs very much to our contemporary theoretical moment and its efforts to broaden the circumference of humanistic inquiry. As an extension of this milieu, rhetorical realism necessarily has one foot in the present and another in the past. This is true of all historical projects, I suppose. But when we turn our sights toward the past and how rhetoricians have negotiated distinctions between humans and nonhumans we assume a certain perspective on the past as well as a rationale for what revisionary histories of these negotiations might mean for the field going forward. As a method of reading the past, rhetorical realism inevitably leads to *speculation*. Not only is the past forever lost to us, but at times the artifacts and realities that influenced the mentalities of past rhetorics do not appear explicitly in the textual (or archaeological) evidence left behind. Examining such absences requires different perspectives and reading styles than those employed in more traditional historical accountings. Throughout this book, theorists such as Immanuel Kant, Martin Heidegger, Bruno Latour, and Emmanuel Levinas serve as pathways for exploring various formations of rhetorical realism. While each of these figures engages history in his own ways, few today would consider them historians as such. Of this group, Heidegger has perhaps written the most about history and the history of philosophy in particular. However, as careful readers quickly learn when exploring Heidegger's lectures on Plato, Aristotle, Parmenides, and the like, his window into the past is very clearly framed by his own interests and motivations. This does not mean that Heidegger is being deliberately irresponsible with the textual evidence he interprets, however. Quite the contrary. Instead, what Heidegger does in these lectures is read the texts in a *crooked* way. The idea of reading history crookedly comes from Hans Kellner, who in *Language and Historical Representation: Getting the Story Crooked* proposes a different way of doing historiography that is more fundamentally a style of reading:

> Learning to write new histories, histories worthy of the remarkable revival of rhetorical consciousness at the present moment, means above all, *to devise new ways of reading*, which will look at the texts as texts not merely as documents, which will look for "other" sources of historical discourse in constant tension with the evidence. What is called for, I think, is "getting the story crooked," looking into the various strands of meaning in a text in such a way as to make the categories, trends, and reliable identities of history a little less inevitable.[53]

This, arguably, is what Heidegger was ultimately after in his readings of significant philosophical thinkers. As a way of reading and writing histories, "getting the story crooked" is what allows Heidegger (and us as well) to "stitch together another story," to assemble other stories—other attunements and mentalities—out of "what is available from the remnants of the past."[54] With respect to rhetorical realism, reading crookedly allows us to pull differently at the threads of rhetoric's realist commitments in order to make something new out of them, something that in turn makes our assumptions about realism "a little less inevitable."

What this means is that this book cannot claim to offer anything like *the definitive history* of rhetorical realism. Such a project may be possible (although I have my doubts), but it is beyond the scope of this study. My focus is necessarily, although regrettably, more restricted, focusing instead on several key epochs in the history of Western rhetoric as a way to demonstrate the viability of revisionary historiography for object-oriented rhetoric and to further cultivate the field's attunements to otherness as such.

This last goal may sound unusual at this point, but in my view it is one of the most important insights rhetoric can learn from the nonhuman turn. The nonhuman turn is often defined by its desire to include ever more objects and beings into our understandings of reality. What is sometimes overlooked in descriptions of this kind is how the inclusion of nonhumans similarly expands the range of ethical concern, compelling us to find ways to accommodate and care for others that share being with us. Such an attunement to otherness—to rhetoric's "other others," we might say—is arguably the most important contribution rhetorical realism stands to offer the field going forward. As both a historical phenomenon and a reading practice, rhetorical realism attunes us as theorists and historians to the alterity and vibrancy of things themselves. As we saw above, one of Thales's greatest mistakes was his inability to see things as more than just objects of knowledge or backdrops for human dramas. Things can be objects of knowledge, of course, and I will treat them as such at various points in the pages ahead. But like anything else—any other other—things cannot be exhausted by our perceptions or epistemological frameworks. There is a depth and mystery to things that exceeds our efforts to grasp or know them as such. It is when we recognize this reality, when we acknowledge the dark and unknowable otherness at the bottom of the well, that we truly begin to care for things and, with them, all kinds of others in the world. By acknowledging the mystery and depths of things, we move one step closer to Theodor Adorno's reassuring claim that "granting the physical world its alterity is the very basis for accepting otherness as such."[55]

* * *

The following chapters comprise a series of historical and theoretical analyses of realist commitments in the Western rhetorical tradition. Throughout these chapters, I argue for a new approach to rhetorical theory and historiography that engages the persistence of realism and realist ideas in the field's various understandings of rhetoric. Rather than perpetuate well-worn distinctions between rhetoric and reality, my readings work within the structures of the distinctions themselves, revealing how mind-independent realities have always held critical roles in the development of rhetorical theory and how an attunement to these realities opens the way to new directions for rhetorical scholarship. Although much of the history of rhetoric predates the philosophical school of realism, I argue that a number of realism's theses and commitments persist throughout rhetoric's long history in the West. Ultimately, however, I argue for a distinctly rhetorical understanding of realism, one related to philosophical versions but rooted squarely within the debates and controversies about language, ethics, and existence specific to rhetorical studies.

Of course, no book can be expected to cover the entire breadth of rhetorical history. And while I argue that versions of rhetorical realism manifest throughout the history of rhetoric, for this study I focus mainly on three epochs in Western rhetorical history: the classical period, the early modern period, and the modern/postmodern periods. I emphasize these specific epochs in part because their engagements with realist ideas have had some of the most lasting effects on present understandings of rhetoric and its complicated history. No doubt, it would be worthwhile to explore how other epochs and figures have engaged rhetoric's realist commitments, for example, the pre-Socratics, Sophists, and Romans, as well as early Christian rhetoricians who attempted to bring classical rhetorical principles into accord with their conception of the divine. I leave these and other potential cases to later projects and other scholars in the field.

Chapter 1 grounds the book's central argument—that realism is nothing new to rhetoric and rhetorical theory, and that it is possible to recover a complex and theoretically robust form of realism from within the structures of the rhetorical tradition itself—by exploring the implications of rhetoric's oftentimes troublesome relationship to "reality." If there is one question that persists throughout the Western rhetorical tradition, it is the question of rhetoric's connection to reality. Setting the agenda for the chapters that follow, this chapter brings the question of reality to the fore by focusing on how realism as a school of thought has been evoked, critiqued, and rejected by rhetorical theorists. The version of realism that is most often referenced in these discussions, however, is but one version among many developed by philosophers over the past several decades. More recent accounts of realism, I argue, offer much more nuanced, and ultimately more rhetorical, forms of realism that avoid the problems of naïve realism while at the same time granting things existence and agency apart from the perceptions and cognitions of human speakers and writers. After introducing these other approaches to realism, the chapter concludes by proposing, after Latour, a methodology of "counter-revolutionary" historiography for examining attunements to reality within the rhetorical tradition.

Chapter 2 begins a series of counter-revolutionary histories of rhetorical realism, starting here with Aristotle's writings on art, nature, and discourse, the intertwining of which, I argue, forms the fabric of his rhetorical realism. Rhetorical theorists have long noted the complex and sometimes contradictory ways in which Aristotle discusses rhetoric and situates it alongside other domains of knowledge (e.g. *epistēmē* and *sophia*). This "official view" of Aristotelian rhetoric and *technē*, however, tends to overemphasize Aristotle's contributions to discursive theories of rhetoric while ignoring his broader metaphysical system which is principally concerned with answering the question, why are there beings at all, and why not rather nothing? When read in terms of this metaphysical system, Aristotle's understanding of rhetoric changes considerably, suggesting that skillful and responsible rhetors must do more than obtain knowledge of audiences, situations, and tropes and figures. Prior to these important understandings, rhetors must first have cultivated an attunement to being and *the being of beings*, to the ways natural, artificial, and human beings move, change, and endure as distinct yet interconnected beings in the world. Drawing on Martin Heidegger's recently translated lectures on the *Rhetoric* as well as other writings of his on the *Physics* and *Metaphysics*, this chapter demonstrates how Aristotle's thinking about being and the being of beings constitutes the essence of his philosophy and thus helps explain his at times conflicted and contradictory accounts of rhetoric, *technē*, and *phusis*.

The next chapter turns its attention to debates about language, reality, and rhetoric in the early modern rhetorical tradition. In many historical accounts, the wake of Ramism and the rise of early modern science in the seventeenth century are said to have spurred the diminution of classical (especially Ciceronian) conceptions of rhetoric and a concomitant privileging of plainness and perspicuity over eloquence and figuration. Historians of rhetoric such as Wilbur Samuel Howell, Brian Vickers, and Tina Skouen have challenged the idea that thinkers like Francis Bacon, John Locke, and the founding members of the Royal Society of London were hostile to rhetoric. According to Howell, the preference for plainness in English prose style in the seventeenth century needs to be understood in the context of the "new science" and its desire to transmit scientific knowledge across cultures and to the general public. In this chapter, I build on these revisionist accounts of early modern rhetoric by examining the realist commitments that underwrite one of the period's more memorable attempts to transcend the ambiguities of natural language, Bishop John Wilkins's *Essay Towards a Real Character and a Philosophical Language* (1668). One of the founding members of the Royal Society, Wilkins authored two important and well-circulated treatises on preaching in 1646 and 1651. He is best remembered today, however, for his ambitious attempt to construct a "*Real universal Character*, that should not signifie *words*, but *things* and *notions*, and consequently might be legible by any Nation in their own Tongue."[56] Famously satirized by Swift in *Gulliver's Travels* and dismissed by twentieth-century theorists such as Stanley Fish as fundamentally anti-rhetorical, Wilkins's project represents an important development in the history of rhetorical realism. In elaborating his universal language, Wilkins reveals how epistemological and ontological rhetorical realisms overlap and mutually inform one another. In addition to seeing language as a means of transmitting knowledge, Wilkins cultivates an attunement to language's ontological status similar to what we find in Aristotle. For Wilkins, language is not only an instrument for symbolically representing concepts in the world; it also has a material dimension of its own that precedes understanding and establishes the conditions of possibility for rhetorical action.

Chapter 4 focuses on rhetorical realism in modern rhetorical theory. It offers a reading of modern rhetoric's epistemic turn and the influence this had on rhetorical theorists' abilities to account for the reality of things in themselves. The revival of rhetoric in the twentieth century is sometimes referred to as the "third sophistic" because of its recuperation of the Sophists's relativist theories of truth and language. This chapter argues for a different source for rhetoric's modern rehabilitation, the German philosopher Immanuel Kant. Despite Kant's critical view of rhetoric, which sees rhetoric as a means of "deceiving by a beautiful show," I argue that it was Kant's famous Copernican Revolution, and its prioritizing of human cognition, that made possible the linguistic turn and that ultimately prepared the way for rhetoric's reemergence as a professional field of study. The influence of Kant's Copernican Revolution is most evident in modern rhetoric's epistemic turn, which similarly emphasizes human cognition as the primary means by which reality comes into being as such. Much like Kant himself, however, proponents of epistemic rhetoric such as Robert L. Scott and Barry Brummett rarely argue that reality is only what human beings make of it. Like Kant, they, too, recognize that there is a noumenal reality that exists but can never be known or grasped directly by human beings. Reading epistemic rhetoric in terms of Kant's *ding an sich* shows that epistemic rhetoric is hardly the anti-realist movement Scott and others claimed it to be. At its core, epistemic rhetoric provides rhetorical theorists an invaluable sense of how things—even things that exceed the limits of knowledge and experience—*matter* and are constitutive of our theories and assumptions about rhetoric.

This book's final chapter builds on the previous chapters' historical analyses to more directly consider rhetorical realism's ethical implications. Taking its cue from Martin Heidegger, Emmanuel Levinas, and Silvia Benso, this chapter explores what it might mean for public deliberation to extend the ideas of care and responsibility to nonhuman beings. While such a move may strike some as anthropomorphism of the worst kind, I argue that such a stance not only makes sense theoretically; it also opens the way to a new sense of responsibility that considers in equal measure the existence, agency, and alterity of nonhuman actors as well as human ones. Chapter 5 explores this sense of responsibility through an analysis of the 2009 BP oil spill. In the wake of the disaster, many on the U.S. Gulf Coast and around the world wanted to know, "How could this have happened?" and, "Who is responsible?" Framing the question in these terms led many to conclude that BP's greed and willingness to cut regulative and financial corners were primarily responsible for the chain of events that led to the explosion on the Deep Water Horizon. While certainly true, the quick acceptance of such conclusions encourages us to ignore some of the larger ethical issues at stake in the event. As I demonstrate in this chapter, reading the event in terms of rhetorical realism enables us to see BP's ethical failure as a failure to understand technological devices as material entities in their own rights and not merely the tools or instrumental resources for human workers and corporations. The ethical issue at the heart of the BP oil spill, therefore, is not unlike the one Aristotle identifies in the *Nicomachean Ethics*: that of living "the good life." As this event makes clear, however, we can no longer continue to think of "the good life" as only what is good *for us*. At the same time, we must also recognize that "the good life is not formed only on the basis of human intentions and ideas but also on the basis of material artifacts and arrangements."[57]

As with any book, this one is limited by the constraints of time and space. As mentioned above, this book cannot claim to offer a full and complete history of rhetorical realism, assuming such a project were even possible. For the sake of depth, I have chosen to focus more narrowly on several cases and several prominent figures in Western rhetorical tradition. Doing so, of course, means that I do not engage with many more figures, epochs, and traditions important to contemporary rhetorical studies. While not

20 *Introduction*

excusing the absence of these voices and traditions, I encourage interested readers to bring their experiences and expertise to bear on the question of rhetorical realism. In particular, much work remains to be done in the areas of pre-sophistic and non-Western rhetorics and how these traditions managed to negotiate places for rhetoric in a wider world of things.[58] As Sarah Hallenbeck has recently shown, feminist rhetoricians may also benefit from examining the roles nonhuman actors have played in the development of women's rights and rhetorics.[59] And in the areas of digital rhetorics and disability studies, rhetoric scholars have long been interested in understanding how new communication technologies and assistive devices have helped shape definitions and attitudes toward media and disability, respectively.[60] Such work can only be further enriched by considering how incorporating even more artifacts into our analyses enables a fuller accounting of the mentalities that produced medial and disability rhetorics in given times and places. The promise such attunements hold for these and other areas suggests that rhetorical realism is not only concerned with the past and the present. It is also very much keyed to the possibilities of future rhetorics to come.

Notes

1. Plato, *Theaetetus*, in *Plato: Complete Works*, ed. John M. Cooper (Indianapolis: Hackett, 1997), 174a.
2. Ibid., 174b.
3. Cicero, *De Re Publica*, trans. C.W. Keyes (Cambridge: Loeb Classical Library, 1928), 1.18.30.; Cicero, *De Divinatione*, trans. W.A. Falconer (Cambridge: Loeb Classical Library, 1923), 2.13.30.
4. Jean de La Fountaine, "The Astrologer Who Stumbled into a Well," *Museé Jean de La Fountaine*, 2007, accessed June 16 2016, http://www.musee-jean-de-la-fontaine.fr/jean-de-la-fontaine-fable-uk-14.html.
5. Aesop provides one of the earliest versions of the Thales story (now numbered 40 in the Perry index): "When Thales the astronomer was gazing up at the sky, he fell into a pit. A Thracian slave woman, who was both wise and witty, is said to have made fun of him for being eager to know what was happening over his head while failing to notice what was right there at his feet." Plato's version, however, has become the canonical one for philosophy since.
6. Herodotus, *The Persian Wars*, trans. A. D Godley (Cambridge: Loeb Classical Library, 1920), 1.73–1.74.
7. G.S. Kirk, J.E. Raven, and M. Schofield, *The Presocratic Philosophers* (Cambridge: Cambridge University Press, 1983), 85.
8. Craig R. Smith, *Rhetoric and Human Consciousness: A History, Fourth Edition* (Long Grove: Waveland Press, 2013), 37–39.
9. Plato, *Theaetetus*, 174c.
10. Although some historians trace the origins of rhetoric as a formal field of study to ancient Greece, and perhaps Plato's engagements with rhetoric in the dialogues where it appears he first coined the word *rhêtorikê*, evidence exists as well for the emergence of rhetorical principles in ancient Mesopotamia. If true, this origin would predate the emergence of philosophy in ancient Greece (although not, of course, in Egypt or Confucian China).

11. Diana Coole and Samantha Frost, "Introducing the New Materialisms," in *New Materialisms: Ontology, Agency, and Politics*, eds. Coole and Frost (Durham: Duke University Press, 2010), 7.
12. Richard Grusin, "Introduction," in *The Nonhuman Turn*, ed. Grusin. (Minneapolis: University of Minnesota Press, 2015), iv.
13. Ian Hacking, *The Social Construction of What?* (Cambridge: Harvard University Press, 2000), 1.
14. Karen Barad, "Posthumanist Performativity: Toward an Understanding of How Matter Comes to Matter," *Signs* 28, no. 3 (2003): 801.
15. Ibid.
16. Coole and Frost, 3.
17. Ibid., 2.
18. Ibid., 9.
19. Scot Barnett, "Toward and Object-Oriented Rhetoric," *Enculturation* 7 (2010), accessed June 16, 2016, http://enculturation.net/toward-an-object-oriented-rhetoric; Scot Barnett, "Chiasms: *Pathos*, Phenomenology, and Object-Oriented Rhetorics," *Enculturation* 20 (2015), accessed June 16, 2016, http://enculturation.net/chiasms-pathos-phenomenology.
20. Debra Hawhee, "Toward a Bestial Rhetoric," *Philosophy and Rhetoric* 44, no. 1 (2011): 83.
21. Kenneth Burke, *A Rhetoric of Motives* (Berkeley: University of California Press, 1969), 23.
22. Wilfred E. Major, "Corax and Tisias," in *Classical Rhetorics and Rhetoricians: Critical Studies and Sources*, eds. Michelle Ballif and Michael G. Moran (Westport: Praeger, 2005), 112.
23. Ibid.
24. Ibid.
25. Silvia Benso, *The Face of Things: A Different Side of Ethics* (Albany: SUNY Press, 2000), xxi.
26. Aristotle, *On Rhetoric: A Theory of Civic Discourse*, trans. George A. Kennedy (New York: Oxford University Press, 1991), 1355b29-31.
27. George A Kennedy, "A Hoot in the Dark: The Evolution of General Rhetoric," *Philosophy and Rhetoric* 25, no. 1 (1992): 2.
28. Hawhee, 85.
29. Ibid.
30. Thomas Rickert, *Ambient Rhetoric: The Attunements of Rhetorical Being* (Pittsburgh: University of Pittsburgh Press, 2013), 223.
31. Ibid.
32. Jennifer Bay and Thomas Rickert, "New Media and the Fourfold," *JAC* 28, no. 1–2 (2008): 213.
33. Ibid., 136.
34. Richard Marback, "Detroit and the Closed Fist: Toward a Theory of Material Rhetoric," *Rhetoric Review* 17, no. 1 (1998): 86.
35. Nathaniel Rivers, "Tracing the Missing Masses: Vibrancy, Symmetry, and Public Rhetoric Pedagogy," *Enculturation* 17 (2014), accessed June 16, 2016, http://enculturation.net/missingmasses.
36. Nathaniel Rivers, "Deep Ambivalence and Wild Objects: Toward a Strange Environmental Rhetoric," *Rhetoric Society Quarterly* 45, no. 5 (2015): 420–440; Paul Lynch, "Composition's New Thing: Bruno Latour and the Apocalyptic Turn," *College English* 74, no. 5 (2012): 458–476.

Introduction

37. Laurie Gries, *Still Life with Rhetoric: A New Materialist Approach for Visual Rhetorics* (Logan: Utah State University Press, 2015).
38. Steve Holmes, "'Can We Name the Tools?' Ontologies of Code, Speculative *Technē*, and Rhetorical Concealment," *Computational Culture* 5 (2016), accessed June 16, 2016, http://computationalculture.net/article/can-we-name-the-tools-ontologies-of-code-speculative-techne-and-rhetorical-concealment.; Alex Reid, "Composing Objects: Prospects for a Digital Rhetoric," *Enculturation* (2012), accessed June 16, 2016, http://enculturation.net/composing-objects.
39. Rivers, "Deep Ambivalence," 423.
40. Ibid., 428.
41. Bruno Latour, "Where are the Missing Masses? The Sociology of a Few Mundane Artifacts," in *Shaping Technology/Building Society: Studies in Sociotechnical Change*, eds. Weibe E. Bijker and John Law (Cambridge: Massachusetts Institute of Technology Press, 1992), 152–153.
42. Ibid.
43. Bruno Latour, *Irreductions*, trans. Alan Sheridan and John Law, in *The Pasteurization of France*, by Latour (Cambridge: Harvard University Press, 1988), 187.
44. Bruno Latour, *We Have Never Been Modern*, trans. Catherine Porter (Cambridge: Harvard University Press, 1993), 62–65.
45. Bruno Latour, "From *Realpolitik* to *Dingpolitik* or How to Make Things Public," in *Making Things Public: Atmospheres of Democracy*, eds. Latour and Peter Weibel (Cambridge: Massachusetts Institute of Technology Press, 2005), 7–12.
46. Nathaniel Rivers, "Tracing the Missing Masses"; Byron Hawk, "Reassembling Post-Process: Toward a Posthuman Theory of Public Rhetoric," in *Beyond Post-Process*, eds. Sidney I. Dobrin, J. A. Rice, and Michael Vastola (Logan: Utah State University Press, 2011).; Paul Lynch and Nathaniel Rivers, eds., *Thinking with Bruno Latour in Rhetoric and Composition* (Carbondale: Southern Illinois University Press, 2015).
47. In "Terministic Screens," Burke notes that, "Even if any given terminology is a *reflection* of reality, by its very nature as a terminology it must be a *selection* of reality; and to this extent it must function also as a *deflection* of reality"; Kenneth Burke, "Terministic Screens," in *Language as Symbolic Action: Essays on Life, Literature, and Method* (Berkeley: University of California Press, 1966), 45. Berlin makes a similar claim with respect to composition pedagogy, writing, "To teach writing is to argue for a version of reality and the best way of knowing and communicating it—to deal […] in the metarhetorical realm of epistemology and linguistics. And all composition teachers are ineluctably operating in this realm, whether or not they consciously chose to do so."; James A. Berlin, "Contemporary Composition: The Major Pedagogical Theories," *College English* 44 (1982): 776.
48. John Muckelbauer, "Domesticating Animal Theory," *Philosophy and Rhetoric* 44, no. 1 (2011): 99.
49. Richard Leo Enos, "Theory, Validity, and the Historiography of Classical Rhetoric: A Discussion of Archaeological Rhetoric," in *Theorizing Histories of Rhetoric*, ed. Michelle Ballif (Carbondale: Southern Illinois University Press, 2013), 14.
50. Ibid., (emphasis added).
51. Ibid.

52. Ibid., 23.
53. Hans Kellner, *Language and Historical Representation: Getting the Story Crooked* (Madison: University of Wisconsin Press, 1989), 32.
54. Byron Hawk, "Stitching Together Events: Of Joints, Folds, and Assemblages," in *Theorizing Histories of Rhetorics*, ed. Michelle Ballif (Carbondale: Southern Illinois University Press, 2013), 109.
55. Theodor Adorno, quoted in Bill Brown, *A Sense of Things: The Object Matter of American Literature* (Chicago: University of Chicago Press, 2004), 18.
56. John Wilkins, *An Essay Toward a Real Character and a Philosophical Language, 1668* (Menston, UK: Scolar, 1968), 13.
57. Peter-Paul Verbeek, *Moralizing Technology: Understanding and Designing the Morality of Things* (Chicago: University of Chicago Press, 2011), 48.
58. In "Parmenides, Ontological Enaction, and the Prehistory of Rhetoric," Rickert explores how pre-Socratic thinkers such as Parmenides developed early rhetorics attuned to the rhetoricity of material environments.
59. Sarah Hallenbeck, *Claiming the Bicycle: Women, Rhetoric, and Technology in Nineteenth-Century America* (Carbondale: Southern Illinois University Press, 2016).
60. In the area of digital rhetoric, Alex Reid and James J. Brown, Jr. have argued for the importance of object-oriented ideas for rethinking our relationships to media and technology. Related, Ben McCorkle and Sean Morey have drawn attention to the ways new developments in information technology affect the classical rhetorical canon of delivery. Finally, Shannon Walters has explored the rhetorical dimensions of touch in the context of disability studies. Drawing on Kenneth Burke and Merleau-Ponty, she develops a rhetorical conception of touch as "a sensation in which, as with identification and division, one may not know for sure where one body or feeling ends and another ends" (40). In her conclusion, Walters speculates on the potentials of touch for rhetorical theory in general. She notes that touch connects us not just to other people but also to the myriad beings in the world, an insight that has far-reaching implications for rhetorical theory: "Beyond language, touch can also create ethical connections not only among people but also among people, animals, technologies, and the various nonhuman entities of the environments" (206).

Bibliography

Aristotle. *On Rhetoric: A Theory of Civic Discourse*. Translated by George A. Kennedy. New York: Oxford University Press, 1991.

Barad, Karen. "Posthumanist Performativity: Toward an Understanding of How Matter Comes to Matter." *Signs* 28, no. 3 (2003): 801–831.

Barnett, Scot. "Chiasms: *Pathos*, Phenomenology, and Object-Oriented Rhetorics." *Enculturation* 20 (2015). Accessed June 16, 2016. http://enculturation.net/chiasms-pathos-phenomenology.

———."Toward an Object-Oriented Rhetoric." *Enculturation* 7 (2010). Accessed June 16, 2016. http://enculturation.net/toward-an-object-oriented-rhetoric.

Bay, Jennifer and Thomas Rickert. "New Media and the Fourfold." *JAC* 28, no. 1–2 (2008): 209–244.

Benso, Silvia. *The Face of Things: A Different Side of Ethics*. Albany: SUNY Press, 2000.

Berlin, James A. "Contemporary Composition: The Major Pedagogical Theories." *College English* 44 (1982): 765–77.

Brown, Bill. *A Sense of Things: The Object Matter of American Literature.* Chicago: University of Chicago Press, 2004.

Brown, James J., Jr. "The Machine that Therefore I Am." *Philosophy and Rhetoric* 47, no. 4 (2014): 494–514.

Burke, Kenneth. *A Rhetoric of Motives.* Berkeley: University of California Press, 1969.

———. "Terministic Screens." In *Language as Symbolic Action: Essays on Life, Literature, and Method*, 44–62. Berkeley: University of California Press, 1966.

Cicero. *De Divinatione.* Translated by W.A. Falconer. Cambridge: Loeb Classical Library, 1923.

———. *De Re Publica.* Translated by C.W. Keyes. Cambridge: Loeb Classical Library, 1928.

Coole, Diana and Samantha Frost. "Introducing the New Materialisms" In *New Materialisms: Ontology, Agency, and Politics*, edited by Coole and Frost, 1–43. Durham: Duke University Press, 2010.

de La Fountaine, Jean. "The Astrologer Who Stumbled into a Well." *Museé Jean de La Fountaine.* 2007. Accessed June 16. 2016. http://www.musee-jean-de-la-fontaine.fr/jean-de-la-fontaine-fable-uk-14.html.

Enos, Richard Leo. "Theory, Validity, and the Historiography of Classical Rhetoric: A Discussion of Archaeological Rhetoric." In *Theorizing Histories of Rhetoric*, edited by Michelle Ballif, 8–24. Carbondale: Southern Illinois University Press, 2013.

Gries, Laurie. *Still Life with Rhetoric: A New Materialist Approach for Visual Rhetorics.* Logan: Utah State University Press, 2015.

Hacking, Ian. *The Social Construction of What?* Cambridge: Harvard University Press, 2000.

Hallenbeck, Sarah. *Claiming the Bicycle: Women, Rhetoric, and Technology in Nineteenth-Century America.* Carbondale: Southern Illinois University Press, 2016.

Hawhee, Debra. "Toward a Bestial Rhetoric." *Philosophy and Rhetoric* 44, no. 1 (2011): 81–87.

Hawk, Byron. "Reassembling Post-Process: Toward a Posthuman Theory of Public Rhetoric." In *Beyond Post-Process*, edited by Sidney I. Dobrin, J. A. Rice, and Michael Vastola, 75–83. Logan: Utah State University Press, 2011.

———. "Stitching Together Events: Of Joints, Folds, and Assemblages." In *Theorizing Histories of Rhetorics*, edited by Michelle Ballif, 106–127. Carbondale: Southern Illinois University Press, 2013.

Herodotus. *The Persian Wars.* Translated by A. D Godley. Cambridge: Loeb Classical Library, 1920.

Holmes, Steve. "'Can We Name the Tools?' Ontologies of Code, Speculative *Technē*, and Rhetorical Concealment." *Computational Culture* 5 (2016). Accessed June 16, 2016. http://computationalculture.net/article/can-we-name-the-tools-ontologies-of-code-speculative-techne-and-rhetorical-concealment.

Kellner, Hans. *Language and Historical Representation: Getting the Story Crooked.* Madison: University of Wisconsin Press, 1989.

Kennedy, George A. "A Hoot in the Dark: The Evolution of General Rhetoric." *Philosophy and Rhetoric* 25, no. 1 (1992): 1–21.

Kirk, G.S., J.E. Raven, and M. Schofield. *The Presocratic Philosophers.* Cambridge: Cambridge University Press, 1983.

Latour, Bruno. "From *Realpolitik* to *Dingpolitik* or How to Make Things Public." In *Making Things Public: Atmospheres of Democracy*, 14–41, edited by Latour and Peter Weibel. Cambridge: Massachusetts Institute of Technology Press, 2005.

———. *Irreductions*. Translated by Alan Sheridan and John Law. In *The Pasteurization of France*, by Latour, 153–236. Cambridge: Harvard University Press, 1988.

———. *Politics of Nature: How to Bring the Sciences into Democracy*. Cambridge: Harvard University Press, 2004.

———. *We Have Never Been Modern*. Translated by Catherine Porter. Cambridge: Harvard University Press, 1993.

———. "Where are the Missing Masses? The Sociology of a Few Mundane Artifacts." In *Shaping Technology/Building Society: Studies in Sociotechnical Change*, edited by Weibe E. Bijker and John Law, 225–258. Cambridge: Massachusetts Institute of Technology Press, 1992.

Lynch, Paul. "Composition's New Thing: Bruno Latour and the Apocalyptic Turn." *College English* 74, no. 5 (2012): 458–476.

Lynch, Paul, and Nathaniel Rivers, eds. *Thinking with Bruno Latour in Rhetoric and Composition*. Carbondale: Southern Illinois University Press, 2015.

McCorkle, Ben. *Rhetorical Delivery as Technological Discourse: A Cross-Historical Study*. Carbondale: Southern Illinois University Press, 2012.

Major, Wilfred E. "Corax and Tisias." In *Classical Rhetorics and Rhetoricians: Critical Studies and Sources*, edited by Michelle Ballif and Michael G. Moran, 111–113. Westport: Praeger, 2005.

Marback, Richard. "Detroit and the Closed Fist: Toward a Theory of Material Rhetoric." *Rhetoric Review* 17, no. 1 (1998): 74–92.

Morey, Sean. *Rhetorical Delivery and Digital Technologies: Networks, Affect, Electracy*. New York: Routledge, 2016.

Muckelbauer, John. "Domesticating Animal Theory." *Philosophy and Rhetoric* 44, no. 1 (2011): 95–100.

Plato. *Theaetetus*. In *Plato: Complete Works*, edited by John M. Cooper, 157–234. Indianapolis: Hackett, 1997.

Reid, Alex. "Composing Objects: Prospects for a Digital Rhetoric." *Enculturation* (2012). Accessed June 16, 2016. http://enculturation.net/composing-objects.

Rickert, Thomas. *Ambient Rhetoric: The Attunements of Rhetorical Being*. Pittsburgh: University of Pittsburgh Press, 2013.

———. "Parmenides, Ontological Enaction, and the Prehistory of Rhetoric." *Philosophy and Rhetoric* 47, no. 4 (2014): 472–493.

Rivers, Nathaniel. "Deep Ambivalence and Wild Objects: Toward a Strange Environmental Rhetoric." *Rhetoric Society Quarterly* 45, no. 5 (2015): 420–440.

———. "Tracing the Missing Masses: Vibrancy, Symmetry, and Public Rhetoric Pedagogy." *Enculturation* 17 (2014). Accessed June 16, 2016. http://enculturation.net/missingmasses.

Smith, Craig R. *Rhetoric and Human Consciousness: A History, Fourth Edition*. Long Grove: Waveland Press, 2013.

Verbeek, Peter-Paul. *Moralizing Technology: Understanding and Designing the Morality of Things*. Chicago: University of Chicago Press, 2011.

Walters, Shannon. *Rhetorical Touch: Disability, Identification, Haptics*. Columbia: University of South Carolina Press, 2014.

Wilkins, John. *An Essay Toward a Real Character and a Philosophical Language, 1668*. Menston, UK: Scolar, 1968.

1 Reclaiming Rhetorical Realism

> The reality of contact with the real world is the inescapable fact of human (or animal) life, and can only be imagined away by erroneous philosophical argument. And it is in virtue of this contact with a common world that we always have something to say to each other, something to point to in disputes about reality.
> —Hubert Dreyfus and Charles Taylor, *Retrieving Realism*

At the center of what is arguably the most famous image ever created of classical thought, the *Scuola di Atene* (*The School of Athens*), stands two figures that have come to represent dual methods for understanding reality. Raphael's famous fresco was commissioned by the Vatican as part of a larger installation depicting the branches of human knowledge that would adorn the walls of the Stanza della Segnatura in the Apostolic Palace, which in the early sixteenth century served as Julius II's personal library. Alongside the other branches of knowledge—theology, poetry, and law—Raphael's masterpiece shows a gathering of twenty-one Greek and Roman philosophers engaged in conversation, work, and games in an ornate school flanked by statues of Apollo and Athena. While the title (which was not Raphael's) implies a harmonious gathering of scholars working together in the pursuit of knowledge, the pairings of certain thinkers suggest a more complex representation of classical thought, one marked by differing and at times opposing views about reality. For instance, standing fairly close to one another we see Socrates and Epicurus, two thinkers whose conceptions of the soul and its immortality could not have been more opposed. And to the left of Heraclitus, the great pre-Socratic philosopher of change, Raphael has placed Parmenides, the Eleatic who argues that nothing changes and that change itself is merely an illusion (one can only imagine what they are talking about!).

Most memorable, however, are the two figures that occupy the middle of the painting. On the left—old, barefooted, and carrying a copy of the *Timaeus*—stands Plato. To his right and slightly ahead stands Plato's greatest student, Aristotle, holding his *Nicomachean Ethics*. In two simple but crucial details, Raphael depicts Plato in the act of pointing above while Aristotle's hand, by contract, hovers over the marble floor below. In these two seemingly minor details, the artist manages to capture not only a key difference between Plato and Aristotle's respective philosophies, but a tension that continues to haunt philosophy (and rhetoric, I will argue) to this day. On the one side, we have a tradition, embodied in the figure of Plato, which presumes that truth exists independent of representational systems and the contingencies of everyday human affairs. Reinforcing this idea is Raphael's inclusion of the *Timaeus*, a dialogue that attempts to explain the beauty of the universe by proposing the existence of a divine Craftsman (*dêmiourgos*) who imposed mathematical order onto chaos and in so doing created the ordered universe (*kosmos*). On the other side, we have the empirical tradition of philosophy characterized by methodological observations of natural, celestial, and social realities. Again, the inclusion of the *Nicomachean Ethics* is revealing as, perhaps more than any of Aristotle's works save perhaps the *Rhetoric*, the *Ethics* conceives of politics, morality, and deliberation—all too human arts—as proper subjects for philosophical investigation. These dual perspectives, allegorized forever in two simple gestures, have been read by scholars in a variety of ways: for instance, as a conflict between mysticism and common sense, as a statement on the importance of religion and science for modern society, and as a depiction of the ultimate compatibility of empiricism and idealism.[1] To this list we can also add the work's anticipation of another conflict to come, that between realism and anti-realism.

The juxtaposition of these two figures no doubt overstates (or at the very least, over simplifies) the differences between Plato and Aristotle. Nonetheless, the famous depictions of Plato and Aristotle in the *Scuola di Atene* are often read as embodying two of the major intellectual traditions to have originated in ancient Athens, traditions that at times led their progenitors to look upwards in search of wisdom while at other times observing the ground below for whatever truth it might reveal. As we saw previously with respect to the Thales myth, such conflicts and differences can be seen in practically every era of philosophical history, from Kant's transcendental idealism, which attempted to reconcile the idealist and realist traditions, to more recent debates over the fate of epistemology in the wake of the linguistic turn's re-conception of truth as, in Nietzsche's terms, "a moveable host of metaphors, metonymies, and anthropomorphisms."[2] Interestingly enough, however, as divergent as these two traditions appear from one another, they have at least one thing in common. At one point or another, each of these traditions has been thought of as "realist" in one way or another.

Of the two traditions allegorized in *Scuolo di Atene*, we see, on the one hand, the Platonic conception of truth as embodied in universal forms and implying a correspondence theory of truth in which what is true corresponds to actually existing structures outside of and independent of the mind. Plato's doctrine of Forms, for example, claims that while our initial encounters with things necessarily occur at the level of perception (as in Plato's famous allegory of the cave), at the same time we have the ability to conceptualize the existence of a different realm where the universal Ideas or

Figure 1.1 *The School of Athens* by Raphael, public domain.

Forms of things, including our own souls, reside. And while it tends to locate truth in more terrestrial places, Aristotle's philosophy similarly presumes the independence and knowability of worldly objects and phenomena. Nature may be chaotic and at times difficult to classify; however, Aristotle never assumes that nature's truths cannot be known, especially if we apply to it the proper reasoning and categorization methods. Underneath both Plato and Aristotle's differing accounts of the world and philosophy's place in the world, in other words, we find similar attunements to reality and to our ability to know reality through specific methods (dialectic for Plato and empiricism for Aristotle). Hence, both philosophies can be said to uphold realist positions, particularly when understood in the context of Alexander Miller's definition of realism:

> There are two general aspects to realism, illustrated by looking at realism about the everyday world of macroscopic objects and their properties. First, there is a claim about *existence*. Tables, rocks, the moon, and so on, all exist, as do the following facts: the table's being square, the rock's being made of granite, and the moon's being spherical and yellow. The second aspect of realism about the everyday world of macroscopic objects and their properties concerns *independence*. The fact that the moon exists and is spherical is independent of anything anyone happens to say or think about the matter.[3]

It is probably safe to assume that realist commitments such as these were not on Raphael's mind when he began to plan *The School of Athens* or when he chose to represent philosophy's approaches to reality in two now famous fingers.[4] Nevertheless, I like to imagine that somewhere outside of the frame of his fresco is a place where these and other thinkers have quietly gathered to congress about the one thing they can all agree upon: that the world is not just what we perceive, wish, or imagine it to be, but is what we each confront and wrangle with every day and that provides the literal ground upon which thought, deliberation, and communication occur in the first place.

The fact that both of these traditions have at some point been thought of as iterations of the same school of thought should beg the question, what, then, does realism mean? As it turns out, this is a surprisingly difficult question to answer in any straightforward way—this, despite the fact that philosophers for centuries have authored innumerable attempts to do precisely this. In rhetoric, however, questions about "the ultimate reality of things,"[5] not to mention the realism-anti-realism debate, have not attracted nearly as much attention as they have in philosophy. Apart from a short period in the 1960s, 70s, and 80s during which rhetoricians debated rhetoric's status as an epistemic art (debates examined in detail in Chapter 4), for the most part realism and anti-realism have appeared as only minor issues for contemporary rhetorical theory. As I discuss throughout this book, there are a number of historical and theoretical explanations for rhetoric's tepid response to realism and related schools of thought. The point I wish to make at the outset, however, is a far more general one. Perhaps one of the reasons why debates over realism have only recently found their way into rhetoric is that, for the better part of rhetoric's history in the West, rhetors and rhetoricians have remained unapologetically committed to understanding and intervening in the "pedestrian" affairs of everyday life.[6] To an extent, rhetoric has always been practiced and understood in reference to a wide range of worldly realities, from audiences that are sometimes inscrutable and thus resistant to certain rhetorical strategies to the argumentative proofs orator invoke in the service of advocating one course of action over others. Whereas philosophy has a long history of forgetting or diminishing realist ideas in pursuit of other aims, rhetoric has an even longer history of accepting and affirming the contingencies of worldliness in its theoretical, praxical, and pedagogical pursuits. Perhaps it is no coincidence, then, that of the two primary figures depicted in *Scuola di Atene* it is Aristotle who authored an important treatise on rhetoric and Plato who often derided rhetors for pandering to public opinion and providing people what is most pleasurable to hear rather than what is best for their souls. As Aristotle proposes near the beginning of the *Nicomachean Ethics*, "we must start from what is known,"[7] which is to say, when addressing issues of ethics, politics, and deliberation (issues very much a part of the rhetorical tradition), we must begin with the common and build up from there. "We must be content," Aristotle says in contrast to his teacher, "if we can indicate the truth roughly and in outline, and if, in dealing with matters that are not amenable to immutable laws, and reasoning from premises that are but probable, we can arrive at probable conclusions."[8] As much as Plato's interests in the Forms makes him suspicious of rhetoric and public opinion (*doxa*), Aristotle's realist commitments are most likely what inspired him to take rhetoric seriously in the first place as a civic practice and a course of study.[9]

Realist commitments about the world are nothing new for rhetoric, in other words, even if explicit engagements with realism are relatively recent phenomena in rhetorical studies. Several years ago while on a campus visit for a position in rhetorical theory, I delivered an early version of one of this book's chapters in which I attempted to associate work in epistemic rhetoric from the 1960s and 70s with more recent ideas in speculative realism. During the question-and-answer period, one faculty member asked a question that I have been pondering ever since. Why, he wondered, if philosophy has not managed to resolve the dispute between realism and anti-realism over the past several centuries would rhetoric now want to get involved in this old and (presumably) tired debate? Needless to say, the question threw me for a loop, and I am sure my answer at the time failed to adequately respond to this person's concerns. In the years since, however, I have found myself repeatedly thinking about this question. If I could answer the question again today, I would tell this person—with just a bit more confidence than I expressed that day—that the reason rhetoric needs to engage realist ideas today is that it has always done so. The history of rhetorical theory is shot through with references to worlds outside of or in excess of language, knowledge, and perception. So much of rhetoric's history, in fact, boils down to anxieties over relationships between word and thing—whether it is best to try to hammer language into shape so that it accords better with our sense of reality, as some early modern rhetoricians suggested, or whether it is better to revel in the inherent incommensurability between signifier and signified, as suggested by some postmodern and poststructuralist philosophers and rhetoricians. In any case, how we understand rhetoric—how we come to understand and define its scope and meaning—follows in large part from the range of possibilities for understanding reality we inherit from our particular historical epochs. As we will see later in this chapter, our current epoch is no different insofar as it enables us to see rhetoric's realist implications in some ways but not others.

But there is a second answer I would offer to the question of why rhetoric would want to dip its toes into the realism debate today, and that is because, unlike philosophy, rhetoric has rarely struggled to accept its realist commitments. If anything, it is anti-realism and its various manifestations as hermeneutics, social constructionism, and deconstruction (among others) that are relatively new to rhetoric, not realism per se. This represents a significant difference from philosophy, particularly in the continental tradition where realism has often been the sounding board against which newer versions of anti-realism are advanced. My answer to the question about rhetoric's stake in realism, then, is twofold. First, I want to argue that it is important to explore realism's place in the rhetorical tradition because, as rhetoricians continue to consider the implications of speculative realism for rhetoric, we will need ways of reading rhetorical history that focus specifically on the realist ideas underwriting many of the field's conceptions of rhetoric. Second, I want to emphasize that, as interest in nonhuman materiality and agency continues to grow in the field, it is important for rhetoricians to understand that such concern need not signal a radical break from past understandings of rhetoric. As with many recent theoretical trends, it is tempting to believe that in the wake of the nonhuman turn and its hostility toward language-centric conceptions of reality that rhetoric, too, must also rethink its commitments to symbolic action as *the* defining feature of rhetorical action. As I explore in more detail throughout this book, such indictments of rhetoric are historically short-sighted insofar as they tend to define rhetoric in distinctly modernist terms and, more specifically, in terms of its reemergence in the twentieth century on the heels of the linguistic and social turns in the humanities and social sciences. Of course, rhetorical history is much older than this, and contemporary theorists who claim that rhetoric is coterminous with human language and symbolic action fail to appreciate how rhetoricians for centuries have defined rhetoric in relation to a wide range of nonhuman agents and agencies including nature, nonbeing, and, even, language itself. If the recent nonhuman turn is to have any lasting significance in rhetorical theory and history, rhetoricians will need to see this moment as an opportunity to explore the presence of nonhuman actors and agencies within the history of rhetoric itself. This book represents one attempt to begin this work. As such, it offers as much a methodological framework for exploring realist commitments in the rhetorical tradition as a contribution to rhetorical theories and histories of nonhuman agents and agencies already underway in the field.

In this chapter, I introduce some definitions and perspectives on realism. Since the majority of the book focuses on specific articulations of realism in rhetorical history, I focus here on realism's larger place in humanistic inquiry, including versions of realism invoked in contemporary accounts of speculative realism, object-oriented ontology, and new materialism.[10] As we will see, realism is hardly a singular idea or worldview. Instead, it is convenient shorthand for a wide range of perspectives that take seriously the existence of things outside of the mind and human experience. This point is especially important for rhetoric and instructive for the historiographic methodology I am attempting to construct here. When we explore realism's place in the rhetorical tradition, we do so not with the aim of defining "rhetorical realism" in any singular, universal sense. In exploring rhetorical realism, rather, we are interested in understanding the various forms realism has taken in rhetorical theory and history and how these forms of realism in turn have shaped assumptions about rhetoric today.

I conclude this chapter with a discussion of my approach toward historiography, which I develop in terms of social theorist Bruno Latour's refiguring of history in the wake of moderns recognition that "we have never been modern." For Latour, modernism as a theoretical construct is characterized by the belief that nature and culture (human and nonhuman) designate distinct ontological zones and that history, as a result, is defined by a steady trajectory of progress moving us (moderns) away from ignorance and toward enlightenment. As I will explain, many scholars in rhetorical studies perpetuate this view of history when they read or teach rhetoric's history as progressive and thus cumulative in one fashion or another. Latour reminds us, however, that history is never as neat or linear as our modernist expectations lead us to believe. For Latour, history instead names the ways different epochs have mixed human and nonhuman actors. It is the mixing that makes the times, not the times that make histories, he argues. This is an important idea for rhetorical theorists today interested in exploring the implications of speculative realism for rhetorical studies. Rather than pushing to reboot rhetoric and/or rebuild it from the ground up, Latour's nonmodern conception of history reminds us of the work still to be done in rhetorical studies—namely, exploring how rhetoricians since antiquity have assembled humans and nonhumans in the service of new definitions of rhetoric and new ways of rhetorically engaging their worlds.

Anti-Realisms

Before exploring realist commitments in the rhetorical tradition, it is useful to situate these commitments within some of the broader debates over realism in rhetoric and philosophy. In turning to philosophy so much at the outset, I do not mean to give the impression that rhetoric is merely playing "catch up" to philosophy or, worse, that rhetoric is of secondary importance to philosophy. On the contrary, one of my claims in this book is that rhetoric has much to teach philosophy about realism, in particular about the prevalence of realist appeals in theories of language and communication more broadly. But in order to explore some of these realist commitments in rhetoric, we first need to understand how theorists have defined realism as both a concept in itself and a concept in relation to various forms of anti-realism. As we will see with respect to rhetoric, realism has come to mean a number of things. Rather than a single school of realism, we find a number of *realisms*, each forwarding sometimes-competing theses on the nature of reality and our abilities to know or represent reality as such. For the sake of conceptual clarity, I will attempt to isolate a few of the key assumptions underwriting some of the more influential versions of realism. When necessary, I will make reference to debates that have shaped understandings of realism in both the analytic and continental philosophical traditions. However, at the risk of being reductive, I will try to keep the bulk of my focus in this and the following section on the broader ideas of realism and anti-realism and the commitments that underlie their claims about the world.

The word realism has experienced a resurgence of late thanks in part to the efforts of speculative realists and other proponents of new materialism and object-oriented ontology. That realist ideas needed recuperating in the first place shows just how strong the backlash to realism has been over the past century. While supporters of realism can be found in both rhetoric and philosophy during this period, for a great many more the word "realism" has come to signify an outdated, old-fashioned, and ultimately naïve worldview. In the wake of post-Kantian idealism and the linguistic turn of the nineteenth and twentieth centuries, philosophy in particular became increasingly anti-realist in its understandings of reality, knowledge, and existence. In his impressive book, *A Thing of This World: A History of Continental Anti-Realism*, Lee Braver follows a line of thought from Immanuel Kant to Jacques Derrida that finds continental philosophers increasingly skeptical of realist claims positing the existence of mind-independent objects and realities. Kant's signature achievement, Braver argues, was to fundamentally reverse philosophy's direction of inquiry away from independent objects of knowledge toward the active mind that organizes and constructs reality. As Kant famously announces in the second preface to the *Critique of Pure Reason*, "Hitherto it has been assumed that all our knowledge must conform to objects. But all attempts to extend our knowledge of objects by establishing something in regard to them *a priori*, by means of concepts, have, on this assumption, ended in failure. We must therefore make trial whether we may not have more success in the tasks of metaphysics, if we suppose that objects must conform to our knowledge."[11] Kant's co-called Copernican Revolution sought to shift the emphasis of philosophical inquiry toward the subject and specifically toward the conscious mind as the new focal point for philosophical analysis. By placing so much emphasis on the active mind, Kant, in effect, succeeded in turning philosophy's commitments away from realism and toward what would eventually become known as anti-realism. As Braver acknowledges, however, and as I explore in Chapter 4 in relation to rhetoric's Kantian turn in the twentieth century, Kant's was not a complete idealism. Throughout the first Critique, Kant repeatedly invokes the idea of a noumenal reality independent of phenomenal experience or sensory data,[12] a curious decision that some commentators see as Kant's attempt to circumvent the excesses of idealism by incorporating limits into what we can know about reality. In any event, Kant's retention of the noumenon would not last long. Over the next century, Hegel and the German Idealists would succeed in transforming Kantian idealism into a full-blown anti-realist epistemology. Although he greatly admired Kant, Hegel was nevertheless skeptical of Kant's decision to retain the noumenon. In Hegel's estimation, it is a fallacy to assert the existence of mind-independent noumena because doing so inevitably makes them objects of knowledge and thus mind-*dependent*. The only way to resolve this problem, he concludes, is to abandon the idea of an in-itself altogether such that the whole of reality effectively becomes "reality for-us," which is to say, immanent to our *Geist* or historical consciousness. As Braver explains,

> By jettisoning the very idea of noumena, Hegel's Objective Idealism takes the scare quotes off of Kant's phenomenal "knowledge," and

it does so without resorting to a God's-eye-view. Without even the conceptual possibility of a world beyond this world, a *meta-physis* realism, this becomes the only one that can sensibly be considered the world, turning knowledge of it into knowledge *simpliciter*.[13]

Hegel's claim that knowledge is necessarily conditioned by the world we experience would soon become one of the hallmarks of many versions of anti-realism. At their core, anti-realisms reject realism's first claim—that things exist independent of our senses or cognitions of them—and in its place posit that knowledge of the world is first and foremost mind-dependent and thus constituted not from without but from within the structures of the active mind.

With respect to modern and postmodern rhetorical theory, anti-realism has become something of a first philosophy, informing a range of theoretical perspectives from epistemic rhetoric and the rhetorics of science and technology to critical rhetorics embracing discursive and constructionist conceptions of rhetoric. In both rhetorical theory and composition studies, the epistemic position in particular has become almost second nature, influencing much of the work in these fields without necessarily being named or analyzed as such any longer. As the name suggests, epistemic rhetoric emphasizes discourse's role in constructing knowledge. From the perspective of epistemic rhetoric, truth and knowledge are not "discovered" out there in the world but rather are constituted through modes of symbolic action and representation. In an article exploring the strengths and weaknesses of epistemic rhetoric, Daniel J. Royer traces some of the historical antecedents for epistemic rhetoric. In particular, he identifies Kant and, to a lesser extent, Ernst Cassirer as key contributors to what would become epistemic rhetoric and social constructionism more generally. According to Royer, epistemic rhetoric "gets both its best ideas and biggest problems from Kant."[14] Kant's philosophy, as we have seen, is predicated upon the notion that people are active rather than passive participants in the production of knowledge. As Royer rightly notes, this idea reflects the "epistemological" thrust of Kant's philosophy that has been so influential for anti-realisms in both rhetoric and philosophy. But there is another aspect to Kant's philosophy that is more "metaphysical" in nature. This aspect is most pronounced in Kant's "perpetuation of the Cartesian notion of two realities: mind and matter, or as Kant more technically called them, 'noumenal' and 'phenomenal' reality."[15] This notion, which I explore in detail in Chapter 4, has been considerably less popular with subsequent philosophers. For example, Royer cites Sean Sayers who criticizes Kant's philosophy for involving "an unbridgeable division—and absolute gulf—between appearances and things-in-themselves; with things-in-themselves placed irretrievably beyond the grasp of our knowledge."[16] The two reality problem Kant perpetuates has carried over to epistemic rhetoric as well, Royer goes on to argue, most notably in epistemic rhetoric's embrace of a representational purview that makes it increasingly difficult to adjudicate the veracity of competing truth claims.[17] As Royer explains, "Given that different people see the 'same thing' differently coupled with Kant's insight that special categories of the mind give shape and meaning to reality, much of modern thought [including epistemic rhetoric] has gone the way of denying that objects of reality exist apart from our thoughts about them including our values, attitudes, and symbolic use of language."[18] This outlook thus results in a rejection of any grounding for "true knowledge about the world" in favor of epistemologies rooted in contingent "coherence" and social consensus.[19] To avoid the problems in anti-realist philosophies, Royer proposes another option besides objectivism and relativism, a "new realism" that would "insist on some kind of unity between the objective and the subjective, between appearance and reality."[20] Such a realism, he concludes, would "better explain the relation of writer, reality, and audience than do those assumptions underlying certain formulations of epistemic rhetoric."[21] Before extending this prospect further in terms of more recent discussions in speculative realism and object-oriented ontology, let us first examine some of the more foundational theses of realism to see what relevance they hold for developing a richer understanding of rhetorical realism.

Realisms

If anti-realism has indeed become the dominant paradigm today (albeit one that has increasingly come under fire by speculative realists), then what, exactly, is realism, this thing we are now supposedly against? As I have suggested already, this is not an easy question to answer in one chapter or even one book for that matter. Realisms are as varied as anti-realisms, taking innumerable forms over the years. Generally speaking, however, we can distinguish two primary forms realism has taken in rhetoric and philosophy. The first form is *global* in nature. Real-world examples of global realism are tough to come by, but global realists resist arguments about reality that locate exigency or meaning in social institutions, histories, or traditions. Proponents of global realism are what we might call realism's "true believers." They are the ones, much like global anti-realists, whose worldviews are shaped exclusively by their realist commitments. The other version of realism is *local* in nature. Proponents of local realism are decidedly more measured in their worldviews. While they believe that there are things that exist independent of the mind, local realists also acknowledge that qualities such as colors, moralities, and identities are immanent to mental, social, and linguistic projections. If we were to conduct a poll about people's realist commitments, it is likely a large majority would identify as local realists rather than global realists. As Stuart Brock and Edwin Mares suggest, when it comes to realism and anti-realism, "most of us are pickers and choosers, some-but-only-someists—that is, most of us are local realists about some entities, but local anti-realists about others."[22] The complexities and contradictions in our attitudes toward realism and anti-realism, while not always the subject of theoretical inquiry, are exactly what make realism a compelling case for rhetorical analysis. After all, on what bases we craft arguments about our world has long been the bread and butter of rhetorical studies. As James Berlin and others remind us, how we understand "reality" makes all the difference in how we think about rhetorical action.[23]

When we encounter the word realism today, however, it is usually referring to a specific version of realism known pejoratively as "naïve realism." Naïve realism is the belief that we can perceive and know reality as it really is without any interference from intermediaries such as language, history, sociality, ideology, and so on. This is the version of realism that gives us the classic philosophical thought experiment about the tree falling in the forest. For the naïve realist, the answer to this infamous question is, yes, the tree makes a noise when it falls even if no one is there to hear it. This conclusion is true, the naïve realist will argue, because objects exist independent of our perceptions or knowledge of them. Moreover, the naïve realist will also assert that the properties of objects—their size, shape, texture, smell, taste, color, and so on—are as objectively real as the objects themselves, meaning that they are not relative to our experiences of them and thus have the potential to be perceived objectively by us under certain conditions. For all of its obvious problems (and there are many problems), naïve realism has at least one advantage: it allows us to justify beliefs about the "real world" without having to appeal to the subjective content of our sense experience. Such justification ensures that when we debate objects of public concern (such as the environment or the economy), we do so under the assumption that, despite our differences, *we are all still talking about the same thing*. Of course, this assumption runs the risk of reintroducing the problem of perspectivism as we must once again account for why so many of us see objects in such different ways in the first place. And, indeed, this problem—predicated on the belief that we can have direct, unmediated contact with things-in-themselves—has helped fuel many of the critiques of realism from Kant to the present. Nevertheless, it is instructive to remember that, despite its argumentative failings, naïve realism has a long history as a serious position in both philosophy and rhetoric.[24] Likewise, naïve realism remains a very popular orientation for laypersons outside of the disciplines of rhetoric and philosophy, from environmentalists who rebuff the skepticism of so-called climate-change deniers by arguing that the "facts speak for themselves" to politicians who claim to be offering voters "the truth" rather than "mere rhetoric." The prevalence of the naïve realism is perhaps one of the reasons why it is sometimes referred to as "common sense realism."

But there is more to realism than what naïve realism would have us believe. To gain a better handle on realism's commitments, we may look to Braver's attempts to map the primary theses of realism in *A Thing of This World*. While relatively few forms of realism accept all of these theses, most are committed to at least one of them. As we will see, this is true in rhetoric as well where we find innumerable commitments to Independence (Braver's R1 thesis) yet fewer commitments to Correspondence (R2). Braver's theses of realism incorporate and build upon Hilary Putnam's canonical definition of "metaphysical (or external) realism." In this definition, Putnam enumerates three intersecting commitments that together make up "a bundle of intimately associated philosophical ideas":

> The world consists of some fixed totality of mind-independent objects. There is exactly one true and complete description of "the way the world is." Truth involves some sort of correspondence relation between words or thought-signs and external things and sets of things. I shall call this perspective the *externalist* perspective, because its favorite point of view is a God's Eye point of view.[25]

To Putnam's three commitments, Braver adds three additional theses that follow from his readings of anti-realism in the continental tradition. Here, then, are Braver's theses on philosophical realism:

R1 Independence: Assertions about the independence of objects tend to be metaphysical in nature. According to Braver, the Independence thesis maintains that "a set of objects or states of affairs, which does not rely upon us in any way, exists [...] The fact that these entities are—and that they are what they are—is unaffected by the facts that and what we are, think or say."[26] Without question, Independence is the most important thesis for any form of realism, and it is arguably the only one of Braver's theses that can be found in all forms of realism from naïve realism and speculative realism to rhetorical realism.

R2 Correspondence: The second thesis of realism is epistemological in that it "defines truth as the correspondence between [...] thoughts, ideas, beliefs, words, propositions, sentences, or languages on the one hand, and things, objects, states of affairs, configurations, reality, or experience on the other."[27] As Braver points out, not all philosophers agree that realism entails a theory of truth. As we will see with respect to rhetorical realism, it is quite possible to accept the metaphysical existence of things (R1) without necessarily accepting a correspondence theory of truth.

R3 Uniqueness: Like R1 and R2, Braver's third thesis is adapted from Putnam's definition of realism quoted above. As Braver summarizes, "If reality has a determinate structure independently of us (R1) and truth consists in capturing that structure (R2), then there will be one and only one way to do so accurately."[28] In other words, while from a realist perspective it may be possible to have partial truths, according to the Uniqueness thesis there can be only one Truth. If the "world is out there," as R1 insists, then Truth must be "the capturing of it, which can only happen in one way."[29] From the perspective of R3, objects are fixed, stable, and self-identical ready-mades that preexist our relations with them but have the potential to be known as such.

R4 Bivalence: The fourth thesis of realism comes not from Putnam but from Michael Dummett, a philosopher who is credited with bringing anti-realism into analytic philosophy. Dummett follows Frege and Wittgenstein in arguing that, in order for a concept to be legitimate, "it must divide in advance all objects into the set it applies to and the set it doesn't; for example, red is meaningful if and only if the universe can be exhaustively split into red and non-red objects."[30] Under this way of thinking, we cannot doubt whether an object falls under a concept; the object must be knowable and verifiable in its entirety. Truth-values, then, must be determinate. According to Braver, "if reality is determined independently of us, then propositions will have determinate truth values regardless of whether we can verify them or not."[31]

R5 Passive Power: The fifth thesis is Braver's own, although, along with the first two theses, it holds true for many realist philosophies. The thesis of the Passive Knower states, "In order to be a realist who thinks there is any chance to attain correspondence truth about the world, there must be a way for the mind to reach reality as it is."[32] This thesis assumes that human beings have access to the thing-itself, an idea most anti-realists since Kant reject. According to Braver, "The mind must be passive and in some sense featureless so as not to distort what comes into it. If it interferes with its input, then, in a metaphor that permeates discussions of realism, the consequence is that (in Francis Bacon's words) 'the human understanding is like a false mirror, which, receiving rays irregularly, distorts and discolors the nature of things by mingling its own nature with it.'"[33] The passive knower thesis has undergone several transformations since Kant and has most recently been adapted to phenomenological conceptions of being-in-the-world.

R6 Realism of the Subject: The final thesis of realism emerges in the context of Braver's analysis of Kant and his insistence on the existence of a transcendental subject that is prior to reality. Unlike the other theses, Realism of the Subject emerges not in defense of realism but in an effort to establish an anti-realist philosophy predicated on the priority of an active, rather than a passive, subject. As Braver argues, however, Kant's attempt to turn philosophy upside down by privileging the subject over objects independent of the subject ultimately backfires in a significant but instructive way. In a key part of Braver's argument as well the argument I am developing here, Braver shows that, in spite of Kant's efforts to transcend realism with a more concerted focus on the human subject and its experiences and cognitions, he winds up affirming some of the other theses of realism. As Braver writes, Kant's transcendental subject claims to be "fixed and universal for all rational beings. It constitutes the unchanging, timeless grid which gives to human experience a uniform conceptual structure."[34] "What is interesting about this transcendental subject," Braver adds, "is that, although it is responsible for undermining two or three of the theses of realism (depending on how one stands on R2 correspondence Truth), it both ensures R3 Uniqueness and *fits the theses of metaphysical realism* [R1] *itself perfectly*. It founds anti-realism, but it is still conceived strictly along the lines of a realist metaphysics. In other words, R1-R3 are true of the transcendental subject, which is why Kant is committed to R6 Realism of the Subject."[35] Along with R1 Independence, R6 Realism of the Subject is one of the most persistent theses of realism we find throughout the rhetorical tradition and especially in the last century as attention in rhetoric has turned to epistemic and constructionist views of reality and their emphases on the (human) subject rather than (nonhuman) objects in relation to the subject.[36]

Braver's account of the theses of realism is hardly definitive or exhaustive. But as a heuristic, it offers a useful way to frame commitments that underlie versions of realism in both rhetoric and philosophy. As mentioned already, realisms vary in their allegiances to these theses, and, indeed, as in the case of R6 Realism of the Subject, some of the theses were not even conceived with defenses of realism in mind. This latter point is instructive for what follows insofar as it recognizes that, in some cases, anti-realisms presuppose one or more realist assumptions about the world and beings in the world. Although anti-realisms often profess to be anti-foundational in their conceptions of reality, Hubert Dreyfus and Charles Taylor have recently argued that many anti-realisms tacitly accept a dichotomy between mind and world that not only places them at odds with realism's doctrine of "direct contact" between self and world, but at the same time perpetuates the same dualism between subject and object that anti-realisms claim to have transcended in the first place. According to Dreyfus and Taylor, many versions of anti-realism adopt a representational theory in which "our contribution to knowing" can be distinguished "from what is out there."[37] In his essay "The Contingency of Language," the American pragmatist Richard Rorty offers (accidentally, one imagines) a perfect illustration of how anti-realists often bolster their epistemological claims while at the same time acknowledging, in true Kantian form, the possibility of a world or thing-in-itself existing independent of thought, language, or experience. While making his case that vocabularies (i.e., historical discourses or situated ways of knowing) shape our perceptions of reality, Rorty finds himself in the awkward position of having to reconcile his version of pragmatism with what common sense tells us about objects in the world. He writes:

> We need to make a distinction between the claim that the world is out there and the claim that the truth is out there. To say that the world is out there, that it is not our creation, is to say, with common sense, that most things in space and time are the effects of causes which do

not include human mental states. To say that the truth is out there is simply to say that where there are no sentences there is no truth, that sentences are elements of human languages, and that human languages are human creations [...] Truth cannot be out there—cannot exist independently of the human mind—because sentences cannot so exist, or be out there. The world is out there, but descriptions of the world are not. Only descriptions of the world can be true and false. The world on its own—unaided by the describing activities of human beings—cannot.[38]

In trying to keep his focus on epistemological rather than metaphysical concerns, Rorty finds himself having to negotiate a delicate balancing act. On the one hand, he clearly wishes to establish a holistic anti-realist theory of truth and language, one he hopes will offer an alternative to representational theories of language and their presumption that speaking about the world is akin to holding a mirror up to nature. At the same time, he feels obligated to say that there are more to things in heaven and earth than are dreamt of in our epistemologies. As we will see in the chapters to come, this recognition of "the world out there" is not just a concession to "common sense," as Rorty suggests, but is a necessary presupposition for his, or indeed any, anti-realist conception of language, knowledge, and things. Despite his eagerness to challenge the epistemological theses of realism (Braver's R2-R5), Rorty affirms, and indeed invokes as a warrant for his own anti-realism, the thesis of R1 Independence. Much more than a specter or placeholder in his particular conception of reality, the "world on its own" functions as the very condition of possibility for his pragmatism, the means by which his anti-realism comes into being and into meaning in the first place. This holds true for other versions of anti-realism as well, including those in rhetoric which, like Rorty's pragmatism, attempt to counter realism by positing an epistemic conception of reality in which writers and speakers understand themselves primarily through discourse rather than through direct contact with things of the world. And yet, as with Rorty, these efforts are emboldened by their tacit acceptance of one or more realist commitments such the existence of mind-independent realities. As Joseph Margolis suggests, at the end of the day, "In an obvious, perhaps even trivial sense, we are all realists—no matter how strenuously we protest."[39] As we will see, this is the case even when our attention is focused directly on language and the role discourse and vocabularies play in shaping our experiences of/in the world.

Speculative Realism

Apart from R1 Independence and R6 Realism of the Subject, Braver's theses of realism couch realism's scope and meaning in decidedly epistemological terms. In the traditional accounts from which Braver draws, realism refers to our abilities to know the world directly through our perceptions or descriptions of it. The critiques of realism we saw above focus primarily on these epistemological assumptions, arguing in response that objects of knowledge are by definition mind-dependent and are thus prone to the contingencies, deflections, and mediations of human minds and social collectives. Most debates about realism and anti-realism in fact presume some epistemological assumptions about what it means to know. One might argue, for instance, that objective knowledge of the world is possible, while another will argue that knowledge is produced by social factors that are relative to historical, cultural, and ideological conditions. Neither, however, is able to gain much headway over the other because, at their core, each argument hinges on differing understandings of the capacities of human beings to know reality rather than on understandings of reality as such.

Our exhaustion with epistemological debates of this kind is perhaps one reason why realism became such a devil term throughout the twentieth century. However, as we have seen already with respect to R1 Independence and R6 Realism of the Subject, realisms often rest upon commitments that are not only epistemological in nature. Indeed, the first and most prevalent thesis of realism, Independence, is not an epistemological thesis at all but rather a metaphysical statement on things that exist apart from or in excess of our abilities to know them. In other words, committing oneself to R1 Independence does not necessarily require one to also believe that mind-independent objects can be known; it simply means that one acknowledges the existence of things that are not objects of knowledge or concern for us. This was Kant's way of avoiding full-blown idealism. It has also been the starting point for recent work in speculative realism, an emerging school of thought that encompasses a range of specialties including object-oriented ontology and new materialism.

The term "speculative realism" first appeared in 2007 in the context of a series of talks given at Goldsmith College, London by Ray Brassier, Iain Hamilton Grant, Graham Harman, and Quentin Meillassoux. The term itself represents an attempt to give a name to a diverse set of interests in contemporary philosophy that "all agree on one thing: that European philosophy since the time of Kant has stopped talking about reality, since it's stuck thinking about how we *know* reality—just endless stuff on demonstrations, discourses, dialectics, and deconstruction."[40] If there is one idea that unifies speculative realists, it is the presumption that in post-Kantian theory reality only has meaning in relation to our epistemological and symbolic conceptions of it. In his short but influential book, *After Finitude*, Meillassoux gives the name "correlationism" to this logic. By "correlation," Meillassoux writes, "we mean the idea according to which we only ever have access to the correlation between thinking and being, and never to either term considered apart from the other."[41] According to Meillassoux, it is possible to say that "every philosophy which disavows naïve realism has become a variant of correlationism."[42] For Meillassoux and other speculative realists, the problem with correlationism is that ensnares us in a circular form of reasoning that renders naïve and illogical any prospect of mind-independent reality. From within the "correlationist circle," it becomes impossible for us to think of anything outside of thought, because once we have thought about it, it is now an object of thought. For the correlationist, to posit anything like a noumenon or thing-in-itself thus constitutes a logical fallacy. While he retains a great deal of respect for correlationism and the thinkers who have espoused it, Meillassoux worries that, by ceding expertise in mind-independent "absolutes," philosophers enable others, such as religious extremists, climate-change deniers, and creationists, to set the terms and conditions for what counts as absolute. His attempt to absolutize contingency such that anything can change at any time, including the laws of physics, can thus be read as an effort to bring philosophy's insights to bear on some of our time's most pressing concerns. It is an effort to make philosophy more rhetorical, we might say.

In tune with these efforts to transcend correlationism or at least inhabit it differently, speculative realists tend to frame their discussions of realism in ontological rather than epistemological terms. In *The Democracy of Objects*, Levi Bryant helpfully distinguishes between what he calls "epistemological realism" and the "ontological realism" favored by himself and fellow speculative realists.

> As such, this book defends a robust realism. Yet, and this is crucial to everything that follows, the realism defended here is not an epistemological realism, but an ontological realism. *Epistemological realism* argues that our representations and language are accurate mirrors of the world as it actually is, regardless of whether or not we exist. It seeks to distinguish between true representations and phantasms. *Ontological realism*, by contrast, is not a thesis about our knowledge of objects, but about the being of objects themselves, whether or not we exist to represent them. It is the thesis that the world is composed of objects, that these objects are varied and include entities as diverse as mind, language, cultural and social entities, and objects independent of humans such as galaxies, stones, quarks, tardigrades and so on.[43]

For Bryant, epistemological realism is equivalent to the naïve realism we encountered above where reality is construed in terms of direct contact between a human mind and the world as it actually is. While it is true that speculative realists accept some of the basic tenets of epistemological (and even naïve) realism, their objection hinges on epistemological realism's focus on the human subject as the primary pathway through which reality comes into being as such. For Bryant and other speculative realists, it is possible to think about objects and object relations without reducing them to their status as objects "for us." Bryant's ontological realism tries to do this by expanding our sense of what counts as an agent (or subject or object, for that matter) while at the same time exploring what it is like to be a thing.

Graham Harman's object-oriented ontology has been the most cited and debated version of speculative realism over the past decade. Beginning with his first book, *Tool-Being: Heidegger and the Metaphysics of Objects*, Harman sets out to revive realism as a viable position for continental philosophy in the wake of poststructuralist theorizing about language and the contingencies of truth and knowledge. Harman was perhaps the first of this new wave of philosophers to reclaim the mantle of realism, albeit a much *weirder* realism than we have seen before. Harman describes his brand of speculative realism as "a frank *realism*," one that "views objects or things as genuine realities deeper than any of the relations in which they might become involved."[44] Harman's realism is not the realism of "objective atoms and billiard balls located outside of the human mind."[45] Instead, it refers to a reality that is "far *weirder* than realists had ever guessed"[46] What makes this version of realism weird, for Harman, is that it rejects traditional realism's focus on epistemology by speculating instead about the being of objects themselves, from their existence as individual and indivisible entities to their relations with other objects.

In terms of his contributions to realism, Harman's ontological descriptions of objects and relationality are perhaps most salient for what follows. Building on Heidegger's phenomenological account of tools and equipment and Edmund Husserl's notion of sensual objects, Harman argues that objects are not the inert stuff we sometimes think they are; nor are they merely the sounding boards against which we come to understand ourselves as subjects. Instead, objects are beings in their own rights, and hence are irreducible to our—or, indeed, any other object's—caricatures of them. In his famous tool-analysis, Heidegger distinguishes between the readiness-to-hand (*zuhandenheit*) of tools and their presence-at-hand (*vorhandenheit*). When we use a tool such as a hammer or, to use a more contemporary example, a computer, we typically focus our attentions on the task itself rather than on the tool we are using to accomplish the task; in its readiness-to-hand, the tool withdraws from our conscious awareness to become part of our work's background contexture. Of course, when our tools break, or when we write theoretical treatises about them, they become conspicuous objects of concern (present-at-hand). Heidegger's point in the tool-analysis was to highlight the ways human Dasein is always already enmeshed in a worldly contexture that is characterized as much by "pre-understanding" and tacit coping as by conscious thought and attention. Thus, for Heidegger, readiness-to-hand becomes something of a privileged term in the sense that presence-at-hand refers to our tendency to assume that theoretical investigation (rather than practical engagement) provides exhaustive knowledge of a thing or phenomena. For Harman, however, Heidegger's insight goes much farther than what it reveals about human being. For one thing, Harman notes that, in spite of Heidegger's deceptively simple model, objects withdraw from our theoretical inspections as much as from our practical engagements.[47] "Our use of the floor as 'equipment for standing' makes no contact with the abundance of extra qualities that dogs or mosquitoes might be able to detect. In short both theory *and* practice are equally guilty of reducing things to presence-at-hand."[48] Regardless of whether we approach them in terms of theory or practice, objects withhold something of themselves from us; in Harman's Heideggerian idiom, they are *withdrawn* from us in some way. But Harman does not stop there. The same process of withdrawal holds true for objects in relation to other objects as well, he argues. To borrow one of Harman's favorite examples, when fire comes into contact with cotton, it does so only at the level of cotton's flammability. While the flame may eventually succeed in consuming the cotton, it will do so irrespective of cotton's numerous other qualities, such as its color, softness, etc. This sense of the object in withdrawal, whether we are talking about objects withdrawing from us (the human ones) or from other objects, is the heart of Harman's speculative realism. Objects exist in a kind of "vacuous actuality," he claims, which ensures that objects are never entirely exhausted by their relations with other objects.

Although many commentators focus on Harman's reading of Heidegger's tool-analysis from *Being and Time*, his most significant contribution, in my view, lies not in the accuracy of his interpretations of Heidegger (which are debatable for some) but in his efforts to shine a light on some of the underappreciated kernels of realism scattered throughout the long history of philosophy. In this sense, Harman offers something of a methodological model for my efforts to reclaim realism's neglected place in the rhetorical tradition. Whether recuperating realist commitments in Leibniz, Husserl, and Levinas, or putting European philosophies in conversation with non-Western conceptions of reality, Harman is at his best when he is reading realism against the grain of contemporary expectations and yet still in response to them. In his many books and articles, the moments that stand out are those where Harman attempts to dig deeper roots for his version of realism within the history of his discipline. At the very least, Harman shows that realism has always had a presence in philosophy, and that these kernels of realism can be reactivated and transformed through readings attuned their presence and to the urgencies of the present moment that compel us to take seriously the realities of things independent of human knowledge and intervention.

Rhetorical Realisms

To date, discussions about realism have mostly been confined to philosophers and theorists working from philosophical principles and traditions. With a few notable exceptions, rhetorical theorists have for the most part tended to avoid the term realism in favor of related concepts such as "ambience," "complexity," and "ecology."[49] Nevertheless, most rhetorical theories presume some of the theses of realism we saw above. As we will see in the chapters to come, realist commitments cut across the rhetorical tradition, from the classical period, which predates the appearance of the word realism by several centuries,[50] through the Enlightenment and into the modern and postmodern periods. While rhetorical realisms on the whole accept to the R1 thesis of Independence, their historical natures (how they emerged at particular times in response to specific exigencies of those times) makes defining rhetorical realism in one sentence challenging if not beside the point. That being said, one way we can begin to understand rhetorical realism—to understand what makes rhetoric *realist* and realism *rhetorical*— is to see it as a specific orientation toward language, knowledge, and reality that begins from the assumption that rhetorical discourse and action always emerge in relation to worlds outside or in excess of knowledge and language. Rhetorical realisms presume, as Dreyfus and Taylor suggest in this chapter's epigraph, that the "reality of contact with the real world is the inescapable fact of human (or animal) life, and can only be imagined away by erroneous philosophical argument. And it is in virtue of this contact with a common world that we always have something to say to each other, something to point to in disputes about reality."[51] When Aristotle says that rhetoric is primarily concerned with contingent topics, because no one deliberates about things that might not be other than they are,[52] he is acknowledging more than rhetoric's difference from other domains of knowledge such as science (*epistēmē*) or philosophy (*sophia*). He is also recognizing how discourse revolves around our contact with a common world—the fact that when we debate, when we attempt to persuade others on a particular course of action, we do so in reference to realities that are shared and independent of what we say or think about them. For Aristotle, a mutual commitment to mind independence is the hallmark of rhetorical interaction, as speaker and audience work together to (re)orient their worldviews in relation to shared (although not always identically perceived) objects of concern. This commitment to mind-independent reality is the hallmark of all of the versions of rhetorical realisms explored in this book. At their most elemental, rhetorical realisms operate under the assumption that objects preexist our knowledge or descriptions of them and as such hold sway in the ways we think about and craft persuasive speech and writing.[53] As such, rhetorical realisms tend to interweave epistemological and ontological concerns, at times emphasizing one over the other but always with the aim of eventually bringing knowledge and existence back into accord with one another. As James W. Hikins suggests, these two properties of realism—existence (ontology) and knowledge (epistemology)—"are inherently interconnected. For if one could not know something about the real world, one could not establish that such a world existed. And, if such a world did not exist, one could not have knowledge of it."[54]

Recent work in rhetorical theory has begun to explore some of these realist commitments, although, again, not always with an eye toward the tradition and multiple meanings of realism. The work of speculative realists such as Harman, Latour, and Jane Bennett has been especially influential in recent years, informing a diverse range of projects in rhetoric from writing pedagogy and historiography to visual analysis and theories of media and technology. As mentioned in this book's introduction, Thomas Rickert's *Ambient Rhetoric* represents one of the most substantial explorations of things in rhetoric to date. In *Ambient Rhetoric*, Rickert builds on Diane Davis's theory of "a primary affectability that emerges before symbolicity"[55] as well as Heidegger's theory of things and worldliness to argue that rhetoric is always already emplaced in the world and thus responsive to our moods and attunements to world. In Rickert's rendering, "rhetoric is a responsive way of revealing the world for others, responding to and put forth through affective, symbolic, and material means, so as to (at least potentially) reattune or otherwise transform how others inhabit the world to an extent that calls for some action."[56] Rather than rhetoric originating from the will of an autonomous human agent, Rickert proposes that rhetoric emerges through collaborations between rhetor and world through which the rhetor crafts meaning by virtue of her specific ways of attuning to the world (for a rhetor who suffers from depression, for example, the world lights up for her differently than for a person who is not so afflicted).

Rickert's *Ambient Rhetoric* finds much of its exigency in Heidegger's fundamental ontology and in recent developments in ubiquitous and pervasive computing. However, he also acknowledges that things have always had an important presence in rhetorical theory. "Rhetoric has always dealt with things," he says, "which is to say that rhetoric has not ignored the material realm."[57] Rickert hastens to add, however, that while rhetoric has embraced various versions of materialism, most notably Marx's dialectical materialism, it has often done so in order to shore up understandings of human subjectivity rather than to explore the susasiveness of matter itself.

> As a long tradition has had it, rhetoric, being one of the seven liberal arts and crucial for the formation of what we call the humanities, is most fundamentally an affair of human beings and their dealings. It is overwhelming discursive, a verbal art. So, yes, things matter, but as objects of concern *for* rhetoric or as part of the infrastructure shaping either how rhetoric is occasioned, pursued, and accomplished or, going further, how it comes into service of material conditions and infrastructures to shape human subjectivity (gender would be a particularly fraught example).[58]

For Rickert, the assumption that rhetoric is fundamentally a human art has encouraged rhetoricians to overlook other material realities including alternative conceptions of language such as Heidegger's notion that language is the "house of being." This assumption has also inhibited rhetoricians from developing fuller accounts of classical concepts such as *kairos* and *chōra* which, as Rickert shows, were much more inclusive of nonhuman actors and agencies than many contemporary versions acknowledge. Ultimately, for Rickert, "persuasion thought ambiently," that is, it terms of its emplacement in and emergence from the environs, "looks to a materialist affectability that sustains our being-in-the-world. An ambient rhetoric will have taken things at world and not just their word."[59]

With his commitments to an ontological conception of rhetoric and his numerous engagements with speculative realist thought in *Ambient Rhetoric*—not to mention his overall interest in Heidegger's notion of worldliness, which emphasizes our original weddedness to world as a condition of our being—one would expect Rickert to strike a sympathetic tone when he arrives at the subject of realism. This is not the case, however. For Rickert, the "tired debates" between realism and anti-realism "are as complicit with each as they are opposed."[60] To truly understand the entanglements of humans and nonhumans, he argues, both positions must be rejected. As the most substantial discussion of realism in recent rhetorical theory, it is worth exploring Rickert's concerns in more detail as they reveal several issues important for what follows. First, from Rickert we can see how the term realism continues to reflect the pejorative connotations that helped conflate realism's multiple meanings with "naïve realism" over the course of the last century. Second, Rickert's dismissal of realism as an option for object-oriented rhetorics indirectly serves to reinforce the argument he makes above about rhetoricians' reliance upon a material realm. While Rickert claims to reject the language and idea of realism, he commits himself to several realist ideas, most prominently R1 Independence and, to a lesser extent, R5 Passive Knower. As will be the case in all of the readings to come in this book, my intention in identifying Rickert's realist commitments is not to debunk Rickert or his notion of an ambient rhetoric. Rather, what I hope to show is that, even in one of the field's most nuanced and measured treatments of things and nonhuman agencies, we still find vestiges of rhetorical realism lurking in its margins and serving as its unstated condition of possibility.

In a section entitled "Realism or Idealism? No Thanks!" Rickert attempts to summarize the debates over realism and idealism as they appear in Richard Cherwitz's edited collection *Rhetoric and Philosophy*. I say "attempts" because, as Rickert confesses at the outset, the back-and-forth interplay in these debates proves wearisome to many readers—himself included.[61] Rickert draws heavily on James Hikins's chapter in this collection to represent the problems with realism and realist approaches to rhetoric. In that chapter, Hikins identifies two core realist theses relevant to rhetoric: 1) that "much of the world does not depend on human (or any other sentient entities) for its existence," and, 2) that "humans are capable of knowing at least some aspects of the real world *as it is in* itself."[62] For Hikins, realism is thus both an ontological and an epistemological theory.[63] "These two properties—existence and knowledge—are inherently interconnected," Hikins argues. "For if one could know something about the real world, one could not establish that such a world existed."[64] An understanding of realism is important for rhetoric in particular, he claims, because "rhetorical practice is ensconced in the pedestrian world."[65] "However esoteric the [rhetorical] theorist's view, it must adequately account for what we know about the natural world in which we all reside."[66] For Hikins, the implications of realism for rhetoric are both significant and incontrovertible. Because human beings have "the ability to know at least some aspects of the natural world in which they live" and because they possess "the ability to communicate that knowledge by use of symbol systems," rhetoric must therefore require realist commitments in order to preserve "intact the world of rhetorical praxis."[67] As Hikins suggests:

> Symbol systems have the capacity to embody both physical and non-physical dimensions of experience, based on meaning, which is in turn grounded in the ontological properties of relations. Thus human experiences, physical, mental, ethical, and aesthetic, are as much a part of the real world as are the human communicators who populate it. Confident that reality is at least in part knowledge, humans weave such knowledge, in the guise of facticity, into their efforts to persuade others, even on contingent issues where the ultimate truth is as yet unattainable. Because rhetoric is in this way anchored in reality, humans are assured at least minimally objective criteria with which to compose discourse, evaluate rhetorical praxis, and generate theory.[68]

For rhetorical action to take place, Hikins suggests that it must do so against a background of shared facts, meanings, and understandings about the world. While disagreements will inevitably arise—as Kenneth Burke argues, "division" is the *raison d'être* for rhetoric—such disputes always turn on differing interpretations of reality rather than on the existence of distinct language games or discourses as postmodern language theorists suggest. "Facticity is a *necessary* component of rhetoric," Hikins insists. "Without facts, rhetoric is either nonexistent or devolves into mere style, adornment, and artifice—'mere rhetoric' in the pejorative sense, divorced from any connection with the natural world in which humans exist."[69]

For Rickert, the problem with Hikins's realist rhetoric centers on its two core realist tenets and Hikins's "waffling" over them. When Hikins hedges his ontological and epistemological theses on realism to suggest that "much of the world" does not depend on human thought and that humans are capable of knowing "at least some aspects of the real world," Rickert argues that he not only softens the uniqueness of the realist position but also opens it up to critiques by idealists.[70] In addition, Hikins's retention of the correspondence thesis has the added effect of placing rhetoric (once again) "under the thumb of philosophy and science" where rhetoric is "notoriously susceptible to charges of wandering far from the well-ordered fields of epistemological certainty. Devalued or even denigrated will be those rhetorical acts that marshal less-secure evidence in favor of other persuasive appeals—to emotion, for instance."[71]

Rickert is not wrong to question Hikins's retention of the correspondence theory of truth. As we will see numerous times in what follows, the assumption that language enables us to access reality and represent it correctly is one of the main reasons realism today has such a bad name. And while rhetorical theory for the most part has tried to distance itself from the correspondence thesis for much of the past century, we can still find its influence in many rhetorical conceptions of language, most notably in the perspicuity movement of the seventeenth and eighteenth centuries, which I examine in more detail in Chapter 3. But it is not only the correspondence theory that gives Rickert pause. He also questions Hikins's first tenet of R1 Independence, which he sees as doubling down on a subject-object dichotomy that has proven so problematic for rhetorical theory. For Rickert, "there is no world 'out there' *fundamentally* distinct from the body and over which humans layer meaning, because there are no humans beings absolved from the world who could do such a thing. The things of the world are already integral to what we mean by human being, making human being a larger, shifting composite of engaged perception, interlocution, and activity."[72] Following Heidegger, Rickert conceives of human being as always already enmeshed in a lived environs; hence, it is impossible to "extricate ourselves from our emplacement so as to get at things from the 'outside.'"[73] As phenomenologists from Husserl to Merleau-Ponty have argued, there is no such thing as a "view from nowhere" for the simple reason that, as beings in the world, we are inextricably bound to our embodied and subjective ways of "having" a world. In Rickert's case, our "holistic entanglements" with world give the lie to the R1 thesis of realism, which he understands as reproducing oppositions between subject and object.

But is this always the case? Does R1 Independence always require us to accept the baggage of the subject-object dichotomy? Or is it possible to have mind-independence without pitting the mind against that which is "outside" of it? Interestingly enough, Rickert's ambient rhetoric offers some clues to this conundrum. For example, in his reading of the ancient Greek concept of *kairos* (often translated as "timeliness" or "opportune moment") Rickert explores some of concept's lesser-known spatial meanings. These spatial dynamics, many of which date back to earliest appearances of the word in Homer, suggest alternative ways of thinking about *kairos* and, with it, rhetorical agency. In many modern renderings of *kairos*, agency is thought to reside mostly in the human subject who possesses the ability to recognize and respond appropriately to "opportune moments." The sense of timing and decorum we find in these notions of *kairos* emboldens the speaker with the power to "master" or "seize upon" gaps or imperfections in the rhetorical situation. But *kairos* also suggests more than these normative and temporal interventions, Rickert argues. Building on Heidegger as well as Mario Untersteiner's and Bernard Miller's fascinating readings of the Sophists and Gorgias's conception of *kairos*, Rickert forwards another notion of *kairos* that disperses responsibility "throughout the situational environs"[74] rather than locating it exclusively within human subjects and agents. Thought ambiently and in terms of its ancient grounding in a strong sense of place, *kairos* for Rickert becomes a situational, and thus entirely inclusive, phenomenon that is "composed of an ensemble of contending elements (including a 'subject')."[75] This kind of *kairos* "is better understood as itself having a kind of vitality, even agency: we do not simply avail ourselves of kairotic opportunities; rather, our words and actions emerge as willed by *kairos*."[76]

The phrase "willed by kairos" is a provocative as well as a telling one for Rickert. While the aim of his reading is to shift conceptions of *kairos* beyond the subject-object dichotomy, the lengths he must go to challenge subjectivist versions of *kairos* ultimately lead Rickert to retain and at times reinforce the importance of mind-independent reality. On the surface, however, Rickert is careful to say that, in rejecting subjectivist readings of *kairos*, he is not endorsing a "deterministic" understanding of *kairos*, one that would situate agency outside the rhetor and thus determinative of what she can say at a given time and place.

> Am I arguing for a new objective determinism? Am I saying that there is no choice, that our actions and words are somehow predetermined or legislated by a mysterious, uncanny, exterior force to which we conveniently give a comforting but still obscurantist label? No, this is assuredly not what I am arguing. Indeed, everything about the Gorgian kairos suggests otherwise, pointing instead to a highly nuanced set of relations among language, environment, and people, relations that Gorgias seemed to view (to the extent that we can assert anything about Gorgias) with an affirmative, inventive eye.[77]

But even in the Gorgian sense, *kairos* retains something of an extra-human, extra-knowable reality. As Rickert explains, for Gorgias "the locus of decision, occasioned by *kairos*, is dispersed rather than seated in the subjective [...] [thus] no rational synthesis can make sense of all the contraries in circulation."[78] While we may not be determined by *kairos* in any objective sense, we are also not fully responsible for its existence. *Kairos* precedes and exceeds our knowledge and understanding of it; in realist terms, it is a set of objects or states of affairs that exists independently of us and hence does not rely upon us in any way.

Rickert's inspired example of the final scene of the film *The Usual Suspects* (1995, dir. Bryan Singer) further illustrates his unstated commitment to R1 Independence. In the film, a disabled patsy named Verbal Kint (Kevin Spacey) is arrested and questioned by police about a series of murders involving the notorious (and thus far unseen) crime lord, Keyser Soze. The film chronicles these events as a series of flashbacks based on Verbal's unfolding testimony while in police custody. It is not until the police finally release Verbal that one of the investigators realizes that the story they (and we the audience) had just heard had been entirely fabricated by Verbal, who had cleverly used fragments of names, faces, and events scattered throughout the investigator's office to weave his compelling but ultimately false testimony.

Reclaiming Rhetorical Realism 51

For Rickert, this climatic twist captures the ways we are both willed by *kairos* and called to co-invent with *kairos* in situational environs. "The film suggests the office space itself to be a coinventor. It thus demonstrates that the environment is always situating us in arrangements that simultaneously unleash some possibilities and forecloses on others. In other worlds, the film suggests that the ambient environs generate various affordances that invent us in kairotic moments."[79] The story Verbal weaves, in other words, could only have emerged from his locatedness in this specific place at this specific time. Who, then, is responsible for the tale that emerges? Rickert argues that it is both Verbal and the office. Subjects such as Verbal "exist not as separate from world but as a complex folding within other complex foldings of material and discursive force."[80] The choice of metaphors here is important, as "foldings" suggest the existence of an inside and an outside or a self and other. While it may be true that subjects such as Verbal are themselves invented at the same time they are inventing with *kairos*, the film also suggests that their abilities to do so emerge in conjunction with realities outside of—or at least separate from—their own knowledge or understanding. Rickert concedes as much in his turn to theories of distributed cognition and the emerging consensus among scientists that the brain is plastic and capable of adapting to new environments and technologies. And yet, while the actions and narratives that emerge from these environs may be "inclusive" of both human beings and the material situation,[81] the engine driving this kind of invention is predicated upon the existence of things whose realities precede and exceed the existence of other things. *The Usual Suspects* is certainly a fantastic illustration of one reading of the Gorgian *kairos*. At the same time, however, it can also be read as dramatizing how rhetorical invention emerges *in response to realities that prefigure and lie beyond our own being and understanding*. While entanglements between us and things (or things and things) permeate and define everyday reality, the film suggests that these entanglements presuppose and are indeed conditioned by a more originary differentiation between inside and outside, self and other.

Rickert is understandably wary of distinctions that appear to harken back to humanism and its subject-object dichotomy. Such oppositions, after all, are not only anathema to Heidegger's more holistic sense of world; they also hinder our abilities to respond effectively to crises involving more than just human agencies and interests. With respect to global warming and issues of sustainability, Rickert rightly finds problematic arguments presuming a fundamental separation between humans and nature. As Rickert recognizes, even so-called "progressive" responses to climate change succumb to this tendency to separate nature from human beings. When we are urged to "go green," for example—to reuse, reduce, and recycle—there is an assumption that doing so is an "individual choice," one "played out against an objective world."[82] These progressive strategies assume that by changing our behaviors we can somehow affect change in the environment while still remaining separate from it, thus disallowing more fundamental insights "into an a priori enmeshment of person and world."[83] For sufficiency and sustainability to take hold, for us to cultivate more ethical relations with world, Rickert claims we will need to see them as "rendered from an ambient attunement rather than a relation of exteriority" that reinforces oppositions between humans and nature.[84]

Again, Rickert is right to worry about divides that quarantine humans and nonhumans into separate and opposing ontological zones. But challenging the subject-object divide does not always require us to do away with the idea of "exteriority" altogether. Emmanuel Levinas, for example, offers another sense of exteriority in his ethics of the Other that may prove useful in considering the kinds of rhetorical entanglements Rickert and I have in mind (I deal with Levinas in more detail in Chapter 5). For Levinas, exteriority is not simply what stands in opposition to "interiority." Rather, it is what precedes and thus makes possible interiority (subjectivity) itself. For Levinas, exteriority is the condition of possibility for face-to-face relations insofar as "Being is exteriority."[85] As Levinas goes on to say, "exteriority is not yet maintained if we affirm a subject insoluble into objectivity, and to which exteriority would be opposed."[86] Exteriority manifests in what Levinas calls the "curvature of the intersubjective space."[87] Whereas "opposition" suggests two interiorities in conflict or at odds with one another, "curvature" (much like Rickert's "folding" metaphor above) suggests a twisting or coiling over of interiority and exteriority such that there is a relation between them without perfect coincidence. In this sense, the exteriority of being constitutes that which exceeds or is in surplus of my being, but which avails itself to me in the face of the Other. For Levinas, it is the exteriority of being that opens in the face of the Other. This exteriority "refuses thematization positively because it is produced in a being who expresses himself."[88] Simply put, for Levinas exteriority is that which constitutes the Other as such, as one whose alterity exceeds my grasp and understanding and yet which summons me forth into an irreducible relation between myself and the Other. In the face of the Other, Levinas says we find the "gleam of exteriority"[89] that is not the appearance of an opposition but the opening to "the experience of something absolutely foreign, a *pure* 'knowledge' or 'experience,' a *traumatism of astonishment.*"[90]

This opening up of alterity and astonishment Levinas sees in exteriority adds an important layer to Rickert's turn to ethics and sufficiency at the close of *Ambient Rhetoric*. As Rickert suggests, when we learn to "dwell ambiently," we understand ourselves not as solitary individuals waging existence against other solitary individuals but as beings whose existence is inextricably bound to other things and beings in the world. Such attunements to world, as I argue in the last chapter of this book, need not preclude the conceptions of otherness and alterity we find in Levinas and other ethical systems. But they do ask us to rethink ideas like exteriority—not so that we can return to an outmoded version of rhetorical humanism, but so that we can devise novel ways to incorporate more sophisticated understandings of exteriority into the growing sense that our being-there is increasingly defined by its relations with other things and beings in the world. If exteriority constitutes a form of R1 Independence, as I argue in this book, then rhetorical realisms have as much to say about ethics as they do our abilities to know realities outside of the mind.

Reading Things Crookedly: Historiography and Rhetorical Realism

As I hope is clear by this point, what I am after in locating realist commitments in rhetorical theory is not the rehabilitation of naïve realism in rhetoric but rather an attunement, if I may borrow this term from Rickert, to beliefs about the world that seem to me to be inextricably entwined with the study and practice of rhetoric as we presently understand it. In identifying and thinking with these commitments, I most certainly am not looking to play a theoretical game of "gotcha." Such a game might be useful, but it is not the one I am interesting in playing here. I am much more interested in exploring how realist commitments in their various guises have informed the development of rhetorical theory at several key moments in its history. My engagements with Rickert above reflect this interest. Although Rickert is dismissive of realism as a position, his ambient rhetoric nevertheless reveals—and indeed depends upon, I would argue—specific realist commitments, most notably the belief in mind-independent reality and, to a lesser extent, the passivity of the subject.[91] In identifying these commitments, I am not suggesting that Rickert's project is flawed or misguided in its conceptualization of rhetoric. Like all of the texts explored here, Rickert's book emerged within a specific historical moment, in this case one where questions about nonhuman and posthuman rhetorics were (and continue to be) pressing issues for rhetorical theory and the humanities at large. But this is not the only version of rhetorical realism available to us. As I argue throughout the book, each epoch in rhetorical history establishes its own relationship to realist ideas and ultimately formulates its understandings of rhetoric in reference to these ideas. Rickert's work is no different in this regard, even if it is the most recent account of things and nonhuman agencies in the field. My goal, then, is not critique but recovery. I want to reclaim rhetorical realisms from the dustbin of history because, at this moment when so much attention is being paid to things and nonhumans in rhetoric and the humanities, it is worthwhile to consider how commitments to exteriority and otherness have long informed understandings of rhetoric from antiquity to the present. I hope to persuade you over the course of these pages that realist commitments are nothing new for rhetoric, and that as long as rhetoric has been tied to the practical affairs of everyday life it has always insisted upon connections between language and world, self and other, word and thing.

Exploring these commitments will require us at times to read beyond the scope of the texts themselves, to in effect *speculate* about the roles realist commitments may have played in a given rhetorician's account. I should say at the outset that my intention is not to recuperate the "truth" of rhetorical history, as if such a thing ever existed in the first place. Instead, it is to read rhetorical history with one eye toward what rhetoricians say about reality and things and another toward what is left unsaid but is nonetheless important to how these rhetoricians come to understand rhetoric. In many cases, my readings will shift from analyses of primary texts toward discussions of their affinities with various theories of realism. The readings that follow, then, are perhaps best read as speculative in (I hope) the best sense: speculative in that they speculate about commitments that are not always present in what the author says, but are nevertheless lurking in the margins of their texts; but speculative, also, in their recognition that no encounter every fully exhausts the meaning of a text or idea. As in Harman's theory of objects, the artifacts of rhetorical history remain inevitably withdrawn from us in one way or another; what remains are the vicarious relations we continue to have with them, the partial connections and associations we cultivate as we attempt to make repeated sense of this thing we call "rhetoric."

If not a linear or "objective" history of realist commitments in rhetoric, then what? One avenue open to us goes through postmodern conceptions of historiography, which understand history as a discursive, and thus partial, construct. This approach to history has paid tremendous dividends in rhetoric over the past several decades, which have seen rhetoricians revisiting a wide range of rhetorical theories and traditions from the Sophists to non-Western rhetorical traditions. In this book's introduction, we saw how historiography, far from obligating us to compose grand narratives of the past, can also benefit from devising different reading styles attuned to the marginal, absent, and forgotten in rhetorical history. Hans Kellner characterizes such approaches as "getting the story crooked," which is to say reorienting our assumptions about the past such that History in the process becomes a little less inevitable. Such approaches to rhetorical history have been enormously valuable for feminist scholars in particular who have had to confront not only the problem of canonization (which has tended to privilege male orators and theorists) but the exclusion—indeed, the literal silence and silencing—of women throughout much of rhetoric's history in the West. Cheryl Glenn among others comments on the challenges feminist historiographers face in attempting to "regender" the rhetorical tradition given that so many women orators have been relegated to the shadows of rhetorical history. Recovering these voices requires more than tradition textual or even archival research methods. Along with these important tools, Glenn argues that feminist historiographers must work to "restory" rhetorical history itself, a process that "entails our rethinking texts, approaches, narrative—and history itself."[92] "Through angular lenses, we catch fragmentary glimpses of the previously unconsidered 'irregularities' that had been smoothed over by the flat surface of received knowledge," Glenn writes.[93] In the case of Aspasia of Miletus, who is mentioned by several classical thinkers including Plutarch and Plato but for whom we have no extant writings of her own, "fragmentary glimpses" are all the historian has to go on. And these glimpses are all the more limited given the fact that Aspasia's considerable contributions to rhetoric "have been directed through a powerful gendered lens."[94] With Kellner, Glenn argues that in order to bring figures such as Aspasia to light, "We must risk [...] getting the story crooked. We must look crookedly, a bit out of focus, into the various strands of meaning in a text in such a way as to make the categories, trends, and reliable identities of history a little less inevitable, less familiar. In short, we need to see what is familiar in a different way, in many different ways, as well as to see beyond the familiar to the unfamiliar, to the unseen."[95]

My methodology builds on these efforts, although it finds more of its inspiration in one of today's most vocal critics of postmodernism, Bruno Latour. Modeled after Latour's historical investigations of scientific artifacts and knowledge, the method of historiography I develop here does not presume a modern understanding of time that "passes as if it were really abolishing the past behind it."[96] Instead, it approaches the history of rhetoric as a series of nonlinear, "counter-revolutionary" practices that have collected and sorted actors irrespective of the modern tendency to divide the world up categorically between nature and culture, human and nonhuman, subject and object, and so on. Following Latour's lead, I am most interested in exploring other methods of accounting for nonhumans *from within the structures of rhetoric's history itself*.

According to Latour, the modern conception of time is characterized by a series of ruptures and revolutions occurring within an otherwise progressive temporal trajectory. This view of history presupposes a movement away from "primitive" understandings of the world, which often confuse what is natural with what is cultural, toward more "mature" worldviews in which nature and culture finally become distinguishable from one another. "The adjective 'modern' designates a new regime, an acceleration, a rupture, a revolution in time," Latour says.[97] This new historical regime makes possible what he calls "the Modern Constitution," a paradoxical logic that enables moderns to distribute power selectively, but no less definitively, among two distinct ontological zones: Nature and Society. The ability to divide the world in this way empowers moderns to mobilize Nature and Society in whatever ways they see fit, even if the results are contradictory. Thus, Latour shows, moderns can argue that "Nature is transcendent and surpasses us infinitely" and Society is "our free construction" while at the same time claiming that Nature is "our artificial construction in the laboratory" and Society "is transcendent."[98] As long as this "work of purification" remains distinct from the "work of mediation" that produces hybrids (quasi-objects that are neither fully social nor fully natural but some mixture thereof), moderns can go on believing they are unique because of their abilities to keep Nature and Society separate and at arm's length.

Latour's thesis in *We Have Never Been Modern* and in many of the works that follow is that this work of purification is no longer sufficient to hide the hybrids produced by the very Constitution that denies their existence.

As a result of global environmental, political, scientific, and economic crises, which force us to confront and deal with myriad hybrid actors that are not easily reducible to the modern axes of Nature/Society and Transcendence/Immanence, the previously distinct works of purification and mediation are becoming increasingly confused. As soon as this happens, as soon as "we direct our attention simultaneously to the work of purification and the work of hybridization, we immediately stop being wholly modern."[99] As a consequence, our past and future begin to change as well: "We become retrospectively aware that the two sets of practices have always already been at work in the historical period that is ending."[100] Once the proliferation of hybrids becomes visible to us, in other words, and once we begin to see in detail how moderns have historically managed to produce hybrids all the while eliminating them from their Constitution, we find, in Latour famous thesis, that *we have never been modern*. No one, in fact, has ever been modern. "Modernity has never begun. There has never been a modern world."[101]

Beginning with the Enlightenment view of scientific progress, moderns imagine science as a story of steady progression that quietly "suppresses the ins and outs of Nature's objects and presents their sudden emergence as if it were miraculous."[102] In his analysis of Robert Boyle's air pump, for example, Latour shows how this exemplar of modern scientific thought relied upon and produced a number of hybrids, from scientists who constructed knowledge in the laboratory but who also "declare[d] that they themselves are not speaking; rather, facts speak for themselves" to Nature itself which became both constructed and transcendent as a result of Boyle's experiments.[103] If the pump constitutes a revolution, then, it is a revolution in our ability to "mobilize Nature, objectify the social, and feel the spiritual presence of God, even while firmly maintaining that Nature escapes us, that Society is our own work, and that God no longer intervenes."[104] Such revolutionary conceptions of history, however, have the tendency to render "the work of mediation that assembles hybrids invisible, unthinkable, unrepresentable."[105] As Latour suggests of Boyle's invention, its apparent "cohesiveness" "is not sufficient to allow a clean break with the past. A whole supplementary work of sorting out, cleaning up and dividing up is required to obtain the impression of a modernization that goes in step with time."[106] Revolutions, those dramatic ruptures within the progressive march of historical time, are thus the "rather neat" solution "moderns have imagined to explain the emergence of the hybrids that their Constitution simultaneously forbids and allows, and in order to avoid another monster: the notion that things themselves have a history."[107]

The history of rhetoric has its own celebrated revolutions, of course, from the flourishing of rhetoric in antiquity, which brought into being more complex ways of producing and theorizing language, to the modern revival of the classical canon of invention following its separation from rhetoric in the wake of Ramist and Enlightenment emphases on logic and perspicuity. Indeed, as anyone who has taught a "history of rhetoric" seminar knows, it is quite easy—and quite tempting, I must confess—to tell rhetoric's history as a story of progress, even if progress has meant, at times, we have had to go two steps backward into order to eventually (and inevitably) push ahead into maturity. But as Latour would argue, this is a particularly modern fable rooted in an asymmetry not only between Nature and Society but between past and future as well: "*The past was the confusion of things and men; the future is what will no longer confuse them.*"[108]

Ironically, the modern historical progression from confusion/immaturity to enlightenment has not constrained our ability to imagine the possibility of nonhuman rhetorics. If anything, this notion of history actually makes the case for the inclusion of nonhumans that much easier, since all the modern rhetorical theorist needs to demonstrate is that the prospect of nonhuman rhetorics constitutes a revolutionary moment in rhetoric's history that will, if properly understood, move the field further along its current path. In this vein, nonhumans simply constitute the next epoch in rhetoric's long story of progress, one that promises to destroy the past behind while at the same charting a future in which we no longer distinguish the symbolic realm of human affairs from the agencies of nonhuman others. While the ends of such efforts may be laudable, the means by which we arrive at this conclusion leaves intact the very logics that were under suspicion in the first place. Thus, Latour's preferred way of challenging the Modern Constitution and its conception of history is not to argue for one more revolution, but to undertake the more complicated task of reading historical events differently. "We have never moved either forward or backward," he concludes. All we have ever done is sort elements and actors belonging to different times. Thus, Latour says, "*It is the sorting [of these actors] that makes the times, not the times that make the sorting.*"[109] In contrast to Kant's Copernican Revolution, which perfected the model "for modernizing explanations" by making the object revolve around and conform to the subject, Latour calls for "a Copernican counter-revolution" in which "[t]he explanations we seek will indeed obtain Nature and Society, but only as a final outcome, not as a beginning."[110] Nature and Society do revolve, but not around one another. Instead, they revolve around "the collective out of which people and things are generated."[111] The historian's task, therefore, becomes one of sorting and collecting rather than breaking and restarting. As Krista Ratcliffe eloquently puts it in *Rhetorical Listening*, historiography in such a key "demonstrates how we may eavesdrop on history, circling through time in order to expose the circling of time."[112] When we eavesdrop in this way, Ratcliffe says, "we not only identify some of our identifications [with/in the cultural structure] but also find ourselves accountable to ourselves and to others not for the *then* but for the *then-that-is-now*."[113]

Building on Latour, Glenn, and Ratcliffe, we can understand the history of rhetoric not as an irreversible advance toward progress, marked by a handful of crises and revolutions, but a series of events in which beings get identified, sorted, and collected. From this perspective, to study histories and theories of rhetoric means studying the ways rhetoricians have constituted, managed, and negotiated distinctions between humans and nonhumans. When we learn to approach events in these terms, we find that the history of rhetoric is no longer simply the history of human speakers and writers. It is the history of natural and artificial things as well.[114] In my view, rhetorical theory today needs to find ways to accommodate and think critically about the implications the nonhuman turn poses for rhetoric. But in so doing, we do not have to jettison all that has come before. As it turns out, rhetorical theory has a very long history of thinking about rhetoric's place in a wider world of things. The challenge today, then, is not to rethink rhetoric from the ground up, but to reclaim those moments in rhetoric's history where theorists and practitioners realized rhetoric as a form of action grounded in our attunements to world and others in the world.

Notes

1. Christiane L. Joost-Gaudier, *Raphael's Stanza della Segnatura: Meaning and Invention* (Cambridge: Cambridge University Press, 2002).
2. Friedrich Nietzsche, "On Truth and Lies in a Nonmoral Sense," in *The Nietzsche Reader*, eds. Keith Ansell Pearson and Duncan Large (Malden: Blackwell, 2006), 117.
3. Alexander Miller, "Realism," *Stanford Encyclopedia of Philosophy*, last modified October 2, 2014, accessed June 16, 2016, http://plato.stanford.edu/entries/realism/.
4. Indeed, if anything, Raphael's conception of classical philosophy as driven by competing visions of reality—one idealist (in the sense of Plato's *eidos*) and the other realist—has had the more lasting influence, helping frame philosophy's disciplinary history as one defined by "questions about the ultimate reality of things," which as Stuart Brock and Edwin Mares note, are questions of the "upmost importance and deeper significance" for philosophy. While the terms themselves are more recent, disputes over the merits of realism and idealism (or anti-realism, as it is also known) have accompanied philosophical inquiry for centuries and have influenced work in both the continental and analytical traditions of modern philosophy. This long legacy makes it possible, although not necessarily easy, to read the history of philosophy, as some of the works referenced below suggest, as an ongoing debate between various understandings of realism and anti-realism.; Stuart Brock and Edwin Mares, *Realism and Anti-Realism* (Montreal and Kingston: McGill-Queen's University Press, 2007), 1.
5. Brock and Mares, 1.
6. The term "pedestrian" comes from James W. Hikins and his attempts to incorporate realist philosophies into contemporary rhetorical theory. As I suggest later, Hikins's work is pioneering in its attempt to bring rhetoric more in tune with theses of realism. However, his commitments to certain realist theses, most prominently the correspondence theory of truth, place him at odds with more recent versions of ontological or speculative realism.
7. Aristotle, *Nicomachean Ethics*, trans. David Ross (New York: Oxford University Press, 1998), 1095b2.
8. Ibid., 1094b19-23.

Reclaiming Rhetorical Realism   59

9. In following Raphael's lead, I do not mean to endorse the view that Plato's position was ultimately anti-rhetorical. In many respects, this remains the accepted interpretation of Plato in rhetorical studies. However, as James L. Kastely has argued convincingly in several places, Plato's dialogues can also be read as developing a conception of rhetoric that is more ammenable to Socratic dialectic. In effect, Kastely reminds rhetoricans to read Plato's dialogues *rhetorically* rather than as treatises on various philosophical themes. When read in this way, dialogues such as the *Gorgias* and *Republic* (both notoriously critical of rhetoric) acquire new relevance for rhetoric as they each attempt to teach "those who will not become philosophers what philosophy still has to offer them" (*Republic*, 134). Kastely's careful readings of Plato further support my position that Plato, far from being rhetoric's most famous detractor, actually establishes an alternative view of rhetoric in reference to already existing material realities such as audiences willing to be won over by flattery rather than reasoned argument. As we will see, this is true for many who have examined rhetoric at some length—including those, like Plato, who seem to dismiss rhetoric out of hand while at the same time managing to integrate rhetoric more fully into their particular conceptions of reality (in particular, see Chapter 3 on Wilkins and Chapter 4 on Kant). See, James L. Kastely, "In Defense of Plato's Gorgias," PMLA 106, no. 1 (1991): 96–109, and, James K. Kastely, *The Rhetoric of Plato's Republic: Democracy and the Philosophical Problem of Persuasion* (Chicago: University of Chicago Press, 2015).

10. For clarity's sake, I will henceforth use "speculative realism" to name work over the past decade that considers the natures of nonhuman agents and agencies. While there are many differences that cut across work in object-oriented ontology, new materialism, and thing theory (to name just three of the most influential schools of thought), "speculative realism" has the advantage of drawing otherwise disparate perspectives together under a single banner while also emphasizing their shared interest in establishing new versions of realism.

11. Kant, Immanuel, *Critique of Pure Reason* (Unified Edition), trans. Werner S. Pluhar (Indianapolis: Hackett, 1996), Bxvi.

12. Lee Braver, "A Brief History of Continental Realism," *Continental Philosophy Review* 45, no. 2 (2012): 262–263.

13. Ibid., 266.

14. Daniel J. Royer, "New Challenges to Epistemic Rhetoric," *Rhetoric Review* 9, no. 2 (1991): 284.

15. Ibid., 285.

16. Sean Sayers, *Reality and Reason: Dialectic and the Theory of Knowledge* (New York: Blackwell, 1985), 22, quoted in Daniel J. Royer, "New Challenges to Epistemic Rhetoric," *Rhetoric Review* 9, no. 2 (1991): 285.

17. Royer, 289.

18. Ibid.

19. Ibid.

20. Ibid., 294.

21. Ibid., 295.

22. Brock and Mare, 11. In his "Realism" entry for the *Stanford Encyclopedia of Philosophy*, Alexander Miller makes a similar point about realism: "Although it would be possible to accept (or reject) realism across the board, it is more common for philosophers to be selectively realist or non-realist about various topics: thus it would be perfectly possible to be a realist about the everyday

60 *Reclaiming Rhetorical Realism*

world of macroscopic objects and their properties, but a non-realist about aesthetic and moral value."

23. See, James Berlin, "Rhetoric and Ideology in the Writing Class," *College English* 50, no. 5 (1988): 477–494., and, James Berlin, *Rhetoric and Reality: Writing Instruction in American Colleges, 1900–1985* (Carbondale: Southern Illinois University Press, 1987).
24. In *Retrieving Realism*, Hubert Dreyfus and Charles Taylor note that, despite its unfashionability among philosophers today, naïve realism has a long and distinguished history in the discipline, going back at least as far as Plato and Aristotle. Of course, they concede, naïve realism "appears terribly unsophisticated and pre-reflective to those who are into the mediational picture. But some rather sophisticated views in our philosophical tradition were contact theories."; Hubert Dreyfus and Charles Taylor, *Retrieving Realism* (Cambridge: Harvard University Press, 2015), 17.
25. Hilary Putnam, *Reason, Truth, and History* (Cambridge: Cambridge University Press, 1981), 49, quoted in Lee Braver, *A Thing of This World: A History of Continental Anti-Realism* (Evanston: Northwestern University Press, 2007), 14.
26. Braver, *A Thing of This World*, 15.
27. Ibid.
28. Ibid., 17.
29. Ibid., 19.
30. Ibid.
31. Ibid., 21.
32. Ibid.
33. Ibid., 22.
34. Ibid., 49.
35. Ibid., 56.
36. Graham Harman adds an additional thesis to Braver's list that encompasses some of his own efforts to recuperate realism in the wake of poststructuralism and postmodernism. Harman calls this thesis R7 Equal Relations. According to Harman, R7 maintains that within realism relations must be on equal footing, meaning that, a la Whitehead, the human-world correlate is just one possible relation among many. See Graham Harman, "What are Speculative Realism and Object-Oriented Ontology?" (presentation, Hello, Everything: Speculative Realism and Object-Oriented Ontology, Los Angeles, CA, December 1, 2010). http://www.ustream.tv/recorded/11193628.
37. Dreyfus and Taylor, 6.
38. Richard Rorty, *Contingency, Irony, and Solidarity* (Cambridge: Cambridge University Press, 1989), 4–5.
39. Joseph Margolis, *Pragmatism Without Foundations: Reconciling Realism and Relativism*, 2nd Edition (New York: Continuum, 2007), xiii.
40. Peter Gratton, *Speculative Realism: Problems and Prospects* (London: Bloomsbury, 2014), 4.
41. Quentin Meillassoux, *After Finitude: An Essay on the Necessity of Contingency*, trans. Ray Brassier (London: Continuum, 2008), 5.
42. Ibid.
43. Levi R. Bryant, *The Democracy of Objects* (Ann Arbor: Open Humanities Press, 2011), 18.
44. Graham Harman, "The Well-Wrought Broken Hammer: Object-Oriented Literary Criticism," *New Literary History* 43 (2012): 196.

45. Ibid., 184.
46. Ibid.
47. Gratton, 87.
48. Graham Harman, *The Quadruple Object* (Alresford: Zero Books, 2011), 38.
49. I address Rickert's work on ambience below. Interest in ecology and complexity theory has a surprisingly long history in rhetoric and composition. See, Marilyn M. Cooper, "The Ecology of Writing," *College English* 48, no.4 (1986): 364–375; Margaret A. Syverson, *The Wealth of Reality: An Ecology of Composition* (Carbondale: Southern Illinois University Press, 1999); Jenny Edbauer, "Unframing Models of Public Distribution: From Rhetorical Situation to Rhetorical Ecologies," *Rhetoric Society Quarterly* 35, no. 4 (2005): 5–24; and, Byron Hawk, *A Counter-History of Composition: Toward Methodologies of Complexity* (Pittsburgh: University of Pittsburgh Press, 2007).
50. According to the Oxford English Dictionary, the word *realism* does not appear in philosophical contexts until the late eighteenth century, with Kant providing one of the first uses, and it is not until the mid-nineteenth and early twentieth centuries that realism begins to gain traction as a philosophical position. Realism's first appearance in rhetoric is harder to measure because of rhetoric's numerous convergences with philosophy over the years. That being said, we can identify the moment when realism first becomes an explicit topic of debate for rhetoric. In the 1960s and 70s, Robert Scott, Richard Cherwitz, James Hikins, Barry Brummett, and others explored some implications of philosophical realism for rhetorical theory in the course of their debates about rhetoric's status as an epistemic art. For more on these debates, see Chapter 4.
51. Dreyfus and Taylor, 107.
52. Aristotle, *On Rhetoric*, 1357a and 1359a.
53. Robert Wess offers a similar take on rhetorical realism in terms of Kenneth Burke's ontological and literal understandings of language ("Whenever we call something a *metaphor*, we mean it *literally*," Burke is said to have argued in a debate with Bernard L. Brock). For Wess, Burke's rhetorical realism "combines theorizing the constructive powers of language with the recognition of language as a reality in its own right, a reality that is not itself a construct, so cannot be understood in constructive terms." Wess's account of Burke and Richard McKeon is a fascinating example of how we can read realist commitments against the grain of grand narratives about rhetoric and philosophy, especially those that retrospectively define the "linguistic turn" as only concerned with constructivist views and language and not the literalness of language.; Robert Wess, "A McKeonist Understanding of Kenneth Burke's Rhetorical Realism in Particular and Constructivism in General, " *KB Journal* 11, no.1 (2015), accessed June 16, 2016, http://kbjournal.org/wess_mckeon.
54. James W. Hikins, "Realism and Its Implications for Rhetorical Theory," in *Rhetoric and Philosophy*, ed. Richard A. Cherwitz (New York: Routledge, 1990), 22.
55. Thomas Rickert, *Ambient Rhetoric: The Attunements of Rhetorical Being* (Pittsburgh: University of Pittsburgh Press, 2013), 15.
56. Ibid., 162.
57. Ibid., 191.
58. Ibid., 191–192.
59. Ibid., 162.
60. Ibid., 193.
61. Rickert, *Ambient Rhetoric*, 193.

62. Hikins, 22. See also, Rickert, *Ambient Rhetoric*, 194.
63. Hikins, 22.
64. Ibid., 22.
65. Ibid., 24.
66. Ibid.
67. Ibid., 68.
68. Ibid., 67.
69. Ibid., 49.
70. Rickert, *Ambient Rhetoric*, 195.
71. Ibid.
72. Ibid., 198–199.
73. Ibid., 199.
74. Ibid., 82.
75. Ibid., 87.
76. Ibid., 91.
77. Ibid.
78. Ibid., 87.
79. Ibid., 96.
80. Ibid., 97.
81. Ibid., 93.
82. Ibid., 251.
83. Ibid., 252.
84. Ibid., 253.
85. Emmanuel Levinas, *Totality and Infinity*, trans. Alphonso Lingis (Pittsburgh: Duquesne University Press, 1969), 290.
86. Ibid.
87. Ibid., 291.
88. Ibid., 296.
89. Ibid., 24.
90. Ibid., 73.
91. When Rickert suggests that subject such as Verbal are "willed by kairos" and "invented in kairotic moments," he opens the door to passive subjectivity, albeit one of "inventive passivity before the ambient environs in which he is immersed" (97) rather than the pure passivity we see in many forms of the R5 Passive Knower thesis.
92. Cheryl Glenn, *Rhetoric Retold: Regendering the Tradition from Antiquity Through the Renaissance* (Carbondale: Southern Illinois University Press, 1997), 3.
93. Ibid., 5.
94. Ibid., 39.
95. Ibid., 7.
96. Bruno Latour, *We Have Never Been Modern*, trans. Catherine Porter (Cambridge: Harvard University Press, 1993), 68.
97. Ibid., 10.
98. Ibid., 32.
99. Ibid., 11.
100. Ibid.
101. Ibid., 47.
102. Ibid., 70.

103. Ibid., 29.
104. Ibid., 34.
105. Ibid.
106. Ibid., 72.
107. Ibid., 70.
108. Ibid., 71. James Berlin offers a similar critique of rhetorical history, noting how "Our 'official' histories of rhetoric—the formulations of George Kennedy (1980a) and Edward P.J. Corbett (1990) and Brian Vickers (1990) and Wilbur Samuel Howell (1971)—for example, depict rhetorical historical trajectory as a march of ideas, ideas characterized as unified, coherent, and rational."; James Berlin, "Revisionary Histories of Rhetoric: Politics, Power, and Plurality," in *Writing Histories of Rhetoric*, ed. Victor J. Vitanza (Carbondale: Southern Illinois University Press, 1994), 112. In *Rereading the Sophists*, Susan Jarratt likewise asserts that the practice of what she calls "sophistic historiography" would entail "the denial of progressive continuity: a conscious attempt to disrupt the metaphor of a complete and full chain of events with a *telos* in the revival of rhetoric in the twentieth century"; Susan C. Jarratt, *Rereading the Sophists: Classical Rhetoric Refigured* (Carbondale: Southern Illinois University Press, 1991), 12.
109. Latour, *We Have Never Been Modern*, 76.
110. Ibid., 79.
111. Ibid.
112. Krista Ratcliffe, *Rhetorical Listening: Identification, Gender, Whiteness* (Carbondale: Southern Illinois University Press, 2005), 107–108.
113. Ibid., 111.
114. Latour, *We Have Never Been Modern*, 82.

Bibliography

Aristotle. *Nicomachean Ethics*. Translated by David Ross. New York: Oxford University Press, 1998.

———. *On Rhetoric: A Theory of Civic Discourse*. Translated by George A. Kennedy. New York: Oxford University Press, 1991.

Berlin, James. "Revisionary Histories of Rhetoric: Politics, Power, and Plurality." In *Writing Histories of Rhetoric*, edited by Victor J. Vitanza, 112–127. Carbondale: Southern Illinois University Press, 1994.

———. "Rhetoric and Ideology in the Writing Class." *College English* 50, no. 5 (1988): 477–494.

———. *Rhetoric and Reality: Writing Instruction in American Colleges, 1900–1985*. Carbondale: Southern Illinois University Press, 1987.

Braver, Lee. "A Brief History of Continental Realism." *Continental Philosophy Review* 45, no. 2 (2012): 261–289.

———. *A Thing of This World: A History of Continental Anti-Realism*. Evanston: Northwestern University Press, 2007.

Brock, Stuart and Edwin Mares. *Realism and Anti-Realism*. Montreal and Kingston: McGill-Queen's University Press, 2007.

Bryant, Levi R. *The Democracy of Objects*. Ann Arbor: Open Humanities Press, 2011.

Cooper, Marilyn M. "The Ecology of Writing." *College English* 48, no.4 (1986): 364–375.

Dreyfus, Hubert, and Charles Taylor. *Retrieving Realism*. Cambridge: Harvard University Press, 2015.
Edbauer, Jenny. "Unframing Models of Public Distribution: From Rhetorical Situation to Rhetorical Ecologies." *Rhetoric Society Quarterly* 35, no. 4 (2005): 5–24.
Glenn, Cheryl. *Rhetoric Retold: Regendering the Tradition from Antiquity Through the Renaissance*. Carbondale: Southern Illinois University Press, 1997.
Gratton, Peter. *Speculative Realism: Problems and Prospects*. London: Bloomsbury, 2014.
Harman, Graham. *The Quadruple Object*. Alresford: Zero Books, 2011.
———. "The Well-Wrought Broken Hammer: Object-Oriented Literary Criticism." *New Literary History* 43 (2012): 183–203.
———. "What are Speculative Realism and Object-Oriented Ontology?" Presentation at Hello, Everything: Speculative Realism and Object-Oriented Ontology, Los Angeles, CA, December 1, 2010. Accessed June 16, 2016. http://www.ustream.tv/recorded/11193628.
Hawk, Byron. *A Counter-History of Composition: Toward Methodologies of Complexity*. Pittsburgh: University of Pittsburgh Press, 2007.
Hikins, James W. "Realism and Its Implications for Rhetorical Theory." In *Rhetoric and Philosophy*, edited by Richard A. Cherwitz, 21–77. New York: Routledge, 1990.
Jarratt, Susan C. *Rereading the Sophists: Classical Rhetoric Refigured*. Carbondale: Southern Illinois University Press, 1991.
Joost-Gaudier, Christiane L. *Raphael's Stanza della Segnatura: Meaning and Invention*. Cambridge: Cambridge University Press, 2002.
Kant, Immanuel. *Critique of Pure Reason* (Unified Edition). Translated by Werner S. Pluhar. Indianapolis: Hackett, 1996.
Kastely, James L. "In Defense of Plato's *Gorgias*." *PMLA* 106, no. 1 (1991): 96–109.
———. *The Rhetoric of Plato's Republic: Democracy and the Philosophical Problem of Persuasion*. Chicago: University of Chicago Press, 2015.
Latour, Bruno. *We Have Never Been Modern*. Translated by Catherine Porter. Cambridge: Harvard University Press, 1993.
Levinas, Emmanuel. *Totality and Infinity*. Translated by Alphonso Lingis. Pittsburgh: Duquesne University Press, 1969.
Margolis, Joseph. *Pragmatism Without Foundations: Reconciling Realism and Relativism*, 2nd Edition. New York: Continuum, 2007.
Meillassoux, Quentin. *After Finitude: An Essay on the Necessity of Contingency*. Translated by Ray Brassier. London: Continuum, 2008.
Miller, Alexander. "Realism." *Stanford Encyclopedia of Philosophy*. Last modified October 2, 2014. Accessed June 16, 2016. http://plato.stanford.edu/entries/realism/.
Nietzsche, Friedrich. "On Truth and Lies in a Nonmoral Sense." In *The Nietzsche Reader*, edited by Keith Ansell Pearson and Duncan Large, 115–123. Malden: Blackwell, 2006.
Putnam, Hilary. *The Many Faces of Realism: The Paul Carus Lectures*. La Salle, IL: Open Court, 1987. Print.
Ratcliffe, Krista. *Rhetorical Listening: Identification, Gender, Whiteness*. Carbondale: Southern Illinois University Press, 2005.
Rickert, Thomas. *Ambient Rhetoric: The Attunements of Rhetorical Being*. Pittsburgh: University of Pittsburgh Press, 2013.

Rorty, Richard. *Contingency, Irony, and Solidarity*. Cambridge: Cambridge University Press, 1989.
Royer, Daniel J. "New Challenges to Epistemic Rhetoric." *Rhetoric Review* 9, no. 2 (1991): 282–297.
Syverson, Margaret A. *The Wealth of Reality: An Ecology of Composition*. Carbondale: Southern Illinois University Press, 1999.
Wess, Robert. "A McKeonist Understanding of Kenneth Burke's Rhetorical Realism in Particular and Constructivism in General." *KB Journal* 11, no.1 (2015). Accessed June 16, 2016. http://kbjournal.org/wess_mckeon.

2 Aristotle's Rhetorical Realism
Technē, *Phusis*, and *Logos*

The central claim of this book is that realist ideas are nothing new for rhetoric. From rhetoric's early formulations in antiquity to postmodern accounts of rhetoric as an epistemic or architectonic art, rhetorical theorists have long sought to position the rhetorical within, alongside, or against the world as it exists apart from or in excess of human agency, consciousness, and language. If the term realism rubs us the wrong way today—if it raises the specter of an outdated and old-fashioned way of thinking—this is because our present moment has tended to privilege the epistemological side of things, the ways, for example, language constructs realities and our perceptions of them. Short of reducing rhetoric's power and limiting its jurisdiction, however, the anti-realist turn in rhetoric has actually, if somewhat paradoxically, helped bolster more recent claims for rhetoric's ubiquity and universality. As Walter J. Ong suggests, the tendency to bracket the thing-in-itself from consideration constitutes one of the greatest triumphs of the linguistic turn insofar it enables humanists to once and for all discredit anything resembling naïve realism and with it the belief that the world accurately conforms to our senses and perceptions of it. "One turns from objectivity to intersubjectivity," Ong says, "not simply because one is overwhelmed and surfeited with objects but because one finds the more central problems really are the intersubjective ones."[1]

Ong's belief that the most central problems facing humanists today are the "intersubjective ones" is shared by a number of scholars in rhetorical studies today who similarly endorse a form of anti-realism in which the phenomenal realm (that which appears to us as human beings) is thought to constitute the only thing about which we can reasonably know or speculate. Much like the continental philosophers whose work helped establish the basic framework of the linguistic turn, however, the overwhelming interest in human knowledge and communication that has defined rhetorical study for the past century has never entirely succeeded in relegating "reality" to what we see, speak, or think it to be. Constructionists we may be, but, to borrow a line from Bruno Latour, we have never been *social* constructionists, at least not in the global sense of the term. In spite of their attempts to enforce distinctions between human beings and the nonhuman things of the world, rhetoricians have always been realists (although not always *naïve* realists) when it comes to their thinking about rhetoric. Far from constituting a liability, the persistence of realism in rhetorical theory and history holds great potential for empowering rhetoric to critically, theoretically, and practically address the challenges of the twenty-first century. As the complexities of life in this century spur us to consider not only the agencies of human beings but those of other actors as well (deteriorating bridges, melting polar icecaps, offshore oil platforms, to name but a few), rhetoricians will need ways to account for such things if they are to fully grasp the rhetorical dimensions at stake in these issues. This is a challenge to be sure, but the good news is we do not have to reboot rhetoric or build it again out of whole cloth in order to reclaim some realist ground for it. We only need to look again, with one eye toward the present, to those moments in rhetoric's history when interest in rhetorical realism peaked and became a topic of serious inquiry and deliberation.

This chapter begins the task of exploring such moments in rhetorical history, focusing here on rhetoric in antiquity and, specifically, Aristotle's inquiries into rhetoric, nature, and metaphysics. Much like the history of Western rhetoric itself, Aristotle's place in the rhetorical tradition has been marked by key moments of rediscovery and rejection. In the early-mid twentieth century, as rhetorical theorists and critics were establishing the theories, methods, and pedagogies that would define the new fields of rhetoric and rhetoric and composition, Aristotle emerged once again as an important authority on rhetoric. As formative as Neo-Aristotelianism was for rhetorical studies, however, it also proved to be short-lived. Even as rhetoricians such as Edwin Black began to question Neo-Aristotelianism on the basis of its simplification of audience and its "restricted view of context,"[2] an increasing number of rhetorical scholars had already begun to move away from—and at times outright resist—Aristotle's influence on the rhetorical tradition. Not coincidentally, this pushback against Aristotle reached its peak in the 1980s and 90s, at roughly the same time as the Sophists and sophistic rhetoric were being rehabilitated and associated ancestrally with poststructuralist theories of language, truth, and subjectivity. In contrast to philosophers such as Plato and Aristotle, the Sophists seemed to many rhetoricians at the time especially prescient given the field's burgeoning interest in rhetoric's symbolic and discursive capacities for constructing understandings of reality. Simply put, as the world around us became postmodern, it was the Sophists, not Aristotle, who appeared to offer the best ways of understanding our status as culturally and linguistically constituted subjects. As Susan Jarratt proposes in the opening pages of *Rereading the Sophists: Classical Rhetoric Refigured*:

> The sophists, taken as an alternative warrant for the conceptualization and practice of rhetoric, offer quite a different epistemic field from that mapped by Aristotle. Rejecting traditional religion as an explanation for natural phenomenon, they evinced a special interest in human

perceptions as the only source of knowledge in all fields, including nature, and emphasized the significance of language in constructing that knowledge.[3]

For Jarratt, what distinguishes sophistic rhetoric and ultimately elevates it over Aristotelian rhetoric is its attunement to language as a constructive and constitutive force in the world. Because language constructs knowledge, and because knowledge of the world is circumscribed by our limitations as perceivers, speakers, and writers, then the only proper grounding for the rhetorical must be (sophistic) epistemology: the study of knowledge and of how we come to know things about the world and things in the world. Given the overwhelming acceptance of the epistemic view in contemporary rhetorical studies, it is little wonder, then, that scholars such as Jarratt would come to look back on Aristotle which such suspicion. If the Sophists were right, if *logos*/rhetoric really is first philosophy and the constitutive force at the center of all human knowledge and communication, then what are we to do with a metaphysics such as Aristotle's, which, as Heidegger explains, "swings back to the basic question of metaphysics: Why are there beings at all, and why not rather nothing?"[4]

Having introduced some of the major theses of realism and their implications for object-oriented rhetorics in the previous chapter, my goal for this chapter is to follow Heidegger's lead by approaching the question of rhetorical realism from a somewhat different angle, one that shifts our orientation toward things from *what we can know* about them to *how such beings are* with respect to their being-in-the-world. As we will see, the oscillations between epistemology and ontology we find in Aristotelian metaphysics follow from the presumption that things exist independent of human perception and cognition (Braver's R1 thesis of mind-independence). At the same time, Aristotelian metaphysics suggests a second, and indeed quite significant, aspect of classical rhetorical realism. Not simply a doctrine about mind-independence or correspondence, Aristotle's rhetorical realism suggests that skillful and responsible rhetors must do more than obtain knowledge of audiences and situations. Prior to these important understandings, Aristotle suggests that rhetors must first have cultivated an attunement to *being* and to *the being of beings*, to the ways natural, artificial, and human beings move, change, and endure as beings in the world.

If "Aristotle's thought is clearly realist," as James W. Hikins suggests,[5] then it behooves us to explore the nature of its realism and the implications it holds for Aristotle's understandings of rhetoric. To be clear, by suggesting that we revisit Aristotle's realist views on rhetoric in light of his writings on *phusis* (φύσις), *technē* (τέχνη), and metaphysics, I am not claiming that doing so offers a more accurate description of classical rhetoric. Rather, my claim is that many of our contemporary engagements with Aristotle and the classical tradition have tended to emphasize their significant contributions to discursive theories of rhetoric, a privileging that, while productive for shaping rhetoric as a modern field of study, has nonetheless tended to abstract and de-contextualize Aristotle's more complicated—indeed, more metaphysical—views on rhetoric. While unsurprising given the constructionist orientation of modern rhetorical theory, the discursive view of rhetoric, particularly when read back into the classical tradition, has more often than not led us to reduce, trivialize, and at times misconstrue the metaphysical worldview in relation to which Aristotelian rhetoric came into being. What we have missed by tending so closely to the discursive aspects of classical rhetoric, in other words, is how many of the ancients and Aristotle in particular managed to situate rhetoric within the complex worldview of their time, a worldview that did not always distinguish rhetoric from reality or from the natural order of things. Protagoras's famous dictum notwithstanding, that "Of all things the measure is man, of things that are that they are, and of things that are not that they are not,"[6] few classical thinkers were the proto-postmodernists we sometimes think them to be. Indeed, for many ancients, things, whether natural or artificial, were never simply the measure of human beings alone. This was certainly the case for Aristotle, who, much to the frustration of modern readers, is often inconsistent in his views on rhetoric and whether art (*technē*) and nature (*phusis*) are truly as distinct as he sometimes claims them to be. In the places where one might expect to find clarification on the relationship between art and nature, such in the *Physics* and the *Metaphysics*, one finds only further questions and speculations, with *technē* and *phusis* being carefully defined and distinguished in one passage only later to be characterized as intertwining in complex ways around the texts' larger questions regarding movement, change, and causation. As I discuss in this chapter, for rhetorical studies the implications of Aristotle's speculations on the relationship between *technē* and *phusis* are quite significant, both for the challenges they pose to studies of classical and Aristotelian rhetorics and for what they reveal about rhetorical realism's place in some ancient accounts of rhetoric and rhetorical theory.

The picture that emerges when we follow key terms such as *technē* and *phusis* across Aristotle's works is one of a highly speculative thinker puzzling over rhetoric's place in a larger universe of things whose actions and interactions exceed the perceptions and interventions of human beings. This more speculative Aristotle has been described by Heidegger in his 1924 lectures on the *Rhetoric* and, more recently, by Joseph Dunne in his impressive study *Back to the Rough Ground: Practical Judgment and the Lure of Technique*. During a series of lecture courses given at Marburg as he was writing what would become *Being and Time*, Heidegger presents Aristotle's *Rhetoric* as having a great deal more to offer contemporary thought than its status as philosophy's first systematic treatise on the art at first indicates. Linking Aristotle's definition of rhetoric to ancient Greek understandings of *logos*, *dunamis*, and *doxa*, Heidegger reads the *Rhetoric* as a significant work of ontology, one mostly in line with Aristotle's views on nature but particularly attuned to the importance of discoursing (*legein*) as the primordial condition through which human being and being-with-one-another are constituted and come into meaning as subjects of interpretation. Short of reducing rhetoric to human speech alone, however, Heidegger's lectures (particularly when read alongside his later discussions of *technē*, *phusis*, and metaphysics in Aristotle's thought) open the way toward another view of Aristotelian rhetoric which finds rhetoric deeply enmeshed in an ontology of things, a view Dunne further supports in his readings of Aristotle's at times contradictory accounts of *technē* and its relations to other key Aristotelian terms. From the vantage of Heidegger and Dunne's discussions of Aristotle, another view of Aristotelian rhetoric comes into focus, one that finds rhetoric interwoven into a metaphysics that, contra some recent interpretations, never truly succeeds in distinguishing the rhetorical from the natural.

By turning to Dunne and Heidegger in particular, I am not claiming to offer the absolute historical truth of Aristotle's views on rhetoric or metaphysics. As many commentators have noted, Heidegger's readings of ancient philosophers, while unquestionably rigorous and attentive to the nuances of the Greek terms, more often than not tend to reveal more about Heidegger and *his* philosophy than about the specific thinker under consideration. This being said, the fact that Heidegger's investigations into the question of Being, of what it means to be and be-with others in the world, led him to revisit Aristotle and rhetoric on several occasions makes Heidegger a useful relay through which to explore rhetorical realism in the classical period. Indeed, Heidegger's work has already begun to inform our understandings of classical rhetorical theory. In his essay "Rhetoric, the Sophists, and the Possible," for example, John Poulakos draws on Heidegger to argue for new sophistic ways of understanding the possible in terms of metaphysics. For Poulakos, Heidegger's project to "destructure" Western metaphysics "inverses the Aristotelian priority of the actual over the possible" and thus "opens a path to the sophistical, whose glory was overshadowed by the imposing dynamics of systematization."[7] In short, Poulakos argues, "Heidegger facilitates the rediscovery of the Sophists."[8] As we will see in this chapter, however, Heidegger owes a great deal more to Aristotelian metaphysics than Poulakos suggests. It is safe to say, I think, that Heidegger learned more from Aristotle, and borrowed more from him, than from anyone else in the Western philosophical tradition (save, perhaps, Nietzsche). And it is Heidegger's interest in Aristotle's metaphysics, I hope to demonstrate, that directly informs his ontological reading of the *Rhetoric* and that, in turn, helps clarify Aristotle's complicated understandings of *technē*, *phusis*, and *logos*, the intertwining of which form the fabric of his rhetorical realism.

The Place of Rhetoric in Aristotelian Metaphysics

The question of rhetoric's place in Aristotle's thought has both intrigued and perplexed classicists, philosophers, and rhetorical theorists and historians. On the one hand, Aristotle provides classical thought its first systematic account of rhetoric as a useful and necessary art, one that, in Cicero's estimation, "did much to improve and adorn this art."[9] At the same time, Aristotle's other writings, particularly those on philosophical topics such as nature, ethics, change, and causation, cast doubt on what exactly he means by rhetoric and how he envisions rhetoric's relationship to these topics. Is rhetoric equivalent to dialectic, or is it a subset or offshoot of dialectic? Or does Aristotle's use of the word "counterpart" (*antistrophos*) in the first chapter of the *Rhetoric* mean that rhetoric is fundamentally opposed to dialectic and therefore inferior to philosophy? Arguments have been made for each of these interpretations and more, from Alexander of Aphrodisias who saw resemblances between the two in terms of theory but not in terms of practice, to Grimaldi and Kennedy who interpret *antistrophos* as indicating a more "correlative" or "parallel" relation between rhetoric and dialectic.[10]

Regardless of where one stands on the issue of rhetoric's place in Aristotelian thought, it is impossible to ignore the complexities and contradictions surrounding his discussions of rhetoric. For Brian Vickers, a majority of these contradictions follow from the composite nature of the *Rhetoric*, which makes it virtually "impossible to form a clear view of Aristotle's final thoughts on the subject".[11] In *Classical Rhetoric and its Christian and Secular Tradition*, George A. Kennedy similarly warns that because the *Rhetoric*, "like Aristotle's other treatises, is a developing work, we should avoid imposing an artificial consistency on it."[12] In addition to having written portions of the work at different times and never having made a complete revision of the whole work, Kennedy observes in the *Prooemion* to his translation of the *Rhetoric* that Aristotle also held a deeply ambivalent attitude toward rhetoric, which perhaps explains why he sometimes changes his views on rhetoric at various points in the text, much to the chagrin of modern readers.[13] And after acknowledging the many inconsistencies in the *Rhetoric* ranging from Aristotle's initial contempt of emotional appeals in the first book to contradictory suggestions about whether rhetoric is a theory (*theoreia*) in the same sense as science (*epistēmē*), Jasper Neel concludes that "as one reads his *Rhetoric* one occupies moments of intellectual clarity, but as one moves from one moment to another the differing moments sometimes compliment, sometimes conflict with, and sometimes negate each other."[14]

While some of these interpretative issues can be traced back to the nature of Aristotle's texts—many of which, including the *Rhetoric*, were assembled after the fact and sometimes from notes taken by students present during Aristotle's lectures—it is just as likely that Aristotle's philosophical pursuits played a significant role in shaping his conflicted understanding of rhetoric. This in part is Neel's position when he suggests that Aristotle's inability to think of a world outside of philosophy, along with his tendency to lecture on rhetoric only in the afternoons "when less intellectually demanding topics were treated," did much to affect his approach to rhetoric vis-à-vis philosophy and his metaphysical worldview. "I believe that this extracurricular, less-than-philosophy, less intellectually demanding conception of rhetoric determined the location that Aristotle gave rhetoric in his system, and I think it laid out the theoretical matrix in which Western metaphysics would always degrade communication so as to elevate what it communicates."[15]

As we continue to build a way toward Aristotle's rhetorical realism, it is worthwhile to explore claims such as this a bit further in order to see how Aristotle's metaphysics may have informed his understandings of rhetoric and communication. To do so, we first need to understand what Aristotle's "system" is and how he positions rhetoric in relation to that system. As Neel observes in his assessment of Aristotle's theoretical commitments, it is commonplace in some circles to lay the burden of Western metaphysics at the feet of Aristotle. After all, it is Aristotle who developed the first significant theories of matter and substance and who speaks at times of natural things as being "essential," "unchangeable," and "eternal."[16] And it is Aristotle as well who frequently defines human beings as superior to animals based on their use of speech or *logos*. For rhetoricians such as Neel and Bradford Vivian, such beliefs do not merely reflect the idiosyncratic views of a particular classical thinker. Rather, they are expressions of "Western metaphysics" as a whole, which, as Vivian defines it, "has been characterized by a fundamental distinction between the *sensible* and the *intelligible*, between the world accessible to our deeply impressionable senses and the realm of eternal truths apprehensible only to the properly trained mind."[17] Along with Neel, Vivian argues that the preservation of the distinction between the sensible and the intelligible has helped define rhetoric "according to the ideal of a knowing and speaking being that personifies the fundamental values of the metaphysical tradition."[18] This, in turn, makes it possible to integrate moral with practical instruction into rhetorical education, a move Vivian says infuses rhetoric with a "moral code" that subsequently emplaces "the ideal of a wise and virtuous rhetor" at the center of rhetorical thought.[19] When considered in these terms and as privileging originary essences and moral certainty, Aristotle seems justly guilty of perpetuating the structures of Western metaphysics. But is this specific brand of metaphysics the same as the one Aristotle developed and dwelled within?

First of all, it is important to remember that Aristotle never uses the term "metaphysics," not even in his treatise of the same name. The *Metaphysics* only received its title from the first century C.E. editor who originally assembled the book out of various fragments of Aristotle's. Nonetheless, the existing title is accurate enough if taken literally to mean "*after* or *above* the *Physics*." The lengthy examinations of substance, actuality, and potentiality that comprise the majority of the *Metaphysics*, in other words, were likely intended to support and elaborate upon Aristotle's previous discussions of nature, causation, and motion in the *Physics*. In this vein, *meta*physics in the Aristotelian sense simply refers to the proper sequence of a course of study, one that proceeds from analyses of the natural body in general to the study of being-qua-being and the fundamental conditions of natural bodies as such. As Heidegger explains in his *Introduction to Metaphysics*, "In Greek, 'away over something,' 'over beyond,' is *meta*. Philosophical questioning about beings as such is *meta ta phusicka*; it questions on beyond beings, it is metaphysics."[20]

At the conceptual level, however, Aristotelian metaphysics is significantly more complex, and it is these complexities that bear directly on the unstable picture of rhetoric we find in the *Rhetoric*. If metaphysics broadly speaking is, as Heidegger suggests, "inquiry beyond or over [*meta*] beings, which aims to recover them as such and as a whole for our grasp,"[21] then Aristotle's metaphysics can also be understood as attempting to grasp the larger conditions of being as such as well as the individual natures of specific beings (the being of such beings), including natural bodies that move and that are moved by other bodies in space and time, artificial things like houses that come into being by virtue of multiple intersecting causes, and substances, comprised of both matter and form, that define the essence of things, be they natural or artificial. When considered these senses, Aristotelian metaphysics can be understood as attempting to conceptualize the universe as a dynamic movement of forces and beings that include humans but is not always reducible to humans' perceptions or cognitions of them. "All things that are capable respectively of affecting and being affected, or of causing motion and being moved," Aristotle says in the *Physics*, "are capable of it not under all conditions, but only when they are in a particular condition and approach one another: so it is on the approach of one thing to another that the one causes and the other is moved, and when they are present under such conditions as rendered the one motive and the other movable."[22] Just because we can observe things moving or at rest, in other words, does not mean that these things have always existed in such states or are in any way knowable exclusively by them. While human beings may eventually arrive at some understanding of the universal principles of motion and change, the comings and goings of beings in the universe will continue to occur outside of (and often in excess of) these epistemological pursuits.

This metaphysical system may seem as first glance worlds away from how Aristotle defines rhetoric with regard to the contingencies of everyday human affairs. Nonetheless, it appears—and is formative—in almost all of his works, including the *Rhetoric*. When Aristotle takes issue with the Sophists and sophistic reasoning, for example, he does so with this metaphysical worldview in mind, one he claims contradicts "the art of the sophist" which offers only "the semblance of wisdom without the reality."[23] Furthermore, in discussing Protagoras's *Homo Mensura* doctrine in the *Metaphysics*, he observes that the doctrine's notion of reality assumes that the sensible world is identical with "that which is."[24] "In general," Aristotle responds, "if only the sensible exists, there would be nothing if animate things were not; for there would be no faculty of sense [...] For sensation is surely not the sensation of itself, but there is something beyond the sensation, which must be prior to the sensation."[25] While appearing at first glance to confirm Neel and Vivian's understandings of Western metaphysics, the distinction Aristotle draws here between the sensible and the intelligible does not assume the existence of an absolute or transcendent truth independent of human beings; it simply assumes the existence of beings as such. Although Aristotle will insist that there is always "something beyond sensation," this "something" does not necessarily designate a realm of eternal truth. More often than not, it simply acknowledges that being precedes human existence and stretches out well past the limits of human knowledge and perception.

More than the static, universal system credited to Aristotle by postmodern and poststructuralist theorists, it is this metaphysical worldview, one overflowing with the actions and movements of all kinds of beings, that ultimately poses the greatest challenge for Aristotle and his understanding of rhetoric. In order to examine rhetoric and its related terminology in relation to his metaphysics, Aristotle must maintain a difficult balancing act, on the one hand keeping rhetoric grounded in previously established understandings of *technē* and *phusis* while at the same time situating these terms within a larger cosmos that is teeming with movements and collisions that may have little or nothing to do with human rhetors and audiences. It is little wonder, then, that the results of these efforts have often come across to readers as "confused," "messy," or, as James Berlin once claimed, "hopelessly conflicted."[26]

Technē and *Phusis* in Aristotle's Scheme of Things: The Official Version

Given the number of inconsistencies and contradictions that pervade Aristotle's writings on rhetoric, *technē*, and metaphysics, it is unlikely we will ever be able to fully reconcile Aristotle's understanding of rhetoric with his metaphysical views of nature. Nonetheless, we can identify moments in the corpus when Aristotle seems to be working productively against the grain of his own thought. This is especially true in his discussions of *technē* and *phusis*, terms Aristotle goes to great lengths to contrast on a number of occasions even as he allows their respective enactments of being to mutually inform one another in other passages scattered across the corpus. Given that Aristotle associates rhetoric with *technē*,[27] these contradictions are quite significant insofar as they document a thinker struggling to determine a place for rhetoric alongside natural things that move and come into being of their own accord. And it is these sometimes perplexing moments of speculation on the relation between art and nature, I want to suggest, that many contemporary rhetoricians have tended to overlook but that point the way toward a uniquely classical form of rhetorical realism lurking in the margins of Aristotle's works. The remainder of this chapter, then, traces Aristotle's metaphysical discussions of *technē* and *phusis*, beginning in this section with his separation of the two on the basis of their differing origins (*archai*) before turning in the following sections to those moments in Aristotle's works where it becomes much less clear where *technē* begins and *phusis* ends.

In *Back to the Rough Ground*, Joseph Dunne identifies two versions of *technē* available to readers of Aristotle's works. The first "official" version can be found in places such as *Nicomachean Ethics* 6.4 and *Metaphysics* 1.1 where Aristotle most clearly attempts to define *technē* in contrast to other forms of knowledge and other domains of being. According to Dunne, these versions of *technē* represent the categorized and instrumental view that Aristotle inherited from Plato and that has more or less dominated understandings of *technē* from classical to contemporary times. The alternative or "unofficial" version, on the other hand, paints of much different picture of *technē* and its place in Aristotelian metaphysics. Assembled from various references to *technē* scattered across the corpus, Dunne's unofficial version suggests that for Aristotle *technē* was not only a mode of knowledge enabling one to have mastery over nature and artificial materials. It was also—and in apparent contradiction to his more celebrated accounts of *technē*—an ontological condition of possibility in its own right, one so entwined with the movements and becomings of *phusis* that it led Aristotle in several places to propose *technē* as the means by which *phusis* comes into presence and into meaning as such.

Since the publication of *Back to the Rough Ground* in 1993, the official version of *technē* has received the most attention in rhetorical studies. The past two decades in particular have seen rhetoricians following Dunne's lead in questioning whether *technē* is indeed merely a means to an end, an assumption that, if true, would indicate that Aristotelian rhetoric is highly instrumental and thus reducible to a speaker's reasoned capacity to craft discourse in aim of some predetermined end or purpose. Working against Aristotle's definition of *technē* in the *Nicomachean Ethics* as a "reasoned state of capacity to make" (*hexis meta logou poiêtikê*), rhetoricians such as Lynn Worsham, Janet Atwill, Byron Hawk, and Kelly Pender have argued for more expansive (what Dunne would call "unofficial") conception of *technē* that acknowledge the extra-rational, material, and environmental factors that hold sway in the production of rhetoric. Short of jettisoning Aristotle altogether, however, these accounts of *technē* attempt to salvage from Aristotle evidence for alternative ways of thinking about *technē* and our relations to it as human speakers and writers. In Hawk's case, this means going farther afield from the *Rhetoric* to consider how Aristotle's fourfold notion of causality, with its emphasis on multiple factors as being co-responsible for a thing's coming into being as such, prepares the way for less instrumental understandings of *technē*. Drawing on Dunne's work, Pender likewise argues for an alternative version of *technē* that harkens back to Aristotelian insights on the instrumentality and teachability of rhetoric. While the question of *technē*'s meaning remains open for debate, one thing is clear from rhetorical theorists' ongoing concerns for rhetoric's status as a *technē*: We do not need to cast Aristotle aside in order to think more expansively about *technē* and rhetoric.

Before turning to some of these unofficial accounts of *technē*, I first want to examine the official version in more detail, particularly with an eye toward how it has informed some contemporary readings of *technē* in Aristotle's thought. As noted above, several of Aristotle's best known discussions of *technē* appear to situate art in opposition to other forms of knowing and domains of being, including nature (*phusis*), science (*epistēmē*), and philosophy. In *Rhetoric Reclaimed*, Janet Atwill notes that for ancients such as Aristotle *technē* "is frequently defined against *physis* (nature), *automaton* (spontaneity), and *tyche* (chance)."[28] Whereas *technē* suggests a form of invention concerned with "situations that yield indeterminacies," *phusis*, *automaton*, and *tyche* represent absolute externalized forces that enable and constrain invention.[29] While there is ample evidence to suggest a more complicated relationship between *technē* and *phusis*, as I discuss below, it is clear in places such as Book 6 of the *Nicomachean Ethics* that Aristotle means to differentiate the two on the basis of their respective ontologies. While *technē* may lead toward the attainment of truth, its *archē* distinguishes it from other modes of thought such as science (*epistēmē*), philosophy (*sophia*), intelligence (*nous*), and practical reasoning (*phronesis*). Put differently, when Aristotle sets out in the *Nicomachean Ethics* to classify the means by which human beings disclose their worlds he does so according to their respective origins or *archai*. The result is an axis separating intellectual reasoning into two distinct capacities that are differently attuned to the ways certain kinds of beings come into existence as such. On the side of those beings that are "invariable" and thus always the same in their being, Aristotle places *epistēmē*, *sophia*, and *nous*. On the other side, with those beings that have the potential to be other than they are, Aristotle places *technē* and *phronesis*. "Let it be assumed that there are two parts which grasp the rational principle," Aristotle writes at the outset of Book 6 of the *Ethics*, "one by which we contemplate the kind of things whose originative causes are invariable, and one by which we contemplate variable things."[30] Because invariable things, per their nature, are eternal and ungenerated by human beings, it makes little sense to approach such things as topics for deliberation, because "no one deliberates about the invariable." For Aristotle, then, the *epistemonikon-logistikon* axis works from the very beginning to classify things ontologically so that we can know "the best state of each of these two parts" and respond to things in kind.

Insofar as *archē* implies cause, Aristotle's axis suggests a further distinction among things on the basis of their relations to agency and purposive human agents in particular. Whereas some things *are* whether human beings act upon them or not, other things come into being as the result of human action. For rhetoric, the consequences of this second distinction could not be more decisive as they suggest that for Aristotle there may be an absolute difference between the contingent realm of everyday human affairs and the natural, eternal domain of being's "highest objects."[31] Here, for example, is how Aristotle characterizes the ends of *epistēmē*:

> We all suppose that what we know is not even capable of being otherwise; of things capable of being otherwise we do not know, when

they have passed outside our observation, whether they exist or not. Therefore the object of scientific knowledge is of necessity. Therefore it is eternal; for things that are of necessity in the unqualified sense are all eternal; and things that are eternal are ungenerated and imperishable.[32]

As knowledge grounded in first principles, axioms, and definitions, *epistēmē* constitutes a demonstrative and apodeictic form of reasoning. Through *epistēmē*, the truth disclosed to the observer is measured according to its correspondence to physical reality, which dwells outside of human invention and intervention. As Barbara Warnick explains, "the purpose of *epistēmē* is to discover knowledge of rules that can apply invariably to all instances within the rubric for which the rule is intended."[33] Once again, deliberation has little role to play given that the state of things here concerns natural principles that hold true for all things at all times.

Like *epistēmē*, *sophia* is directed toward the invariable. Its focus, however, is on the broader elements of being that are eternal and changeless rather than on the necessary truths evidenced in physical reality. Aristotle designates *sophia* as "the most finished of the forms of knowledge," the one that combines the intuitive reason of *nous* with *epistēmē*'s scientific knowledge.[34] According to Aristotle, *sophia* is the form of wisdom best suited to the study of metaphysics, of being and beings as such—what Aristotle calls "the things that are highest by nature."[35] Based on this logic, politics and *phronesis* are distinct from *sophia* because they address questions specific to human existence, which, as Aristotle says, "is not the best thing in the world" and thus not the proper grounding for *sophia*.[36] From the perspective of *sophia*, then, human being is overshadowed by the eternal conditions of possibility that constitute the being of all beings, human and nonhuman alike: "If the argument be that man is the best of the animals, this makes no difference; for there are other things much more divine in their nature even than man, e.g., most conspicuously, the bodies of which the heavens are framed."[37]

It is *technē*'s immersion in the realm of human affairs that distinguishes it from *epistēmē* and *sophia*.[38] Aristotle defines *technē* as "a state of capacity to make, involving a true course of reasoning."[39] Unlike *phronesis*, which enables practitioners to act responsibly "with regard to the things that are good or bad for man,"[40] *technē* refers to a producer's "know-how" to make or bring a thing into being. In terms of rhetoric, this means having the knowledge and experience to observe the available means of persuasion and determine how best to deploy those means for a given audience and with a specific end in mind. As is the case with other *technai* such as shipbuilding and medicine, an effective rhetor must be able to anticipate the desired end of her efforts (a sea-worthy ship or a patient's good health, in the case of shipbuilding and medicine) and work methodically toward that end. *Technai* thus require producers to have knowledge of both the general and the particular, of the general form a thing must take and the particular actions required *in situ* to produce that form. The point of emphasis for *technē*, therefore, is on the maker and her reasoned capacity to produce rather than on the thing made:

> All art is concerned with coming into being, i.e. with contriving and considering how something may come into being which is capable of either being or not being, and whose origin is in the maker and not in the thing made; for is concerned neither with things that are, or come into being, by necessity, nor with things that do so in accordance with nature (since these have their origin in themselves).[41]

In clear contrast to *epistēmē*, *sophia*, and *phusis*, *technē* deals exclusively with things that are contingent rather than necessary and that have their *archē* in human beings rather than in the things themselves. Because the affairs of human life are never fixed or eternal, *technai* such as rhetoric guide human beings to deliberate and take action on uncertain matters because, as Aristotle observes in the *Rhetoric*, "we debate about things that seem capable of admitting two possibilities; for no one debates things incapable of being different either in part or future or present."[42]

The division of faculties Aristotle presents in the *Nicomachean Ethics* thus breaks down along two related fronts. On the one hand, Aristotle draws distinctions between the modes of thought based on the specific kinds of beings each reveals, with *epistēmē*, *sophia*, and *nous* dealing with things that are invariable and unchangeable and *technē* and *phronesis* with those that might be other than they are. At the same time, Aristotle introduces another related distinction based on the agent responsible for the beings' existence as such. In the case of *epistēmē* and *sophia*, which deal primarily with the objects and forces of nature, the *archē* of a thing lies within the thing itself. An acorn, for example, carries within itself the potential to become a mighty oak tree. This potential, however, does not require an external mover or agent to ensure its actuality; it simply requires the proper conditions and time to be what it is already becoming. A chalice or persuasive speech, on the other hand, *does* require the force of an external agent in order to come into being as such, in this case a human artist or rhetor equipped with the appropriate knowledge, experience, and technique. The boundaries between *phusis* and *technē* appear then to be set. In Aristotle's rendering, *phusis* becomes "a source or cause of being moved and of being at rest in that to which it belongs primarily, in virtue of itself and not in virtue of a concomitant attribute."[43] In contrast, *technē* deals exclusively with the artificial object that does not have "in itself the source of its own production."[44] Taken in these terms, the official view situates *technē* in contrast to other domains of being under the assumption that the scope of *technē* is limited only to those things whose existence can be traced directly back to the interventions of human beings.

Strange as it may seem, this official view, and with it the distinctions Aristotle inscribes between *technē* and *phusis*, has actually helped improve rhetoric's standing as a term and a scholarly field of study, especially in the wake of the linguistic and postmodern turns. By accepting the classical period's sometimes opposing views of nature and art, contemporary rhetorical theorists have been able to defend a discursive view of rhetoric—one that effectively eschews any connection to objective reality—based on rhetoric's status as a *technē*, which, per Aristotle's definition, concerns the contingencies of everyday human affairs. In *Rereading the Sophists*, for example, Jarratt endorses this official view of *technē*, in this case using it as a warrant to justify epistemological differences between Aristotelian and sophistic rhetorics:

> In Aristotle's worlds as well [as Plato's], realms of knowledge are divided; "rhetoric" is a faculty (a process or method) functioning only in fields of probable knowledge, i.e. politics, ethics and law (*Rhetoric* I. iv. 5). He specifies that knowledge of the natural world or of metaphysics—indeed of any specific "science"—is out of the scope of rhetoric's powers (I. v. 6–7). Studies of first causes of objects in the world require a different process of discovery and logical framework for articulation, namely induction and syllogism.[45]

Poulakos offer a similar assessment of Aristotle and his treatment of the Sophists. Like Jarratt, Poulakos worries that Aristotle and his "metaphysical perspective" has too heavily influenced our contemporary view of rhetoric. In order to understand the Sophists as fully as possible, Poulakos argues, "we need a framework to keep us away from an Aristotelian understanding of sophistical rhetoric. Similarly, to understand the possible in the spirit of the Sophists we must operate free from Aristotle's influence, or from a pre- or non-metaphysical perspective."[46] Likewise, if more polemically, Diane Davis concludes that "Plato and Aristotle assume that the world is naturally orderly, and, like good protostructuralists, they go about fitting everything into their (obsessive-compulsive) structural schemes—what can't be fit in gets erased."[47] And while he acknowledges the messy ways in which Aristotle defines *technē* across his writings, Kennedy nonetheless follows Book 6 of the *Ethics* in suggesting that art "is a capacity to realize a potential by reasoning and operates in the realm of the probable. It is not concerned with things that exist by nature or by necessity, but rather with 'the coming into being of something which is capable of being or not being.'"[48]

Furthermore, in her extensive historical and pedagogical account of *technē* in the humanist tradition, Atwill not only acknowledges but accepts many of Aristotle's categorical distinctions, including those between the major domains of knowledge: theoretical, practical, and productive. Atwill argues that aligning rhetoric with the theoretical (*epistēmē*), as Grimaldi and others attempt, tends to equate rhetoric with philosophy and metaphysics, a move that effectively ignores the productive role Aristotle gives to *technai* such as rhetoric. To truly grasp the full meaning and implications of Aristotle's *technē*, Atwill argues that we must go beyond the reductive conceptions of *technē* inherited from the classical handbook tradition. Following Aristotle's lead, she proposes a definition of *technē* that positions it "against the forces of necessity, spontaneity, experience, chance, compulsion, and force."[49] In contrast to philosophical and practical knowledge, *technē*, for Atwill, is a form of productive knowledge that "neither represents reality nor encompasses a set of deductive postulates."[50] Conceived in such terms, rhetoric qua *technē* defines a discursive power that encourages us to locate the human subject at the center of rhetorical production and education, even if that subject is not necessarily the fixed and stable one we associate with humanist rhetorics and philosophies.

Again, these readings of Aristotle are not in themselves inaccurate or unconvincing. In fact, their problem may be that they have been entirely *too convincing*, allowing us to accept the idea that Aristotle never cared to involve rhetoric in the metaphysical system he was inventing and describing. What has been lost in our efforts to blame or improve upon Aristotle, in other words, is the degree to which he actively puzzles over the place of rhetoric in a wider world of artificial and natural beings. While it is true that Aristotle may never have succeeded in finding a harmonious place for rhetoric alongside his understanding of nature, he does attempt on multiple occasions to place *technē* and *phusis* on more equal footing. It is to these other, less official accounts that I turn to next.

Technē and *Phusis*: The Intertwining

In his essay "On the Essence and Concept of *Phusis* in Aristotle's *Physics B, I*," Heidegger singles out *phusis*'s relationship to *technē* as the essential grounding for Aristotle's metaphysical system. As much a lesson in how to read and listen to ancient thinkers as it is a close analysis of one particular book of the *Physics*, Heidegger's essay works meticulously to reassemble Aristotle's thinking about *phusis* and *technē* so that the original nature of each term shines forth. This move toward the ontological, or more precisely toward the conditions of possibility for being and beings as such, is a common one for Heidegger, one he repeats often when dealing with classical thinkers and concepts. For Heidegger, the philosopher's primary task is to practice a kind of thinking that opens the way toward being. According to Heidegger, thinking does not occur in vacuum—spatial, temporal, or otherwise—but is rather always already grounded in the "worldhood" of Dasein's being-in-the-world. And worldhood, in Heidegger's view, is inextricably bound up with language, with the fact that we are born into and dwell continuously with/in language. In order to understand the full scope and depth of Aristotle's writings on *phusis* and *technē*, then, Heidegger insists that readers must do more than simply decode or interpret existing texts because doing so often leaves the respective worlds of those texts hidden and uninvestigated. The better approach, he suggests, is to attempt to reconstruct the world within which that thinker dwelled so as to see whether the concepts he employed still bear a trace of the world we have long since lost or forgotten.

In Heidegger's work, this "destructive" approach often takes the form of close etymological analyses of the Greek terms themselves. In the case of *phusis*, Heidegger begins by noting that our modern word "nature," which derives from the Latin *natura*, hardly captures the full ontological resonance of the original Greek word *phusis*. In the Western metaphysical worldview that emerged after the Greeks, the term nature would come to designate a distinct realm lying apart from or in opposition to other pursuits such as art, history, and spirit.[51] While such oppositions are not necessarily foreign to the Greeks, Heidegger suggests that for contemporary readers there is a temptation to project this modern sense of nature back into Aristotle's works, as if *phusis* and "nature" were indeed the same thing for Aristotle. As Heidegger's careful reading of the *Physics* demonstrates, however, for Aristotle *phusis* is anything but a place or a specific entity. In fact, it is precisely this confusion about nature—that *phusis* designates a singular being or substance—that Aristotle means to confront.

So what does Aristotle mean by *phusis* and *technē*? According to the official view described above, *phusis* and *technē* designate different things or beings that have (or whose existence is owed to) different *archē*. A natural thing such as a tree has inside of itself its own source of movement and change, whereas an artificial thing such as a wooden bench does not possess that same potential; its existence is owed directly to the reasoned theories and interventions of an external mover, in this case a master craftsperson. As we saw above, while not incorrect, the official view of *technē* and *phusis* nonetheless encourages us to accept sharp distinctions between *phusis* and *technē*, to in effect see artifacts and natural beings as entirely different kinds of beings. This orientation may serve to empower rhetoricians to claim rhetoric's jurisdiction as only what human beings can know or produce themselves. However, as Heidegger, Dunne, and others have suggested, the official view represents only one aspect of Aristotle's thinking about *phusis* and *technē*. For all of his attempts to distinguish *phusis* and *technē*, there are nearly as many passages where Aristotle seems willing to reject these distinctions in order explore alternative ways of thinking about *phusis* and *technē*. The results of these speculations, while complicated and at times lacking the same precision Aristotle demonstrates in his treatments of other subjects, suggest that for Aristotle *technē* and *phusis* are not distinct at all but are rather entwined with one another around the larger question that is ultimately at the heart of Aristotle's writings on metaphysics: *what is being, and why are there beings at all instead of nothing?*[52]

In contrast to Platonists and pre-Socratics such as Parmenides and Antiphon for whom being constitutes something fixed and essential, Aristotle conceives of being in somewhat paradoxical terms as *enduring change*. According to Aristotle, beings are to the extent that they emerge into presence and preserve themselves in appearance: "For the Greeks [...] 'being' means: *presencing into the unhidden*."[53] While *ousia* is often translated as "substance" or "actuality," Heidegger contends that neither of these words fully captures the Greek understanding of the being of beings, which goes "beyond the givenness and availability of beings [...] to look into the horizon that gives rise to the advent of beings."[54] Metaphysics loses its way, then, when it assumes that specific beings define or represent the whole of being as such. For both Aristotle and Heidegger, conflating being and beings in this way not only makes the question of being all-but unthinkable (thus, Heidegger's well-known argument about modernity's tendency to "forget being"); it also reinforces a misconception that associates being with the absolute and unchangeable essence at the heart of beings in the world. This is not what Aristotle means by being or *ousia*. For Aristotle, *ousia* does not refer to any particular being per se but instead indicates the ways in which beings lie forth and endure as beings, the ways beings have for presencing and holding themselves together in presence.[55] Hence, at the heart of Aristotle's understanding of being is presencing and movement—the kind of being beings have to change and endure as changeable things.

When Aristotle turns his attention to *phusis* and *technē* in the *Physics* and the *Metaphysics*, he does so with this larger understanding of being in mind. Rather than accept the categorical views of art and nature, which tend to define natural and artificial beings in the simplest of terms, Aristotle works ontologically from the reality of particular beings in order to understand the horizons that give rise to their beingness as such. As he says in the *Physics*, *phusis* is being itself (*ouisa*), "a lying forth from out of itself."[56] As we saw above, unlike artifacts whose movedness originates from something else, natural beings have "the *archē* of their movedness *not* in another being but in the beings that they themselves are (to the degree that they are these beings)."[57] In Aristotle's metaphysics, *phusis*—and *technē* as well, as we will soon see—refers to the presencing of beings through the *kinesis* that belongs to their nature as beings, and not, as is often assumed, to any specific beings or places that happen today to bear to name "nature."

> *Phusis*, therefore, is what has been said. Everything that possesses this kind of origin and ordering "has" *phusis*. And all these things *are* (have being) of the type called beingness. *Phusis* is, in each case, such as lies present of and by itself, and is always *in* a thing that lies present in this way (constituting its lying-present). In accordance with *phusis*, however, are these things as well as everything that belongs to these things in themselves, of and by themselves, as, e.g., it belongs to fire to be borne upward. In point of fact this (being borne upward) is not *phusis*, nor does it possess *phusis*, but it certainly is from *phusis* and in accordance with *phusis*. So now it has been settled what *phusis* is, as well as what is meant by "from *phusis*," and "in accordance with *phusis*."[58]

Beings, in other words, *are not phusis* but are rather "from *phusis*" or "in accordance with *phusis*,"[59] and it is this dynamic (the way things such as fire are borne upward) that the metaphysician seeks to understand. Only once we have accepted this fundamental point, Heidegger insists,

> can we understand *phusis* in its essence as the *origin and ordering of the movedness of what moves from out of itself* and toward itself. Thus it is clear in principle that the question about the *phusis* of natural beings is not a search for ontic properties to be found *in* beings of this sort, but rather an inquiry into the being of those beings, from which being gets determined antecedently in what way beings of this kind of being can have properties at all."[60]

In the same way that natural beings are in accordance with *phusis*, so too are artifacts in accordance with *technē*. This is perhaps a more difficult idea to grasp because in our everyday dealings with things we tend the focus more on the properties of artifacts—the sturdiness of a wooden bedstead, for example—rather than on the *way* artifacts *are* in their being, which is to say, what constitutes their movedness, presencing, and enduring as beings in the world. This aspect of *technē*, however, is precisely the one Aristotle seeks to uncover in his discussions of the term. For instance, early in the second book of the *Physics* he offers what on surface seems like a relatively clear rehearsal of the differences between *technē* and *phusis*:

> All [natural] things mentioned present a feature in which they differ from things which are *not* constituted by nature. Each of them has *within itself* a principle of motion and of stationariness (in respect of place or of growth and decrease, or by way of alteration). On the other hand, a bed and a coat and anything else of that sort, *qua* receiving these designations—i.e. in so far as they are products of art—have no innate impulse to change. But in so far as they happen to be composed of stone or of earth or of a mixture of the two, they *do* have such an impulse, and just to that extent—which seems to indicate that *nature is a source or cause of being moved and of being at rest in what to which it belongs primarily*, in virtue of itself and not in virtue of a concomitant attribute.[61]

Once again, we hear the same distinction made numerous other times in works such as the *Physics*, *Metaphysics*, and *Nicomachean Ethics*—that *technē* and *phusis* are distinguishable on the basis of their differing *archē*. A closer look at the passage, however, shows that even as he attempts to make this point yet again, at the same time, Aristotle is attempting to understand *technē* and *phusis* in more ontological terms with respect to their particular ways of movedness and rest. In his reading of this passage, Heidegger proposes that the claim made here that artifacts "have no innate impulse

84   *Aristotle's Rhetorical Realism*

to change" contradicts Aristotle's already established arguments on change and rest. As Aristotle suggests elsewhere in the *Physics*, there is no such thing as "rest" in the sense of not-moving or not-having-been-moved. For Aristotle, all things move and undergo change in some fundamental ways; this is what it means "to be," after all. Thus, Heidegger is left to wonder, "are bedsteads and garments, shields and houses moving things? Indeed they are, but usually we encounter them in the kind of movement that typifies things at rest and therefore is hard to perceive. Their 'rest' has the character of having-been completed, having-been produced, and, on the basis of *these* determinations, as standing 'there' and lying present before us."[62] We tend to overlook this kind of rest, Heidegger says, because in our modern way of thinking about being "we are addicted to thinking of beings as *objects* and allowing the being of beings to be exhausted in the objectivity of the object. But for Aristotle, the issue here is to show that artifacts *are what* they are and *how* they are precisely in the movedness of production and thus in the rest of having-been produced."[63] Unlike the inert objects that dominate our modern thinking about things, artificial things in Aristotelian metaphysics *move*—they have their way of being in movedness and rest—to no less a degree than natural beings.

Moreover, like *phusis*, *technē* enacts a form of presencing or bringing-forth. In "The Question Concerning Technology," Heidegger draws attention to similarities between *technē* and *phusis* on the basis of their capacities for "bringing-forth" (*poiesis*). "*Physis* is indeed *poiesis* in the highest sense," he says, "For what presences by means of *physis* has the bursting open belonging to bringing-forth, e.g., the bursting of a blossom into bloom, in itself."[64] Similarly, the artifact from *technē* has "the bursting open belonging to bringing-forth," albeit not in itself but rather in the craftsperson or artist.[65] On a purely ontological level, however, *technē* is a form of presencing or revealing, a movedness that enables certain beings to be in their beingness.

> Thus what is decisive in *technē* does not lie at all in making and manipulating nor in the using of means, but rather in the aforementioned revealing. It is as revealing, and not as manufacturing, that *technē* is a bringing-forth.[66]

Much like *phusis*, *technē* involves "a bringing forth of beings in that it *brings forth* present beings as such beings *out of* concealedness and specifically *into* the unconcealedness of the appearance."[67] When understood in this way, *technē* ceases to be the foil for *phusis* that some readers take it to be. As a mode of presencing, *technē* shares a critical place alongside *phusis* in Aristotle's metaphysical system because, like *phusis*, it provides insight into the fundamental question at the core of Aristotelian metaphysics: what is being, and why are there beings at all instead of nothing?

That *technē* and *phusis* intertwine with another, and thus constitute two of the primary ways we have for understanding being as enduring presence, perhaps explains why Aristotle only rarely discusses *technē* in and of itself. As Dunne observes, individual treatments of *technē* are rare in Aristotle's writings, appearing only in *Nicomachean Ethics* 6.4 and *Metaphysics* 1.1. By far, Aristotle's preferred way of discussing *technē* is in relation to other topics such as *phusis*, change (*genesis*), and life or soul (*psuche*).[68] With respect to *phusis*, Aristotle frequently draws on the more accessible realm of *technē* to understand the beingness of nature.[69] In Book 2 of the *Physics*, for example, where Aristotle raises the topic of potentiality (*dunamis*), we find a more complicated relationship between *technē* and *phusis*, one that does not necessarily indicate an equivalence (Aristotle, like Heidegger after him, will never go this far) but rather a shared connection to *dunamis*, to the capacity of things to be other than they are and work toward some end:

> Now intelligent action is for the sake of an end; therefore the nature of things also is so. Thus if a house, e.g., had been a thing made by nature, it would have been made in the same way as it is now by art; and if things made by nature were made also by art, they would come to be in the same way as by nature. Each step then in the series is for the sake of the next; and generally art partly completes what nature cannot bring to a finish, and partly imitates her. If, therefore, artificial products are for the sake of an end, so clearly also are natural products. The relation of the later to the earlier terms of the series is the same in both.[70]

Later in the same chapter, Aristotle offers a second analogy between *technē* and *phusis*:

> It is absurd to suppose that purpose is not present because we do not observe the agent deliberating. Art does not deliberate. If the ship-building art were in the wood, it would produce the same result *by nature*. If, therefore, purpose is present in art, it is present also in nature. The best illustration is a doctor doctoring himself: nature is like that.[71]

The logic of the analogies developed here is quite complex. As Dunne suggests, "there seems to be as much encouragement [in these two passages] to think of *technē* as naturelike as to think of nature as technical."[72] The reluctance on Aristotle's part to keep *technē* and *phusis* separate raises a number of interpretive problems, Pender adds. If Aristotle's conception of nature builds from his understanding of *technē*, what then in nature, asks Pender, "could warrant a different understanding of *technē* if it is through *technē* that Aristotle already understood nature?"[73] While the two analogies seem intended to clarify distinctions already made between *technē* and *phusis*, they actually serve to complicate the relationship to such an extent that it becomes increasingly unclear where *technē* begins and *phusis* ends. The first passage begins with Aristotle wondering what might happen if nature itself built a house. At this point, Aristotle seems well on tract to keeping the analysis grounded in *phusis*, specifically, in understanding how nature produces beings and toward what ends. By the time he arrives at the passage's concluding syllogism, however, which inverts the direction of imitation so that nature is understood in terms of the "for-sake-of-which" characteristic of artificial products, Aristotle has long since lost the focus of the initial proposition, leaving the analogy teetering to the point that it begins to fold back on itself. The resulting chiasmus reaches its highest point in the second analogy, which moves from a relatively clear point about the differing origins of artifacts and natural beings to a conclusion that locates purpose and movement in both *phusis* and *technē*.

Furthermore, while the image of a doctor "doctoring himself" works well to illustrate *phusis* and *technē's* comparable ways of *kinesis*, the decision to link a *technites* such as a doctor to nature further raises the possibility of *technē* having within itself its own source of movedness and change. A doctor, after all, can be the source and receiver of his own medical know-how. The second analogy, then, suggests two notable turns in Aristotle's thinking about *technē*. First, it significantly complicates the understanding of *technē* put forward earlier in the *Physics*. There, Aristotle suggests as well that "a man who is a doctor might cure himself."[74] Even as he grants this possibility, however, Aristotle is quick to point out in this earlier passage that the doctor's ability to serve as both patient and doctor shares little in common with nature's ways of movedness and rest, because these capacities "belong" to natural beings "primarily" and "in virtue" of themselves whereas the doctor's *technē* is enacted only "in virtue of a concomitant attribute."[75] In other words, the art of medicine may cause a change, whether in the doctor himself or in another person, but it does so only because medical knowledge is an attribute acquired after or in excess of what nature otherwise produces in virtue of itself.[76] When we arrive at the "doctor doctoring himself" analogy later in the same book, however, this previous distinction between essence and attribute has all but disappeared. In its place we find the possibility that *phusis* and *technē* may in fact possess similar sources of *kinesis* and change. For Dunne, this leads to the somewhat surprising implication:

> both *technē* and nature are generative and work toward an end; nature already shows its resourcefulness by brining to completion, in an orderly process, its own natural product. It therefore requires no impossible stretch of the imagination to suppose that in the case of *artificial* products, the *technē* might be in the material, i.e., the material might somehow be able to assemble itself into the finished *ergon*. If this were the case, the process would be just as orderly and sequenced as it is now when it is indebted to the *technē* of the craftsman, but, in fact, with the removal of the craftsman, *technē* as an immanent potentiality of the material would not *be phusis*.[77]

According to Dunne, the force of Aristotle's analogies is clear: "They encourage us not to be so impressed by the intervention of the *technites* as to suppose that it inaugurates a new realm that is entirely different from *phusis*."[78] By suggesting that a house can be made in the same way as by nature, or that a being's purpose is present equally in *technē* and in *phusis*, Aristotle seems eager to leave the question of *technē* and *phusis* undecided, or at least open to further investigation.

The second shift evident in the two analogies speaks directly to the metaphysical questions that so extensively inform Aristotle's treatments of *technē* and *phusis*. For Aristotle, *technē* and *phusis* are in the end comparable ways by which we experience and come to understand the being of beings. While certainly not equivalent to *phusis*, *technē* constitutes a crucial aspect of Aristotle's metaphysical system. Never simply the instrumental form of knowledge enabling human beings to produce things with an eye toward some desired end, *technē* for Aristotle is inextricably linked to the conditions of being that make possible the enduring presencing of beings as such. In a practical sense, this suggests that for Aristotle it is not enough for *technites* to possess "know-how" or "reasoned capacity to make." Long before they can think about taking chisel to stone, hammer to wood, or pen to paper, *technites* must also possess (or, more accurately, must also have cultivated) *an attunement to the being of beings*, to the beingness of stone and wood, for example. "When *technē* handles a natural being for the sake of producing something, it produces something other than the being it found there. It is able to do so because, in advance, it has taken into consideration the categorical ways these beings are and can be."[79] This is why Aristotle says in *Metaphysics* 1.1 that the master craftsman is the one who can *see* the essence that allows a natural being to be as the being it is, rather the one who simply makes or does things:[80] "For men of experience know that the thing is so, but do not know why, while others know the 'why' and the cause [...] thus we view them [the master-workers] as being wiser not in virtue of being able to act, but of having the theory for themselves and knowing the cause."[81] The expertise the master craftsman gains from producing things such as houses and benches goes far beyond mastering some specific techniques. As Heidegger suggests, the strength of the *technites'* expertise lies fundamentally in her ontological attunement, her responsiveness to being and how particular beings are in their beingness:

> A cabinetmaker's apprentice, someone who is learning to build cabinets and the like, will serve as an example. His learning is not mere practice, to gain facility in the use of tools. Nor does he merely gather knowledge about the customary forms of the things he is to build. If he is to become a true cabinetmaker, he makes himself answer and respond above all to the different kinds of wood and to the shapes slumbering within wood—to wood as it enters into man's dwelling

with all the hidden riches of its essence. In fact, this relatedness to wood is what maintains the whole craft. Without that relatedness, the craft will never be anything but empty busywork, and occupation with it will be determined exclusively by business concerns. Every handicraft, all human dealings, are constantly in that danger. The writing of poetry is no more exempt from it than is thinking.[82]

Simply put, in the Aristotelian sense, "*technē* presupposes an awareness of the being of beings."[83] And it is precisely this awareness that constitutes the core of Aristotle's rhetorical realism. Just like the metaphysician, homebuilder, or cabinetmaker, the master rhetor must have awareness of the being of beings, of the ways the wooden ships of an opposing army will respond to the country's seasonal temperature changes or how the architectural features of an assembly hall will affect the tenor of one's deliberative speech.[84] In the wake of Aristotle's entwining of *technē* and *phusis*, "the ability of human beings to produce beings has been shown to be founded on a prior and presupposed awareness of the being of natural beings. It is though [sic] this familiarity with the world in which beings emerge that humans are able to be productive."[85] As Heidegger argues in his recently translated lectures on the *Rhetoric*, it is this view of things—this attunement to the being of beings—that most directly informs Aristotle's understanding of rhetoric and that makes the *Rhetoric*, in his view, one of Aristotle's most significant works on ontology. As always, however, the issue modern readers have with this text lies with the worldviews they bring to it, worldviews that often assume a dialectical relationship between subjects and objects, art and nature. As Heidegger is quick to remind readers, however, "for the Greeks, human beings are never subjects, and therefore non-human beings can never have the character of objects (things that stand-over-against)."[86] In order to fully grasp Aristotle's rhetorical realism, therefore, we must first agree to let go of the modern subject-object dichotomy and learn (again) how to answer and respond to the being of beings—to let beings be in their beingness, as Heidegger says.

Aristotle's Rhetorical Realism

I began this chapter by acknowledging the confusing and sometimes contentious place of rhetoric in Aristotle's metaphysical system. While the preceding discussions of *technē* and *phusis* may have done little to resolve Aristotle's understanding of rhetoric, one thing should be clear: In order to understand what Aristotle means by rhetoric, we need to look beyond what the *Rhetoric* has to teach us. As Alan G. Gross has argued, even when our question concerns Aristotle's definition of rhetoric, "the *Rhetoric* offers us only limited help." In order to truly get Aristotle, Gross believes, we are better advised to proceed by indirection: "We must start from the Aristotelian corpus as a whole and work inward, hoping that this circuitous and extended journey will provide us with the constraints we need to capture the meaning we're after."[87] Over the course of this chapter, I have tried to follow Gross's advice. In the case of Aristotle's understanding of the relationship between *technē* and *phusis*, such indirection has yielded another, more speculative way of reading Aristotelian metaphysics, one that opens the way toward an under-acknowledged but nonetheless fundamental possibility at the heart of his thinking about *technē* and *phusis*: the attunement to being and the being of beings that is available to metaphysician and craftsman alike who understand art and nature not as distinct beings or separate realms of existence but as comparable ways beings have for presencing and enduring in the world.

The question that still remains, however, is how Aristotle's metaphysical view of *technē* and *phusis* informs his understanding of rhetoric as an art of speaking or discoursing with others. What happens when we return to the *Rhetoric* with the awareness of the being of beings Aristotle cultivates in his other works? This is precisely the question that frames Heidegger's 1924 lectures on the *Rhetoric*, translated in 2009 as *Basic Concepts of Aristotelian Philosophy*. While Heidegger's perhaps best-known discussion of the *Rhetoric* appears in his treatment of moods in *Being and Time*, it is in this earlier lecture course where we find him truly making good on his intriguing evaluation of the work in 1927's *Being and Time*. In that book, Heidegger commends the *Rhetoric* for offering one of the first substantial treatments of Dasein's way of being-in-the-world, which, in Heidegger's interpretation of Aristotle, is always already *being-with-others* in the world. "Contrary to the traditional orientation, according to which rhetoric is conceived as the kind of thing we 'learn in school', this work of Aristotle must be taken as the first systematic hermeneutic of the everydayness of Being with one another."[88] His appreciation notwithstanding, by the time Heidegger returns to the *Rhetoric* in *Being and Time* his interest in the work has narrowed considerably, with the second book's discussion of the emotions now occupying the bulk of his commentary on rhetoric. Three years earlier, however, Heidegger presents a much more expansive interpretation of the *Rhetoric*, one aimed to introduce Heidegger's students to the *Rhetoric*'s major concepts and themes, from the nature of speech as *logos* to the ontological significance of *doxa* or public opinion and the question of whether rhetoric is indeed a *technē* as Aristotle claims.

Unsurprisingly, what grounds Heidegger's explication of the *Rhetoric* in the Marburg lectures is his sense of Aristotle as a metaphysician concerned with the question of being and the being of beings. While Aristotle may explicitly define rhetoric as "an ability [*dunamis*], in each [particular] case, to see the available means of persuasion," Heidegger argues that the true meaning of rhetoric for Aristotle precedes this ability and, in fact, constitutes rhetoric's condition of possibility as such. Before a speaker can ever proceed to see the available means of persuasion, she must first have encountered others as beings who share existence with her. As Aristotle suggests in *Politics* when he defines "man" as "the political animal," and as Heidegger argues in these lectures, there is no way to understand human being without understanding it as situated in the world and thus in relation to other beings in the world. In Heidegger's terminology, the being of Dasein is always being-in-the-world, meaning that Dasein is always already rooted in the concrete and practical relations it has with spaces, things, and others in the world. With respect to rhetoric, this is a crucial point because rhetoric assumes, and perhaps even requires, the presence of other human beings who share similar capacities to speak, listen, and communicate in a community or polis. For Heidegger, this suggests that at the core of Aristotle's thinking about rhetoric lies a larger question concerning being and the being of human (qua speaking/discoursing) beings.

Of course, few if any of these metaphysical issues appear directly in the *Rhetoric* itself. On the surface at least, Aristotle's concern throughout much of this work lies with the practical and ethical issues rhetors must understand before speaking on matters of public concern. Nonetheless, Heidegger maintains that it is not only possible to read the *Rhetoric* in same way one would read the *Physics* or *Metaphysics*, but that it is absolutely critical that we should do so if we want to appreciate Aristotle's contributions to ontology and metaphysics. As he goes on to demonstrate, when approached as work of ontology, the *Rhetoric* reveals itself to be nothing less than an exploration of *logos* as the condition of possibility for human being-there. As Heidegger explains, for Aristotle speaking is not something that comes after the fact, as a supplement to or prosthesis for human existence. In other words, *logos* is not simply a tool human beings consciously employ or may choose to ignore or "join in on later, so that only then would it become a speaking with others. Rather, speaking is, in itself and as such, self-expressing, speaking-with-one-another where others are themselves speaking; and therefore speaking is, according to its being, the fundament of *koinonia*."[89] *Logos* is the essential ground upon which human being comes into being as such, not as an isolated or autonomous individual but as one whose existence is constituted by her speaking-with-one-another. This notion of being as speaking-with-one-another does not mean simply "being-situated-alongside-one-another."[90] More than that, it suggests an active, concernful, and relational mode of being that has as its fundamental character "*being-as-speaking-with-one-another* through communication, refuting, confronting."[91] "[T]he basic determination of [*Dasein's*] being itself is being-with-one-another," Heidegger asserts. "This being-with-one-another has its basic possibility in speaking that is, in speaking-with-one-another, speaking as expressing-oneself in speaking-about-something."[92]

With *logos* understood as the basic determination for human being-there as speaking-with-one-another, Heidegger turns his attention back to the *Rhetoric* itself. More than its peculiar relations to politics and dialectic, and perhaps even more than its status as an art or mode of formal discourse, rhetoric becomes in light of this original sense of *logos* the very means by which human beings experience and come to understand the everydayness of being-there as being-in-the-world. According to Heidegger, only a rhetoric rooted in an understanding of the *logos* has the potential to recognize and disclose average everydayness as the fundamental way in which Dasein is in the world. While being-in-the-world and being-with others constitute the basic determinations of human existence, this does not mean that we must always spend our time in reflexive contemplation of these conditions. More often than not, we are simply immersed in our daily activities and concerns, an immersion Heidegger describes as Dasein's average everydayness. Far from being the impoverished state of passive existence it is sometimes made out to be, average everydayness is, for Heidegger, "a positive phenomenal characteristic of this entity." "Out of this kind of Being—and back into it again," he insists, "is all existing, such as it is."[93]

Over the course of his reading of the *Rhetoric*, Heidegger identifies several aspects of Aristotelian rhetoric that facilitate the "discoveredness" of average everydayness. In his explication of the three species of rhetoric, for example, Heidegger suggests that the different temporal structures audiences experience while listening to deliberative, forensic, and epideictic speeches have the potential to exhibit the concreteness of Dasein's being-in-the-world. "The characters of the being-there of the environing world, how they come to language in everydayness, are characterized, at the same time, in relation to temporality [...] Being in itself as concern and concernful speaking is *temporal*, concerns the *not-yet-present*, speaks about what *has-happened-already*, treats the *existing-there-right-now*."[94] Heidegger singles out rhetoricians' willingness to engage *doxa* as a genuine way of being as similarly enabling the disclosedness of "how human being-there *initially has its world there in an average way*."[95] *Doxa*, Heidegger says, "is the *genuine discoveredness of being-with-one-another-in-the-world*. The world is therefore for us as what-is-with-one-another in discoveredness, insofar as we live in *doxa*. Living in a *doxa* means having it *with others*. That *others also* have it belongs to opinion."[96] In *doxa*, we are always already in the world with others in some essential but provisional way. While it provides essential grounding for Dasein's being-in-the-world, *doxa* remains "uncertain, unfinished, and subject to desire." And so, Daniel M. Gross adds, "[w]e must make do in a world of the merely probable and thus we are always susceptible to affect and change."[97] As rhetoricians have long understood, uncertainty in the face of contingent states of affairs is exactly what defines the realm of rhetoric and sets forth the possibilities for speaking and making things otherwise. The fact that we must "make due" with uncertainty in the first place, even in cases when the uncertainty of one's future life often leads to anxiety, speaks to the ontological grounding in which Dasein finds itself, existing temporally and thus subject to change over time.

For all of its particular advice about the *topoi*, *pathē*, and *pisteis*, the *Rhetoric* at its core is a treatise on human being, on how human beings are with respect to their being-in-the-world. Just as the *Physics* and *Metaphysics* work to cultivate an attunement to the being of beings—of natural and artificial beings—the *Rhetoric* attempts to bring into focus the being of human beings and to establish an attunement to human beings as they are in their average everydayness. While rhetoric is still the ability to see the available means of persuasion, it is also a great deal more. When considered in terms of Aristotle's metaphysical system, rhetoric, as Heidegger puts it,

> *is nothing other than the interpretation of concrete being-there, the hermeneutic of being-there itself.* That is the intended sense of Aristotle's rhetoric. Speaking in the mode of speaking-in-discourse—in public meetings, before the court, at celebratory occasions—these possibilities of speaking are definitively expounded instances of customary speaking, of how being-there itself speaks.[98]

In its own ways, the *Rhetoric* offers an answer to the question at the heart of Aristotle's metaphysics: why are there beings at all, and what is the being of such beings? To study and practice rhetoric means first cultivating an attunement to the being of beings, in particular, the being of human being. And this attunement to the concrete everydayness of human being-there, Aristotle suggests, can be enriched when we undertake similar interpretations of other beings, including natural and artificial beings. What Aristotle ultimately demonstrates is that when we approach things metaphysically we not only learn to appreciate the distinctiveness of beings as they are in the world (how, for example, a bedstead differs from an oak tree on the basis of different *archai*, or how a human rhetor differs from an animal whose being is not in the same way as Dasein's speaking-with-one-another), but also the ways beings and their ways of being oftentimes overlap and intertwine with one another.

In his reading of the Marburg lectures, Daniel Gross makes a striking observation that in my view perfectly captures the twofold way Aristotle and Heidegger have for understanding how beings are in the world. As Heidegger weaves his way through Aristotle's corpus over his three-month lecture course—along the way touching on the *Metaphysics, Politics, Nicomachean Ethics, Rhetoric, Topics, De anima, De mutu animalium,* and *Physics*—it is *pathos*, that key term from the *Rhetoric*, that Gross argues "provides the transfer point between social and naturo-physical phenomena" in Aristotle's metaphysical view of things.[99]

> According to Heidegger's reading of Aristotle, Being-with-one-another turns out to be only one way of being among many—living and nonliving, human and nonhuman. The shared ontology of all Being, claims Heidegger, is grounded in the categories of Aristotle's *Physics* (284). The pathos of a stone allows it to become part of a wall, the pathos of a plant to grow, the pathos of an animal to perceive imminent danger and to shriek a warning to others. Unique to human pathos is a

dependence on *nous poietikos*: the human faculty that allows us to extend into every domain of being and be moved even by things that are not there in body. Thinking allows us to be with others in a manner unattainable for other animals [...] Though only human being is moved to discourse, or *logos*, Being-moved is essential to all [...] What we share with things of all sorts is body-in-movement, a movement characterized by pathos.[100]

That it may be possible to consider the "*pathos* of a stone" suggests that for Aristotle rhetoric is epitomized by—and yet cannot be fully reduced to—the *logos* of human beings. As we saw above, for Aristotle even artificial things have their being in movedness and rest. Perhaps what distinguishes rhetoric, then, is its capacity to see and reveal not only how beings are in their beingness but also, and as important, how beings relate to and affect one another as similar "bodies-in-movement." At the core of Aristotle's rhetorical realism, then, lies both an attunement to the being of beings (living and nonliving, human and nonhuman) and an understanding—or more accurately *a desire to understand*—that such beings move and are moved by one another.

Beings That Matter

What Heidegger demonstrates over the course of his 1924 Marburg lectures is that Aristotle's inquiry into rhetoric is nothing less than an inquiry into human being-there—into the "*how of being*," or the ways human beings have for being-with-one-another.[101] As in his analyses of *technē* and *phusis*, Heidegger encourages us to approach the *Rhetoric* from within the structures of Aristotelian metaphysics, rather than as a more theoretical version of the *technē logōn* or *technē rhētorikē* that were popular in Aristotle's time. The advantage of such an approach is that it enables us to identify a characteristically Aristotelian preoccupation at the heart of the *Rhetoric*: a concern for the being of beings and the desire to cultivate an attunement to beings and the ways beings are in their beingness. When Aristotle turns his attention to the particulars of rhetoric, to the *pisteis*, *pathē*, enthymemes, and species of rhetoric (all of which Heidegger carefully explains to his students over the course of these lectures), he does so in concert with his goal of understanding human being-in-the-world as speaking-with-one-another.

As we have seen, this move toward understanding the being of beings is precisely the same move that frames Aristotle's writings on *technē* and *phusis* in the *Physics* and *Metaphysics*. For Aristotle, the focus must always be on the question of being and of how inquiry into the being of beings should attempt "to go beyond the givenness and availability of beings and to look into the horizon that gives rise to the advent of beings."[102] When we trace key terms across the corpus and take into account Aristotle's particular version of metaphysics, what we find is a series of comparable investigations that collectively suggest ways of thinking that take seriously "the how of

94 *Aristotle's Rhetorical Realism*

being," the ways natural and artificial things are with respect to their *archē* and movednesss and, equally, the ways the *zoōn logon echon* is in its being-with-one-another. Coupled with his willingness to intertwine and sometimes confuse distinctions between *technē*, *phusis*, and human being, the belief on Aristotle's part in ontology's applicability to all areas of inquiry exemplifies a particular form of realism at play in his rhetoric, one that acknowledges the existence and vibrancy of other beings—human, technical, and/or natural—and that works accordingly to cultivate an attunement to the being of such beings so that we no longer mistakenly equate their givenness to us with the meaning of their being as such.

Certainly, this form of realism is not one Heidegger would have named as such or associated with Aristotle. For all of his insight and prescience on matters ranging from ontology to technology, Heidegger remains a philosopher of the early-mid twentieth century. This explains, I believe, his eventual dismissal of the philosophical debate between realism and idealism near the end of the first division of *Being and Time*. While he initially commends realism for its ability to ground thinking in one's everyday being-in-the-world, Heidegger eventually concludes that realism, at least in its more traditional formulations, lacks an "ontological understanding" of reality and the real.[103] This is because realism tends to approach "the problem of Reality" epistemologically, assuming, for example, that "the Reality of the 'world' not only needs to be proved but also is capable of proof."[104] In the existential analytic Heidegger seeks to develop, beings can never be reduced to their status or value as provable objects. The same objection holds for idealism, which, despite its closer affinities to Heidegger's analysis of Dasein, also tends to treat beings epistemologically, only in this case as entities located "in consciousness" rather in an external world independent of thought or perception. Like realism, then, idealism neglects "any existential analytic of Dasein,"[105] which must account for how Dasein is in the world, including how Dasein experiences and is driven to care for its existence. "As long as idealism fails to clarify what this very understanding of Being means ontologically, or how this understanding is possible, or that it belongs to Dasein's state of Being, the Interpretation of Reality which idealism constructs is an empty one."[106] While Heidegger never revisits or attempts to revise these understandings of realism and idealism, his existential analytic of Dasein suggests at the very least that "reality" needs to be retained as an ontological term, because it is "one that relates to entities within-the-world."[107] In order to properly understand human being-there, one must account for what "reality" means for Dasein, for the fact that "*'Consciousness of Reality' is itself a way of Being-in-the-world*."[108] At the same time, Heidegger insists that we must also understand how reality—that is, how other beings are in the world—disclose themselves to Dasein and in so doing set Dasein on its way toward understanding the conditions and possibilities for being as such. While this insight may not obtain from traditional philosophical realism, it is very much in keeping with the ways Aristotle understands reality and how beings come to relate to one another as beings in the world.

It is reasonable to suggest, then, that Aristotle helps Heidegger understand that realism and idealism can potentially constitute different words for the same form of analysis that questions after the being of beings. Importantly, this insight reaches its fullest resonance for Heidegger not in his readings of the *Physics* or *Metaphysics* but in his interpretation of the *Rhetoric*, where the question of human being-there receives its first serious treatment. For Heidegger the culmination of Aristotle's thought is the *Rhetoric*, because this is the place where the methods and insights of his metaphysical system come finally to bear on the average everydayness of human existence. Aristotle's rhetorical realism thus turns out to be the final, critical piece that builds a way toward an analysis and understanding of being as the being of beings. And because it does not ignore, bracket, or dismiss the human—just as it does not ignore, bracket, or dismiss the reality of nonhuman beings—Aristotle's rhetorical realism offers Heidegger the perfect example of what it means to understand beings not in isolation from one another but as relational to other beings in the world, as being-with-others in the world. As he says in his *Introduction to Metaphysics*,

> We do mean beings as a whole, but without any particular preference. Still, it is remarkable that *one* being always keeps coming to the fore in this questioning [about why there are beings at all instead of nothing]: the human beings who pose this question. And yet the question should not be about some particular, individual being. Given the unrestricted range of the question, every being counts as much as any other. Some elephant in some jungle in India is in being just as much as some chemical oxidation process on the planet Mars, and whatever else you please. Thus if we properly pursue the question "Why are there beings at all instead of nothing?" in its sense as a question, we must avoid emphasizing any particular, individual being, not even focusing on the human being.[109]

When we approach things differently, when we oscillate our orientation between the epistemological to the ontological—when we learn to see things as rhetorical realists, in other words—we find that beings are not just multiple but that they *matter* as much as all other beings. This is how Aristotle tries to imagine the world and rhetoric's place in that world. For Aristotle, understanding a speaker's ability to persuasively communicate about things barely scratches the surface of what rhetoric is. While he undeniably privileges speech as essential to human beings' way of being in the world, this does not mean that Aristotle is the direct precursor to the discursive rhetorics of the twentieth and twenty-first centuries. Because *logos* constitutes for Aristotle the way humans have for disclosing other beings and questioning after the being of beings, rhetoric cannot be defined by nor reduced to the particular tools human speakers employ to affect audiences or the specific messages they communicate through speech.

Ultimately, rhetoric for Aristotle is best understood as the practice and study of beings whose way of being is being-with-one-another in the world. To be rhetorical is to already be in the world and to have an attunement toward other beings, be they fellow interlocutors, distant relatives, or some jungle in India. This is perhaps the most fundamental insight rhetorical realism stands to learn from Aristotle. When read indirectly and at times against the grain of his own thought, Aristotle invites rhetoricians to reconsider the ways human and nonhuman beings exist together and in so doing produce the conditions of possibility for rhetorical action. Of course, such an attunement to the being of beings raises a number of ethical questions about what it means to live with others and to care responsibly for other beings. As Heidegger says, "In Being-with-one-another we have with an Other the same world. Being-with-one-another is at the same time *having the same world with an Other*."[110] We will explore this and other ethical issues in more detail in Chapter 5. In the meantime, let us further explore the realist territory opened up through Aristotle by considering rhetorical realism's place in early modern conceptions of language (Chapter 3) and its bearings on modern and postmodern conceptions of knowledge and its limits in the face of unknowable realities (Chapter 4).

Notes

1. Walter J. Ong, "Religion, Scholarship, and the Resituation of Man," *Daedalus* 91, no. 2 (1962): 425.
2. Edwin Black, *Rhetorical Criticism: A Study in Method* (Madison: University of Wisconsin Press, 1965), 39.
3. Susan C. Jarratt, *Rereading the Sophists: Classical Rhetoric Refigured* (Carbondale: Southern Illinois University Press, 1991), xviii.
4. Martin Heidegger, "What is Metaphysics?" in *Basic Writings*, ed. David Farrell Krell (New York: HarperCollings, 1993), 110.
5. James W. Hikins, "Realism and Its Implications for Rhetorical Theory," in *Rhetoric and Philosophy*, ed. Richard A. Cherwitz (New York: Routledge, 1990), 24.
6. Sextus. *Against the Schoolmasters*, in *The Older Sophists*, ed. Rosamond Kent Sprague (Indianapolis: Hackett, 2001), 18.
7. John Poulakos, "Rhetoric, the Sophists, and the Possible," *Communication Monographs* 51 (1984): 216.
8. Ibid., 217.
9. Cicero, *De Inventione*, trans. H.M. Hubbell (Cambridge: Loeb Classical Library, 1949), 1.7.
10. Jasper Neel, *Aristotle's Voice: Rhetoric, Theory, and Writing in America* (Carbondale: Southern Illinois University Press, 1994), 40–48. See also, George A. Kennedy, *Classical Rhetoric and its Christian and Secular Tradition: From Ancient to Contemporary Times, 2nd Edition* (Chapel Hill: University of North Carolina Press, 1999), 79–80.

Aristotle's Rhetorical Realism 97

11. Brian Vickers, In *Defense of Rhetoric* (Clarendon Press, 1988), 18.
12. Kennedy, *Classical Rhetoric and its Christian and Secular Tradition*, 63–64.
13. George A. Kennedy, prooemion to Aristotle's *On Rhetoric*, ed. Kennedy (New York: Oxford University Press, 1991), xi.
14. Neel, 91.
15. Ibid., 50.
16. Aristotle, *Nicomachean Ethics*, trans. David Ross (New York: Oxford University Press, 1998), 1139b18–32.
17. Bradford Vivian, *Being Made Strange: Rhetoric Beyond Representation* (Albany: SUNY Press, 2004), 25.
18. Ibid., 24.
19. Ibid., 4.
20. Martin Heidegger, *Introduction to Metaphysics*, trans. Gregory Fried and Richard Polt (New Haven: Yale University Press, 2000), 18.
21. Heidegger, "What is Metaphysics?" 106.
22. Aristotle, *Physics*, trans by R.P. Hardie and R.K. Gaye, in *The Basic Works of Aristotle*, ed. Richard McKeon (New York: Random House, 2001), 251b1–7.
23. Aristotle, *Sophistical Refutations*, trans. Jonathan Barnes, in *The Complete Works of Aristotle, Vol. 1*, ed. Barnes (Princeton: Princeton University Press, 1984), 165a20–22. See also, Aristotle, *Metaphysics*, 1004b18–23.
24. Aristotle, *Metaphysics*, trans W.D. Ross, in *The Basic Works of Aristotle*, ed Richard McKeon (New York: Random House, 2001), 1010a1–6.
25. Ibid., 1010b31–1011a3.
26. James A. Berlin, "Aristotle's Rhetoric in Context: Interpreting Historically," in *A Rhetoric of Doing: Essays on Written Disocurse in Honor of James L. Kinneavy*, eds. Stephen P. Witte, Neil Nakadate, and Roger D. Cherry (Carbondale: Southern Illinois University Press, 1992), 55.
27. Aristotle, *On Rhetoric: A Theory of Civic Discourse*, trans George A. Kennedy (New York: Oxford University Press, 1991), 1354a3.
28. Janet Atwill, *Rhetoric Reclaimed: Aristotle and the Liberal Arts Tradition* (Ithaca: Cornell University Press, 1998), 70–71.
29. Ibid.
30. Aristotle, *Nicomachean Ethics*, 1138b7–10.
31. Ibid., 1141a19.
32. Ibid., 1139a20–27.
33. Barbara Warnick, "Judgment, Probability, and Aristotle's Rhetoric," *Quarterly Journal of Speech* 9 (1989): 304. See also, Michael Bernard-Donals, *The Practice of Theory: Rhetoric, Knowledge, and Pedagogy in the Academy* (Cambridge: Cambridge University Press, 1998), 39–46.
34. Aristotle, *Nicomachean Ethics*, 1141a7–8.
35. Ibid., 1141b2–3.
36. Ibid., 1141a23.
37. Ibid., 1141a35.
38. Warnick, 304.
39. Aristotle, *Nicomachean Ethics*, 1140a10–11.
40. Ibid., 1140b5–7.
41. Ibid., 1140a11–18.
42. Aristotle, *On Rhetoric*, 1357a4–7.
43. Aristotle, *Physics*, 192b21–22.
44. Ibid., 192b28–29. See also, Atwill, 85.

98   *Aristotle's Rhetorical Realism*

45. Jarratt, xvi.
46. Poulakos, 216.
47. Diane Davis, *Breaking Up [at] Totality: A Rhetoric of Laughter* (Carbondale: Southern Illinois University Press, 2000), 84.
48. Kennedy, *Classical Rhetoric and Its Christian and Secular Tradition*, 77.
49. Atwill, 7.
50. Ibid.
51. Martin Heidegger, "On the Essence and Concept of *Phusis* in Aristotle's *Physics* B, I," in *Pathmarks*, trans. Thomas Sheehan (Cambridge: Cambridge University Press, 1998), 183.
52. Aristotle, *Metaphysics*, 1028b3–5.
53. Heidegger, "On the Essence and Concept of *Phusis* in Aristotle's *Physics B*, I," 206.
54. Walter A. Brogan, *Heidegger and Aristotle: The Twofoldness of Being* (Albany: SUNY Press, 2005), 49.
55. Ibid., 34.
56. Aristotle, *Physics*, 192b33–39.
57. Heidegger, "On the Essence and Concept of *Phusis* in Aristotle's *Physics B*, I," 193.
58. Aristotle, *Physics*, 192b32–193a2, quoted in (and translated by) Heidegger, "On the Essence and Concept of *Phusis* in Aristotle's *Physics B*, I," 198.
59. See Brogan, 49–50.
60. Heidegger, "On the Essence and Concept of *Phusis* in Aristotle's *Physics B*, I," 200.
61. Aristotle, *Physics*, 192b12–25.
62. Heidegger, "On the Essence and Concept of *Phusis* in Aristotle's *Physics B*, I," 192.
63. Ibid., 192.
64. Martin Heidegger, "The Question Concerning Technology," in *The Question Concerning Technology and Other Essays*, trans. William Lovitt (New York: Harper, 1977), 10.
65. Ibid., 11.
66. Ibid., 13.
67. Martin Heidegger, "The Origin of the Work of Art," in *Poetry, Language, Thought*, trans. Albert Hofstadter (New York, Harper, 2001), 57.
68. Dunne, 251.
69. Ibid., 336. See also Brogan, 31.
70. Aristotle, *Physics*, 199a11–19.
71. Ibid., 199b26–30.
72. Dunne, 337.
73. Kelly Pender, *Techne: From Neoclassicism to Postmodernism* (Anderson: Parlor Press, 2011), 129.
74. Aristotle, *Physics*, 192b24.
75. Ibid., 192b22–23.
76. Ibid., 192b30–32.
77. Dunne, 337.
78. Ibid., 338.
79. Brogan, 45.
80. Ibid., 44.
81. Aristotle, *Physics*, 981a-981b.

82. Martin Heidegger, *What is Called Thinking?* trans. J. Glenn Gray (New York: Harper and Row, 1968), 14–15.
83. Brogan, 46.
84. See Aristotle, *On Rhetoric*, 1359b–1360b.
85. Brogan, 45.
86. Heidegger, "On the Essence and Concept of *Phusis* in Aristotle's *Physics B, I*," 189.
87. Alan G. Gross, "What Aristotle Meant by Rhetoric," in *Rereading Aristotle's Rhetoric*, eds. Gross and Arthur Walzer (Carbondale: Southern Illinois University Press, 2000), 26–27.
88. Martin Heidegger, *Being and Time*, trans. John Macquarrie and Edward Robinson (New York: Harper and Row, 1962), 178.
89. Martin Heidegger, *Basic Concepts of Aristotelian Philosophy*, trans. Robert D. Metcalf and Mark B Tanser (Bloomington: Indiana University Press, 2009), 35–36.
90. Ibid., 33.
91. Ibid.
92. Ibid., 71–72.
93. Heidegger, *Being and Time*, 69.
94. Heidegger, *Basic Concepts of Aristotelian Philosophy*, 89–90.
95. Ibid., 101.
96. Ibid.
97. Daniel M. Gross, "Introduction: Being-Moved: The Pathos of Heidegger's Rhetorical Ontology," in *Heidegger and Rhetoric*, eds. Gross and Ansgar Kemmann (Albany: SUNY Press, 2005), 32.
98. Heidegger, *Basic Concepts of Aristotelian Philosophy*, 75–76.
99. Daniel M. Gross, 12.
100. Ibid., 13.
101. Heidegger, *Basic Concepts of Aristotelian Philosophy*, 45.
102. Brogan, 49.
103. Heidegger, *Being and Time*, 251.
104. Ibid.
105. Ibid., 250.
106. Ibid., 251.
107. Ibid., 254.
108. Ibid.
109. Heidegger, *Introduction to Metaphysics*, 4.
110. Heidegger, *Basic Concepts of Aristotelian Philosophy*, 162 (Daniel M. Gross's translation).

Bibliography

Aristotle. *Metaphysics*. Translated by W.D. Ross. In *The Basic Works of Aristotle*, edited by Richard McKeon, 682–926. New York: Random House, 2001.
———. *Nicomachean Ethics*. Translated by David Ross. New York: Oxford University Press, 1998.
———. *On Rhetoric: A Theory of Civic Discourse*. Translated by George A. Kennedy. New York: Oxford University Press, 1991.

———. *Physics*. Translated by R.P. Hardie and R.K. Gaye. In *The Basic Works of Aristotle*, edited by Richard McKeon, 214–394. New York: Random House, 2001.

———. *Sophistical Refutations*. Translated by Jonathan Barnes. In *The Complete Works of Aristotle, Vol. 1*, edited by Barnes, 278–314. Princeton: Princeton University Press, 1984.

Atwill, Janet. *Rhetoric Reclaimed: Aristotle and the Liberal Arts Tradition*. Ithaca: Cornell University Press, 1998.

Berlin, James A. "Aristotle's Rhetoric in Context: Interpreting Historically." In *A Rhetoric of Doing: Essays on Written Disocurse in Honor of James L. Kinneavy*, edited by Stephen P. Witte, Neil Nakadate, and Roger D. Cherry, 55–64. Carbondale: Southern Illinois University Press, 1992.

Bernard-Donals, Michael. *The Practice of Theory: Rhetoric, Knowledge, and Pedagogy in the Academy*. Cambridge: Cambridge University Press, 1998.

Black, Edwin. *Rhetorical Criticism: A Study in Method*. Madison: University of Wisconsin Press, 1965.

Brogan, Walter A. *Heidegger and Aristotle: The Twofoldness of Being*. Albany: SUNY Press, 2005.

Cicero. *De Divinatione*. Translated by W.A. Falconer. Cambridge: Loeb Classical Library, 1923.

Davis, Diane. *Breaking Up [at] Totality: A Rhetoric of Laughter*. Carbondale: Southern Illinois University Press, 2000.

Dunne, Joseph. *Back to the Rough Ground: Practical Judgment and the Lure of Technique*. Notre Dame: Notre Dame University Press, 1993.

Gross, Alan G. "What Aristotle Meant by Rhetoric." In *Rereading Aristotle's Rhetoric*, edited by Gross and Arthur Walzer, 24–37. Carbondale: Southern Illinois University Press, 2000.

Gross, Daniel M. "Introduction: Being-Moved: The Pathos of Heidegger's Rhetorical Ontology." In *Heidegger and Rhetoric*, edited by Gross and Ansgar Kemmann, 1–46. Albany: SUNY Press, 2005.

Heidegger, Martin. *Basic Concepts of Aristotelian Philosophy*. Translated by Robert D. Metcalf and Mark B Tanser. Bloomington: Indiana University Press, 2009.

———. *Being and Time*. Translated by John Macquarrie and Edward Robinson. New York: Harper and Row, 1962.

———. *Introduction to Metaphysics*. Translated by Gregory Fried and Richard Polt. New Haven: Yale University Press, 2000.

———. "On the Essence and Concept of *Phusis* in Aristotle's *Physics B*, I." Translated by Thomas Sheehan. In *Pathmarks*, edited by William McNeill, 183–230. Cambridge: Cambridge University Press, 1998.

———. "The Origin of the Work of Art." Translated by Albert Hofstadter. In *Poetry, Language, Thought*, edited by Hofstadter, 15–86. New York, Harper, 2001.

———. "The Question Concerning Technology." Translated by William Lovitt. In *The Question Concerning Technology and Other Essays*, edited by Lovitt, 3–35. New York: Harper, 1977.

———. *What is Called Thinking?* Translated by J. Glenn Gray. New York: Harper and Row, 1968.

———. "What is Metaphysics?" In *Basic Writings*, edited by David Farrell Krell, 89–110. New York: HarperCollings, 1993. 89–110.

Hikins, James W. "Realism and Its Implications for Rhetorical Theory." In *Rhetoric and Philosophy*, edited by Richard A. Cherwitz, 21–77. New York: Routledge, 1990.

Jarratt, Susan C. *Rereading the Sophists: Classical Rhetoric Refigured.* Carbondale: Southern Illinois University Press, 1991.

Kennedy, George A. *Classical Rhetoric and its Christian and Secular Tradition: From Ancient to Contemporary Times, 2nd Edition.* Chapel Hill: University of North Carolina Press, 1999.

———. Prooemion to Aristotle's *On Rhetoric*, edited by Kennedy. New York: Oxford University Press, 1991.

Neep, Jasper. *Aristotle's Voice: Rhetoric, Theory, and Writing in America.* Carbondale: Southern Illinois University Press, 1994.

Ong, Walter J. "Religion, Scholarship, and the Resituation of Man." *Daedalus* 91, no. 2 (1962): 418–436.

Pender, Kelly. *Techne: From Neoclassicism to Postmodernism.* Anderson: Parlor Press, 2011.

Poulakos, John. "Rhetoric, the Sophists, and the Possible." *Communication Monographs* 51 (1984): 215–226.

Sextus. *Against the Schoolmasters.* In *The Older Sophists*, edited by Rosamond Kent Sprague, 18–19. Indianapolis: Hackett, 2001.

Vickers, Brian. In *Defense of Rhetoric.* Clarendon Press, 1988.

Vivian, Bradford. *Being Made Strange: Rhetoric Beyond Representation.* Albany: SUNY Press, 2004.

Warnick, Barbara. "Judgment, Probability, and Aristotle's Rhetoric." *Quarterly Journal of Speech* 9 (1989): 299–311.

3 Speaking with Things
Early Modern Rhetoric and the Dream of a Common Language

As we learned in the previous chapters, realist commitments vary in their assumptions about reality and about how rhetoric engages with, embodies, and animates the things of the world. This has certainly been the case when rhetoricians have turned their attentions to language, which of all of rhetoric's subject matters lends itself most immediately to realist questions and concerns. Whereas sophistic and postmodern rhetorics tend to forward a tragic view of *logos* in which, through speaking, we come face-to-face with the limits of language to represent reality,[1] Aristotle, as we saw in the previous chapter, offers a sense of *logos* as emerging out of an intertwining relationship between art (*technē*) and nature (*phusis*). Aristotle's conception of *logos* is less concerned with representation than revelation—*logos* is the way human beings are; it is our primary way of disclosing our worlds *as worlds*, as places of meaningful relation with others and of concernful dwelling and deliberation. For Aristotle, *logos* cannot be anything tragic because it constitutes the condition of possibility for human beings and communities, making possible our being-with one another. For all of their differences, however, each of these conceptions of language (representational and revelatory) rests upon similar realist assumptions about the world. In particular, each assumes that language and knowledge take shape in response to the recalcitrance of things and forces outside of the control of human beings. For representational conceptions of language, this recalcitrance takes the form of linguistic constraints limiting language's capacity to capture the full plentitude of reality through speech and discourse. In revelatory conceptions such as Aristotle's, recalcitrance emerges out of the existential horizons that make possible speaking as such. For Aristotle, language reveals things—it allows the world to light up for us in different ways—but it never reveals things completely; something is always missed or held in reserve when the *logos* manifests worlds. In other words, while they each share a sense of the recalcitrance of *logos*, the representational and revelatory accounts of language arrive at this realization from different directions, one grounded in epistemology and the other in ontological claims about the nature of human being and being-with others. These two inflections of rhetorical realism, while complimentary, make a great deal of difference for how proponents of either approach come to understand rhetoric and language: whether it is tragic to not know or whether it is enough to disclose our worlds, however imperfectly, to others through speaking or discoursing. Epistemological and ontological forms of realism yield different results depending on how rhetoricians inhabit and think within them.

In spite of the important differences between representational and revelatory conceptions of *logos*, it is important to remember that versions of realism rarely, if ever, align perfectly with either epistemology or ontology. As we saw in Chapter 1, in almost all cases realisms weave together concerns about knowledge and being such that questions about the limits of knowledge often accompany questions about the nature of being and beings as such. This is certainly true of Aristotle, who adopts an ontological approach to reality and yet conceives of rhetoric—within the contours of his ontology—as the ability to see (*theōrēsai*) the available means of persuasion. This indicates that even as one approach (epistemological or ontological) sometimes takes precedence over the other, realisms often appear as hybrid entities, intertwining notions of being and knowing into different configurations depending on the exigencies of the time. Building on Bruno Latour's idiom, we might say, then, that realisms are "quasi-objects" mixing traditions, perspectives, and presumptions about reality. And similar to Latour's quasi-objects, rhetorical realisms are networks of discourses and actants that "circulate in our hands and define our social bond by their very circulation."[2] They "are narrated, historical, passionate, and peopled with actants of autonomous forms. They are unstable and hazardous, existential, and never forget Being."[3] The inherent complexity and instability of these networks makes them challenging to see if not to study as well. Nonetheless, it is important that we learn to see historical events not just in terms of fixed essences or stables categories but as fluid and shifting movements that variously mix and assemble worlds. Bringing such a counter-revolutionary approach to realism's legacies in the rhetorical tradition helps us see anew what we thought we already knew about rhetoric and "the history of rhetoric."

Nowhere is this counter-revolutionary historiographic methodology more appropriate, and arguably more necessary, than in the field's perceptions of the early modern period and, specifically, British rhetoricians' obsessions with language and the plain style. The mid-late seventeenth century was a period of renewed attention to rhetoric during which grammarians, theologians, and philosophers enthusiastically explored language's role in the dissemination of knowledge across cultures and disciplines. In the wake of Ramism and its reduction of rhetoric's scope to style and delivery, rhetorical inquiry in the seventeenth century turned increasingly toward language and the problems natural languages pose for representing reality to one's fellows. As H. Lewis Ulman suggests in *Things, Thoughts, Words, and Actions: The Problem of Language in Late Eighteenth-Century Rhetorical Theory*, one of the leading concerns during the seventeenth and eighteenth centuries was whether words map onto or "graphically resemble […] the things to which they refer."[4] As we will see, one of the ways early modern rhetoricians attempted to resolve the issues of referentiality was to invent new language systems that attempted to bypass the problems of natural language by making language more fixed, orderly, and, arguably, more universal. If a new language could be devised, one that all rational people, irrespective of nationality or linguistic heritage, could learn and use in their writing if not their speech as well, then, the reasoning went, it might be possible finally bring an end to the curse of Babel and the imperfections that have plagued human languages for millennia. As we will see, these efforts to construct new universal languages were closely tied to early modern assumptions about language and reality (the relationship between *word* and *thing*), assumptions rooted in Braver's R2 thesis of realism: the correspondence theory of truth.

As in my previous engagements of Aristotle, I believe there is something important we can learn about rhetoric and rhetorical realism from this period in rhetoric's history. Although historians over the past several decades have begun to flesh out a fuller picture of rhetorical theory in the early modern period, its legacy remains a contentious one in contemporary rhetorical studies. For some critics and historians, the period's obsession with the plain style and its penchant for developing new language systems succeeded only in diminishing rhetoric's importance by intensifying the Ramist reduction of rhetoric to the stylistic dressing of thought. In their introduction to Enlightenment rhetoric in *The Rhetorical Tradition*, Patricia Bizzell and Bruce Herzberg note how members of the British Royal Society "envisioned a world without rhetoric, a world where people would speak of things as they really were, without the colorings of style, in plain language as clear as glass—so many words for so many things."[5] According to Bizzell and Herzberg, for early Society fellows, rhetoric and eloquence were of limited value to the more important work of discovering truth and knowledge, work they saw as intersecting more significantly with the domains of science, philosophy, and dialectic than with rhetoric. *If* rhetoric would have any role to play in the new sciences, it would only be to provide scholars the tools to communicate—as plainly and transparently as possible—knowledge obtained through these other means. As a generalization of a specific period in history, this is a powerful and persuasive narrative. And as we will see, one does not have to look far to find pejorative accounts of rhetoric and eloquence in the writings of early modern thinkers such as Francis Bacon, John Wilkins, Thomas Sprat, and others.

However, there are other ways we can understand the contributions of early modern language scholars to rhetorical theory. Here, again, I believe, the vantage of rhetorical realism offers some insight. The early modern period is a particularly noteworthy one in the development of rhetorical realism as this was one of the first periods in which concerns about correspondence (language's abilities to capture the truth and plenitude of reality) arose in response to nascent forms of scientific realism in which things were being increasingly understood as objects of knowledge and (more mysterious and elusive) things in themselves. While concerns about correspondence have never been far removed from debates about rhetoric, it is not until the late Renaissance and early Enlightenment that we find rhetoric fully implicated in a conception of epistemological realism predicated upon a correspondence theory of truth. This historical convergence of rhetoric and realism, I believe, has served to color contemporary rhetorical theory's perceptions of the era and its sense of what rhetoric meant—or could have meant—for early modern scholars. In this chapter, I attempt to re-open the caskets of early modern rhetoric in order to see what artifacts and objects remain lingering in the dust. My readings of the Royal Society, Bishop John Wilkins, and their realist rhetorics build on the work of historians of early modern rhetoric including Brian Vickers, Wilbur Samuel Howell, Ryan J. Stark, and Robert Markley. While early Society fellows were unquestionably critical of rhetoric and eloquence, I argue that they practiced and examined rhetoric in quite profound and oftentimes explicit ways. Much like Immanuel Kant, whom I discuss in detail in the next chapter, Bacon and later Society members engaged in a "rhetoric against rhetoric," the implications of which point to a much more complicated and conflicted attitude toward rhetoric than some of our accounts of the era suggest. Building on these readings of seventeenth-century British rhetoric, I add another layer to their nuanced understanding of the period by highlighting how some early Society figures attempted to redefine rhetoric to better suit the realist paradigm of the age. This paradigm, I argue, was primarily epistemological in nature, although not exclusively so. The emphasis on plainness that runs through the writings of early Society members reflects a commitment to an epistemological form of realism in which objects of knowledge exist independent of us, thus implying that language, as a consequence, serves as our means of accessing and understandings these objects. This thesis is not especially controversial among historians. However, I suggest that in the writings of early Society members, especially Bishop John Wilkins, we find an accompanying concern with the ontological status of both objects and language itself. For Society fellows like Wilkins, epistemology and ontology were hardly separate matters of concern. For Wilkins in particular, the most pressing questions concerning language and rhetoric were simultaneously epistemological and ontological: What is this thing we are talking about, and how is it related to other things in the world?

In what follows, I attempt to reconstruct the distinct version of rhetorical realism that emerged in early modern Britain and eventually became dominant in much subsequent rhetorical theory. As I suggest in the early sections of this chapter, one of the ways early modern rhetoricians attempted to resolve the imperfections of natural language was to advocate for the adoption of a plain style that would alleviate the jargon and ambiguities that had come to define scholarly writing of the period. As several commentators have noted, advocacy of the plain style, while often combative in tone and highly suspicious of persuasive and figurative language, was not necessarily anti-rhetorical. Rather, advocacy for the plain style reflected a decidedly rhetorical understanding of reality and language's role in accessing and disseminating potential objects of knowledge. After tracing some of these early accounts of the plain style, I turn to the central case study of this chapter, Bishop John Wilkins's attempt to construct a universal language system. A founding member of the British Royal Society, Wilkins authored two important treatises on preaching in 1646 and 1651. He is best remembered today, however, for his unfinished attempt to construct a "*Real universal Character*, that should not signifie *words*, but *things* and *notions*, and consequently might be legible by any Nation in their own Tongue."[6] Although rhetorical theorists and historians have often mentioned Wilkins's *Essay Towards a Real Character, and a Philosophical Language* (1668), no rhetorician to my knowledge has ever examined Wilkins's notorious—and notoriously difficult—book in any substantial detail. Where we do find references to the *Essay*, these references usually serve as cautionary tales or as evidence of the period's obsession with plainness at the expense of rhetoric. To be sure, the *Essay* is a strange text, one overflowing with assumptions about the world and about the distinctly Western notion of reason Wilkins believed to lie in the heart of all human beings. But for all of its obvious problems and errors, the *Essay* is also an extraordinary and fascinating case study of rhetorical realism in action during the early modern period. In the course of explaining his universal language, Wilkins shows how, at the beginnings of modern rhetoric, epistemological and ontological realisms could be productively brought together in mutually informative ways. In addition to seeing language as a means of transmitting knowledge and corresponding to mind-independent realities, Wilkins asks his readers to cultivate an attunement to language's ontological status, to its material existence and constitutive power—in short, its *thingness*, its ways of gathering and emplacing us in new worlds and new ways of seeing and thinking of ourselves in the world. Ultimately, for Wilkins language is not only an instrument for representing things in the world (although it certainly has this potential); it also carries considerable material weight of its own that precedes understanding and establishes the ontological conditions for communing with one's fellows.

The British Royal Society and the Case Against Rhetoric

As one of the founding members of the Royal Society, Wilkins (1614–1672) played a significant role in shaping not only the Society's view of rhetoric but its attitude toward natural philosophy as well. Along with John Wallis and Robert Boyle, Wilkins helped to organize a series of informal meetings in London that eventually led to the drafting of the first charter for the Royal Society in 1662. These early Society fellows were drawn together by their shared enthusiasm for the new science and their "conviction that the inductive method as propounded by Francis Bacon was destined to create a new order of human knowledge and bring about vast improvements in the conditions of human life."[7] By 1668, the Society had already established its second charter and had welcomed a new class of members into its ranks, most notably Thomas Sprat, who would go on to write the definitive early history of the organization, Joseph Glanvill, a Latitudiniarian and champion of English natural philosophy, and a young Oxford student named John Locke. While the interests of the Society fellows varied, each remained true in their own ways to Royal Society's motto, *Nullius in Verba*: "On the word of no one," "in the words of no one else," or, "take nobody's word for it." The Society's motto is widely understood to have been an allusion to a line from Horace's *Epistles* where Horace proudly declares, "*nullius addictus iurara in verba magistri*" ("I am bound to swear in the words of no master").[8] As its motto suggests, the Society prided itself on its skepticism and its progressive stance toward authority and established knowledge. As one of the most visible signifiers of the organization, *Nullius in Verba* epitomized the Royal Society's desire "to renounce the authority of the past and to assert the right of the present to a fresh look at the facts and to truth to be derived from them."[9]

As an organization made up of clergymen, grammarians, philosophers, and natural scientists, the Society commissioned numerous opinions and treatises on a wide range of issues. With respect to language and rhetoric, the Society focused most of its energies contesting what Sprat in his *History of the Royal Society* contemptuously calls "the easie vanity of *fine speaking*."[10] The plain style celebrated by Society fellows sought to provide an alternative to the age's abuses of rhetoric and eloquence by transcending the "sophism of all sophisms" that, as Bacon says, is "equivocation or ambiguity of words and phrase, specially of such words as are most general and intervene in every inquiry."[11] If language could be brought into sharper accord with reality, the Royal Society argued, it might be possible to transcend the ambiguities and imperfections that accompany the use of words and phrases in natural languages. In this assumption lies the core of the early modern form of rhetorical realism.

The influence of Francis Bacon, and to a lesser extent Ramism, on the Society's attitudes toward rhetoric, language, and reality cannot be overstated. Bacon's philosophy—so essential to the governing philosophy of the early Royal Society—was itself a response to debates in Britain over the meaning and legacy of continental Ramism. In late sixteenth-century Britain, most accounts of language, rhetoric, and logic leaned heavily on Ramism and its method of delineating topics in terms of a progression from general to particular. With respect to rhetoric, Ramus and his followers advocated a radical overhaul of the classical conception of rhetoric and, with it, rhetoric's five interconnected canons that serve to guide the production of persuasive speech and writing: invention (*inventio*), arrangement (*dispositio*), style (*pronuntiatio*), memory (*memoria*), and delivery (*elocutio*). In an effort to simplify the traditional teaching disciplines, Ramus broke apart the five classical parts of rhetoric, assigning *inventio* and *dispositio* to dialectic, *elocutio* and *pronuntiatio* to rhetoric, and omitting *memoria* altogether. "There are two universal general gifts bestowed upon man, Reason and Speech," Ramus proclaims in *Arguments in Rhetoric Against Quintilian*, "dialectic is the theory of the former, grammar and rhetoric of the latter."[12] Whereas dialectic draws its power from the exercise of human reason, rhetoric, according to Ramus, only demonstrates "the embellishment of speech first in tropes and figures, second in dignified delivery."[13] Ramus's diminution of rhetoric to style and delivery looms large in Britain's fascination with the plain style, or what Walter J. Ong calls, somewhat contemptuously, the "nonrhetorical style."[14] Ramists in England and on the continent became known for advocating a simplified conception of language that could be stripped down to its barest essentials in order to facilitate the easy transmission of knowledge from one person to another. "Plaine delivery of the Word without painted eloquence," as the Puritan (and Ramist) ideal of preaching from axioms had it.

Although the influence of Ramism on early modern accounts of rhetoric is undeniable, it is less certain to what extent seventeenth-century British rhetoric represents a departure or a modification of Ramist rhetoric. In *The Advancement of Learning*, Bacon extends but also challenges the Ramist conception of method as relevant only to studies dealing with logic and judgment.[15] In contrast to Ramus and his followers, Bacon sees method as applicable to a wide range of knowledge-making practices including the "handling of knowledge by Assertions and their Proofs, or by the Questions and their Determinations" and the "delivery of the Mathematics, which are the most abstracted of knowledges, and Policy [Politics], which is the most immersed."[16] Apart from his account of the diversity of method, however, Bacon hews closely to the Ramist and scholastic conceptions of logic and rhetoric, a decision that, in Wilbur Samuel Howell's estimation, makes Bacon more of a "composite of scholasticism, of Ramism, and of something that looks to the future" (i.e., Descartes' focus upon inquiry).[17] Evidence of this can be found in Bacon's reading of invention, which he sees as separate from rhetoric and argument. "The invention of speech or argument is not properly an invention," Bacon claims, "for to invent is to discover that we know not, and not to recover or resummons that which we already know."[18] The kind of "invention" we get with rhetoric and argument is little more than "Remembrance or Suggestion," which needs to be distinguished from actual invention that results in new knowledge not previously possessed. Thus, Bacon concludes, "the scope and end of this invention [the kind associated with rhetoric] is readiness and present use of our knowledge, and not addition or amplification thereof."[19] For Bacon as well as for Ramus, rhetoric needs to be distinguished from other domains of knowledge—in particular logic and morality—because rhetoric deals primarily with the styles of thought that engage the imagination in ways that supplement the ends of logic and morality which are, respectively, to "teach a form of argument to secure reason, and not to entrap it" and "to procure the affections to obey reason, and not to invade it."[20] While he acknowledges the need for "Eloquence of Persuasions" in procuring the ends of reason, and in this sense aligns himself more with Aristotle and Cicero than with Plato, Bacon never manages to fully escape the shadow of Ramist rhetoric, which arrived in earnest in England in the late sixteenth century when Ramist ideals began to inform new approaches to teaching rhetoric, logic, and philosophy and continued to exert influence well into the next century.[21]

Bacon's excision of invention from rhetoric sheds further light on his view of language and its role in communicating knowledge "invented" (or discovered) through other means. In his famous account of the "idols of the marketplace," Bacon describes words and language as "the biggest nuisance of all" because words enforce themselves on the understanding and in so doing influence how we understand the world and things in the world.[22] Paolo Rossi, in his study of the search for a universal language, suggests that in order for Bacon to "get closer to things" it was necessary "to reject those terms which do not correspond to real things, and to learn to construct words which do correspond to the effective reality of things."[23] Certain idols or illusions associated with words are easy to get rid of, Bacon claims. However, things become more complicated when we are dealing with "the names of things which exist but are confused and badly defined, being abstracted from things rashly and unevenly."[24] The example Bacon gives is the word "wet." Rather than signify a specific object in the world, "wet" "is simply an undiscriminating token for different actions which have no constancy or common denominator."[25] "Wet" can signify multiple states of being, from being damp to being totally drenched and saturated with liquid. Bacon recognizes that there are "various degrees of deficiency and error in words," ranging from the class of proper names to the names of actions and, finally, the names of qualities, which are most likely to lead to ambiguity and misunderstanding in communication. As he suggests in *The Advancement of Learning*, words have the power to produce "false appearances [...] which are framed and applied according to the conceit and capacities of the vulgar sort."[26] While we may never be able to fully escape the prisonhouse of language,[27] Bacon believes we can learn to appreciate the threat words pose to representations of reality and, ultimately, the production of knowledge through induction and the exercise of reason and imagination in the pursuit of truth.

The impact of Bacon's work on the Royal Society can be felt in many of the Society members' writings—including Wilkins's, as we will soon see.[28] To get a clearer sense of how some Society fellows took up Bacon's concerns about rhetoric, and how the Society eventually came to accept a realist approach to language and rhetoric, it is useful to consider Thomas Sprat's *History of the Royal Society of London, For the Improving of Natural Knowledge*. Published in 1667 and most likely commissioned by the

Society itself, Sprat's *History* sought to defend many of the philosophical positions espoused by the Society's earliest members. Its biased origins notwithstanding, Sprat's *History* remains one of the definitive accounts of the early Royal Society, and as a contemporaneous window into the Society's thinking it is a valuable resource for rhetorical theorists interested in the period's attitudes toward rhetoric and the reasoning behind its privileging of the plain style. According to Sprat, the Society's interest in the plain style sprung from a shared contempt for "the luxury and redundance of *Speech*" evident in many understandings and treatises on rhetoric. Sprat's tone in the famous section of part two where he describes the Society's attitude toward style is one of fury and contempt, a noticeable change, Vickers notes, in his otherwise "generally balanced manner" throughout the rest of the work.[29] In his defense of the plain style, Sprat focuses the most on the "corrupt" and "wicked" forms of eloquence the Society hoped to replace:

> The ill effects of this superfluity of talking, have already overwhelm'd most other *Arts* and *Professions*; insomuch, that when I consider the means of *happy living*, and the causes of their corruption, I can hardly forbear recanting what I said before; and concluding, that *eloquence* ought to be banish'd out of all *civil Societies*, as a thing fatal to Peace and good Manners. To this opinion I should wholly incline; if I did not find, that it is a Weapon, which may be as easily procur'd by *bad* men, as *good*: and that, if these should onely cast it away, and those retain it; the *naked Innocence* of vertue, would be upon all occasions expos'd to the *armed Malice* of the wicked. This is the chief reason, that should now keep up the Ornaments of Speaking, in any request: since they are so much degenerated from their original usefulness.[30]

These new discourses of eloquence and fancy, Sprat goes on to say, "are in the open defiance against *Reason*; professing, not to hold much correspondence with that."[31] "Who can behold, without indignation, how much mists and uncertainties, these specious *Tropes* and *Figures* have brought to our Knowledge? [...] And, in few words, I dare say; that of all the Studies of men, nothing may be sooner obtain'd, than this vicious abundance of *Phrase*, this trick of *Metaphors*, this volubility of *Tongue*, which makes so great a noise in the world."[32] For Sprat, the "constant Resolution" of the Society was "to reject all the amplifications, digressions, and swellings of style; to return back to the primitive purity, and shortness, when men deliver'd so many *things*, almost in an equal number of *words*."[33] What exactly this meant for Sprat or the Royal Society is not always clear. In place of specifics, what we are left with is an inspired indictment of certain rhetorical practices that, in Sprat's estimation, served only to amplify and embellish thought rather than "deliver" things in as "pure" a way as possible.[34]

While Sprat's words are often cited as evidence of the Royal Society's hostility toward rhetoric, the degree to which his and the Society's attitudes toward rhetoric were universally negative is still an open question. If we take Sprat's words seriously (and no one has suggested we should not), the Royal Society certainly appears to have been openly antagonistic to rhetoric. However, as Brian Vickers and Ryan J. Stark suggest, it may also have been the case that early Society members were merely resisting certain uses or understandings of rhetoric and not necessarily looking to reject rhetoric altogether. Both Vickers and Stark argue that while Sprat and other Society fellows were clearly opposed to linguistic embellishment, they were not anti-rhetorical in their understanding (and use) of language. In their view, the main concern for the Society was not rhetoric per se, but rather the misuses of rhetoric among Society fellows' religious and political enemies that only served to exasperate ambiguities and indeterminacies in their rivals' published works. According to Vickers, "In effect the Church of England [and the Royal Society] propagandists constructed a self-validating myth of their plain style and rational proceeding. Yet, as Glanvill himself wrote, plainness is 'a Character of great latitude'; that is, it is a relative concept."[35] Stark suggests something similar in his reading of seventeenth-century rhetoric and science as responding to "the arcane worlds of wonderment and incantation."[36] According to Stark, the paradigm shift from enchantment (a theistic, magical, or charmed rhetoric) to plainness evident in seventeenth-century England reflected a cultural and philosophical shift in the country toward more empirical—and ultimately more realist—accounts of the world. Rather than try to do away with rhetoric altogether, Vickers and Stark suggest that Sprat and the Royal Society may simply have been objecting to certain rhetorical styles, all the while using many of the traditional tools of rhetoric—metaphor and amplification, for instance—to their own advantage. As Vickers argues of Sprat, it is possible these so-called anti-rhetorical prophets were not attempting to "abolish language but [to] bring it into some kind of economical relation to its subject matter"[37]—to in effect bring rhetoric into closer accord with things as they exist outside of language. If this is the case, then the early members of the Royal Society would have been following in a long line of rhetorical realists who, for centuries, have attempted to bring world, word, and self back together again.

"A Puerile Worded Rhetorick:" Bishop John Wilkins and the Rhetorical Art of Preaching

Of the Society fellows who inspired Sprat's account of rhetoric and language, John Wilkins stands out not only for the important role he had in leading the Society in its early years but for his broadly circulated writings on preaching and his attempt to construct a real character and philosophical language. A clergyman, linguist, and natural philosopher, Wilkins helped to popularize the Society's plain style, most prominently in his writings on religious oratory that merged Ramism, Ciceronianism, and new attitudes toward scientific knowledge. Like many of his Society colleagues, Wilkins was a scholar of wide-ranging interests and abilities. In addition to his work on the rhetoric of preaching and his universal language, Wilkins proposed new transportation technologies and designed several noteworthy scientific experiments. As Arika Okrent recounts in his history of universal languages:

> He [Wilkins] drew up plans for land-water vehicles and flying machines. He designed an early odometer and a rainbow-producing fountain. He built a hollowed-out statue for playing practical jokes on people; he would speak through the statue's mouth by means of a long pipe that allowed him to stand at a distance and observe the bewildered reactions of his targets. He constructed an elaborate glass beehive, outfitted like a palace with tiny decorations. Whimsical but also practical, it permitted the scientific observation of bee behavior.[38]

In one of his earliest works, *A Discourse Concerning a New World and Another Planet in 2 Books* (1640), Wilkins attempted to prove that the moon is habitable and that people can engineer ways to get to the moon by applying wings to their bodies or "training some huge bird to carry [them] or by constructing a flying chariot which would be capable of ascending into space 'beyond the sphere of the earths magneticall vigor.'"[39] Needless to say, Wilkins's interests ran far and wide, and it is in part due to his incredible breadth of imagination that he deserves a place in any account of rhetoric and rhetorical realism in particular.

Among rhetoricians, Wilkins is perhaps best remembered for his attempt to devise a real character and universal language capable of resolving the imperfections inherent in natural languages. This is an interesting legacy because, while several rhetorical theorists and historians mention Wilkins's language in their accounts of the early modern period, none has tried to explore the complicated taxonomies and assumptions that underwrite his new language. In effect, Wilkins's name and real character have been invoked to demonstrate how philosophers of the seventeenth century attempted to marginalize rhetoric's status as a knowledge-producing art. In his essay "Rhetoric," for example, Stanley Fish excoriates Wilkins for trying to devise a language system that "faithfully reflects or reports on matters of act uncolored by any personal or partisan agenda or desire."[40] For Fish, projects such as Wilkins's constitute nothing less than a rejection of rhetoric, a rejection born from long-standing suspicions about rhetoric's tendency to privilege "charm" and "style" over the straightforward matter-of-factness of the sciences.

> The idea [behind Wilkins's project] is that such a language, purged of ambiguity, redundancy, and indirection, will be an appropriate instrument for the registering of an independent reality, and that if men will only submit themselves to that language and remain within the structure of its stipulated definitions and exclusions, they will be incapable

of formulating and expressing wayward, subjective thoughts and will cease to be a danger either to themselves or to those who hearken to them. In this way, says Wilkins, they will be returned to that original state in which the language spoken was the language God gave Adam, a language in which every word perfectly expressed its referent.[41]

In Fish's view, Wilkins's desire to return to an Edenic state when word, self, and world were coincident with one another epitomizes the anti-rhetorical bias widespread among philosophers and natural scientists in the early modern period. Denise Tillery is similarly skeptical of invented languages such as Wilkins's. She argues that the form of interpretive control that obtains from the plain style in which readers are empowered to accurately discern differences between "metaphors" and "reality" was, in fact, "designed to standardize meaning" and thus minimize the "subversive tendencies of language." "To the Royal Society plain stylists," she claims, "the reader's subjective responses to elaborate language are sources of error and must be eliminated."[42] And as we saw above, Bizzell and Herzberg associate Wilkins's project with the era's attacks on rhetoric and the effects these attacks had on rhetoric's reputation during and after the early modern period.

To further underscore the absurdity of the plain style and Wilkins's dream of a universal language, Bizzell and Herzberg cite Jonathan Swift's satirical account of the language invention movement. In Book III of *Gulliver's Travels*, Swift's Gulliver finds himself at the Grand Academy of Lagado where scientists are performing a series of strange and comical experiments. In one laboratory, a chemist is attempting to extract sunlight from cucumbers. In another, an "ingenious architect" is celebrating his new way to build houses beginning with the roof and working down to the foundation. When Gulliver enters the School of Languages, he finds three professors of differing nationalities working to correct the imperfections of natural language. Swift describes their first experiment as attempting to "shorten discourse, by cutting polysyllables into one, and leaving out verbs and participles."[43] Their second project is considerably more ambitious, both in scope and presumption. Rather than work within the structures of existing discourse, the professors devise "a scheme for entirely abolishing all words whatsoever."[44] Because words are only names for things, the professors reason it would make more sense—and would help alleviate misunderstandings brought about as a result of natural language—if people simply expressed themselves through things themselves rather than through symbolic representations:

> many of the most learned and wise adhere to the new scheme of expressing themselves by things; which has only this inconvenience attending it, that if a man's business be very great, and of various kinds, he must be obliged, in proportion, to carry a greater bundle of things upon his back, unless he can afford one or two strong servants to attend him. I have often beheld two of those sages almost sinking

under the weight of their packs, like pedlars among us, who, when they met in the street, would lay down their loads, open their sacks, and hold conversation for an hour together; then put up their implements, help each other to resume their burdens, and take their leave.[45]

Even though this new way of communicating makes longer discourses more difficult and less practical, the professors agree that it is well suited for shorter conversations, particularly in one's home where one "cannot be at a loss:"[46] "The room where company meet who practise this art, is full of all things, ready at hand, requisite to furnish matter for this kind of artificial converse."[47] In Swift's biting satire, the absurdity of projects such as Wilkins's boils down to their assumption that communication is best undertaken through the exchange of actual things rather than through the more economical process of symbolic action. In the School of Languages—as well as in the Royal Society, Swift implies—speaking with things constitutes our best bet for ensuring absolute commensurability between speakers and listeners.

Such satirical accounts of the Royal Society and Wilkins's real character continue to resonate with contemporary historical accounts of the plain language movement in rhetorical theory, which, as suggested above, have tended to treat Wilkins as a cautionary tale reflective of a broader distrust of rhetoric in the early modern period. Although some of the textual evidence warrants such a view, it is also the case that when we fixate on the perceived anti-rhetorical bias in early modern rhetorics we risk overlooking some of the ways these thinkers were attempting to assemble their world into new— and newly useful—configurations. In the case of Wilkins and other language philosophers of the late seventeenth century, these configurations were both ontological and epistemological; while granting language a discrete weight and rhetorical agency of its own (a "thingness" that is not simply reducible to symbolic expression), Wilkins and his colleagues believed that language systems could be simplified in order to maximize correspondence between symbols and referents. As we will see, these two missions, while distinct in their respective emphases, were ultimately seen by their proponents as two sides of the same coin. As Wilkins's real character suggests, when we grant language ontological standing we expand language's communicative function and thus facilitate the dissemination of knowledge across cultures. Teasing out the realist commitments underwriting Wilkins's work, then, is important not only for what it adds to our historical understanding of early modern rhetoric but for what it suggests about the entangled ways ontology and epistemology consistently guide (and continue to shape) conceptions of rhetoric and rhetorical realism.

Interestingly, much of the fascination and perplexity surrounding Wilkins's project today was already anticipated in the reactions of his contemporaries, including some of his Society colleagues. (Like Sprat's *History*, Wilkins's *Essay* was supported and most likely commissioned by the Royal

Society itself.[48]) According to Robert Markley, Wilkins's contemporary readers were most likely to be drawn to the *Essay's* "aesthetic vocabulary of gentlemanly compliment."[49] For instance, an anonymous author in the early eighteenth century writes that Wilkins's real character "is Natural, Graceful, and Easie, containing a lively Picture, Description, or indeed Definition of the thing it represents; the Language [is] numerous, Copious and Noble [...] and more full and expressive than any extant."[50] Despite much of the praise given to the *Essay*, however, neither Wilkins nor many of his contemporaries truly believed it possible to institute a real character or a universal language. As Wilkins himself acknowledges in his Dedicatory Epistle, he has "*but very slender expectations*" of bringing a real character "*into Common use.*"[51] Ten years after the *Essay's* publication, Society fellow John Wallis, a professor of geometry at Oxford, offered a similar assessment of Wilkins's project:

> Not that [Wilkins] did expect, this *Real Character* of his, and his *Philosophical Language*, should universally obtain; and all Books be translated into it: But, to shew the thing to be fesible; and divers Advantages which might arise thence, if it could so obtain. And to demonstrate the thing it self to be Practicable; He was pleased (when his Book was newly made publick) to write a letter to me, in his *Real Character*; to which I return'd an Answer in his *Philosophical Language*: And we did perfectly understand one another, as if written in our own Language.[52]

These admissions cast doubt on some of the accounts of the language invention movement. If neither Wilkins nor his readers believed such a feat were possible, then, contra Fish and others, theirs was not a rejection of rhetoric or natural language but a distinctly rhetorical project designed to cultivate new understandings of the relations between symbols and things. The complicated but largely praiseworthy reception of Wilkins's *Essay* perhaps speaks less to its feasibility, then, than to its ability to diagnose and think creatively about problems of signification that were on the minds of many scholars in early modern Britain.

Perhaps we are getting ahead of ourselves, however. Prior to the publication of the *Essay*, Wilkins was already well known for his writings on preaching and the art of the using rhetoric to guide one's duties in the pulpit.[53] These works deserve a chapter or more of their own, and I direct readers' attentions to Stark and Howell for their careful readings of Wilkins's religious writings. For the present purposes, it is most relevant to consider how Wilkins's early works on preaching anticipate some of the claims he makes in the *Essay* and how these claims further our understanding of rhetorical realism in the early modern period. Outside of the *Essay*, it is in Wilkins's religious writings that we find his most explicit references to rhetoric and his support for the plain style. In *Ecclesiastes, or, A Discourse Concerning the Gift of Preaching as it Fals Under the Rules of Art* (1646), Wilkins claims that "The greatest learning is to be seen in the greatest plainness," a lesson he views as essential for anyone attempting to preach the Word of God to everyday people. One of the more noteworthy legacies of *Ecclesiastes* is that it contains one of the earliest uses of the word "elocution" as a synonym for rhetorical delivery (rather than as rhetorical style).[54] However, it would be inaccurate to label Wilkins an elocutionist, at least in the ways we typically understand the elocutionary movement. Unlike for the later elocutionists, for Wilkins delivery or elocution could not be easily separated from content.[55] In fact, Howell notes that for Wilkins delivery "was to be treated only as the fulfillment of a content and a form" discussed at length earlier in *Ecclesiastes*.[56] While he may have held a different view of the relationship between delivery and content, Wilkins shared with his contemporaries the desire to square his understanding of rhetoric with the influence of British and continental Ramism. Rather than reject Ramism outright, Wilkins tried to marry Ramist ideas with his own sense of rhetoric's importance in the pulpit and in the delivery of God's message to the masses. From the Ramists Wilkins learned "the practice of separating a whole into two or three major divisions, and of proceeding systematically to break those divisions up into parts, and those parts into subparts, until only indivisible units remained."[57] This practice plays out in his discussions of the processes for developing a sermon, which focus on proofs drawn from Scripture as well as from reason.[58] We also see this practice of separating and dividing in his taxonomical approach to language in the *Essay* where his method is to systematically break down the whole into smaller and smaller subparts.

In spite of the complicated ways he understood invention and its place in religious rhetoric, Wilkins nonetheless seems to have held a more conventional understanding of style and language, an understanding that would eventually feed into the development of his universal language. "The *phrase* should be plain, full, wholesome, and affectionate," Wilkins writes in the third part of *Ecclesiastes*.[59] He goes to say that the new rhetorical style

> must be *plain* and naturall, not being darkened with the affectation of *Scholasticall* harshness, or *Rhetoricall* flourishes [...] The greatest learning is to be seen in the greatest plainness. The more clearly we understand any thing our selves, the more easily can we expound it to others [...] How unsuitable is it to the expectation of a hungry soul, who comes unto this ordinance with a desire of spirituall comfort and instruction, and there to hear only a starched speech full of a puerile worded Rhetorick? [...] Our expressions should be so *close*, that they may not be *obscure*, and so *plain*, that they may not seem vain and *tedious*. To deliver things in a crude confused manner, without digesting of them by previous meditations, will nauseate the hearers, and is improper for the edification of the minde, as raw meet is for the nourishment of the body.[60]

It is hard to ignore the use of metaphoric language here, particularly for someone who is criticizing rhetoric for embellishing and distorting the true meanings of words and phrases. Is Wilkins simply being hypocritical? Perhaps not, as Stark and Vickers have argued. In any case, Wilkins's attitude toward language is suggestive for how it anticipates where he eventually goes in the *Essay* and how, in crafting his universal language, he hopes to bring rhetoric, reality, and knowledge back together again. Expressions should be "so close" and "so plain" that they do not obscure the nature of thing being expressed, he argues. From the perspective of plainness, the goal of language should not be to *represent* the world but to *deliver things* in such a way that they are not weighted down with "previous meditations" and can therefore provide the body something truly nourishing (the echoes to Plato's analogy of rhetoric to cookery in the *Gorgias* are especially striking in this passage).

For Wilkins, then, the aim is not representation, which implies a translation of one thing into another (object into word, for example), but the possibility of delivering things in such a way that they effectively speak for themselves, free of any "starched speech full of a puerile worded Rhetorick." As we saw above, this dream was shared by many of Wilkins's contemporaries. However, the dream of a common language in which things speak for themselves was not restricted to the Royal Society. Over the centuries, this dream has inspired numerous attempts to overcome the perceived corruptions of natural language. When Wilkins finally turned his attention to the goal of developing a real character and universal language, he was in effect following a long line of philosophers and grammarians who have dreamed of inventing the one true "universal" language. That all of these previous attempts failed to replace natural language did not discourage Wilkins. Indeed, he appears to have found inspiration in their failures, seeing them as opportunities to learn more about what makes natural language work and, by extension, how best to apply our understanding of natural language to the invention of a new universal and philosophical language. Ultimately, however, the genius of Wilkins's real character was not its complexity (it, too, failed to replace natural language, of course) but its attempt to establish a new rhetorical language for delivering things in ways adherent to the patterns of logic and natural language. The result is a fascinating case study of the ways some early moderns attempted to marry rhetoric and realist ideas into new configurations adaptable to the multiple exigencies (scientific, political, religious) of their time.

Wilkins's Dream of a Common Language

Wilkins opens his *Essay* by rehearsing one of the key inspirations behind the language invention movement: the desire to find a solution to Babel—to "remedy the Curse of the Confusion," as he writes in his Dedicatory Epistle.[61] Given his background and prior work on religious oratory, it makes sense that Wilkins would attempt to justify his real character on the basis of long-standing scriptural concerns. However, as Umberto Eco suggests in *The Search for the Perfect Language*, the biblical language Wilkins employs at times in the *Essay* may not have been as consequential to him (or to his readers) as one might expect. Prior the seventeenth century, the search for a perfect language "arose from profound tensions of a religious nature," Eco explains.[62] With advent of a priori philosophical languages in the seventeenth century, however, the religious impetus became increasingly tempered by a more secular aim: the elimination of "the *idola* responsible for clouding the minds of men and for keeping them afar from the progress of science."[63] As Eco further suggests, for seventeenth-century language inventors such as Wilkins, there was no longer "any question of discovering the lost language of humanity." Instead, "the new language was to be a new and totally artificial language, founded upon philosophic principles, and capable of realizing, by rational means, that which the various purported holy languages (always dreamt of, never really discovered) had sought but failed to find."[64] Alongside references to biblical mandate, Wilkins emphasizes how a new philosophical language could help facilitate "mutual Commerce, amongst the several Nations of the World, and the improving of all Natural knowledge."[65] According to Wilkins, languages such as English had undergone tremendous change over just a few centuries—so much change, Wilkins insists, that the English language spoken in his time would be virtually unrecognizable to English speakers from just a century previous. The reasons for these changes are complex, of course. Among other things, Wilkins credits the infusion of colonial languages into European languages as well as the addition of new words and other embellishments of language that were introduced simply "for the more easie and graceful sound."[66] Ultimately, however, Wilkins insists that every change in language "is a *gradual corruption*"[67] of the language, a further deterioration of language's abilities to approximate the reality of things outside of its representational and communicative functions. Thus, Wilkins predicts that in order to facilitate "mutual Commerce" and the dissemination of knowledge across cultures, a new language must be devised, one simple, methodical, and universal enough to provide for "more easy conversing with those of other Nations."[68]

Given his view of language and language change, it stands to reason that Wilkins would see his real character as a cure for the corruptions of his own and other natural languages. Indeed, one place where we see this problem-solution logic most clearly is in the overall arrangement of the *Essay* itself. Following the dedicatory epistle and a note to the reader, Wilkins offers a prolegomena that specifies the origins and corruptions of natural languages and prescribes a new philosophical language capable of rectifying these problems. The *Essay's* second part introduces the "universal philosophy" of Wilkins's real character, which includes numerous tables (discussed below) representing the genus of things arranged according to "their natural order, dependence, and relations."[69] The third part explores what Wilkins calls his system's "philosophical grammar" (including particles, prepositions, syntax, and orthography). Finally, in the fourth part, Wilkins offers some examples and discussions of his real character, most notably transcriptions of the Lord's Prayer and the Creed into his new written language.

In this final section, Wilkins also appends a dictionary of English words that can be "sufficiently expressed of the Philosophical Tables" contained in the *Essay*.[70]

As his title indicates, Wilkins is primarily concerned with developing a "real character" that is at once systematic and universal. Wilkins's use of the term "real character" echoes Bacon's distinction in the *Advancement of Learning* and *De augmentis scientiarum* between hieroglyphs and "Characters Real." In Bacon's view, hieroglyphs "have evermore [...] an affinity with the things signified."[71] Real characters, on the other hand, are "not at all emblematic," but are instead artificially constructed characters that, through custom and usage, have become agreed upon representations of "things and notions."[72] Unlike their alphabetic counterparts, real characters "represent not just letters or words, but things and notions."[73] Bacon points to Chinese ideograms as instances of real characters. Rather than represent distinct sounds, Chinese characters "stand directly for a signified notion without the mediation of a verbal language."[74] As such, Chinese characters enable speakers from different dialect groups to communicate and understand one another through writing. The potential benefit of developing analogous real characters in Europe was not lost on Bacon. However, Bacon recognizes that inventing a language of this order would require a vast number of new characters. For such a new universal language to function efficiently, he cautions, "there ought to be as many [characters] as there are radical words."[75] While Wilkins does not share Bacon's skepticism regarding the feasibility of developing a universal language, he accepts Bacon's conception of real characters, describing the function of his own "universal real character" in similar terms as different from ordinary notions of language because it would not "signfie *words*, but *things* and *notions*, and consequently might be legible by any Nation in their own Tongue."[76] As Wilkins further explains:

> If to every thing and notion there were assigned a distinct *Mark*, together with some *provision* to express Grammatical *Derivations* and *Inflexions*; this might suffice as to one great end of a *Real Character*, namely, the expression of our Conceptions by *Marks* which should signifie *things*, and not *words*. And so likewise if several distinct *words* were assigned for the *names* of such things, with certain invariable *Rules* for all such Grammatics *Derivations* and *Inflexions*, and such onely, as are natural and necessary; this would make a much more easie and convenient Language then is yet in being.[77]

Like Bacon, Wilkins saw in real characters the potential for transcending the constraints of natural language and facilitating communication (and commerce) across cultures and nationalities.

Although Bacon himself never tried his hand at developing a new language of real characters, a number of his contemporaries did. In fact, according to Arika Okrent, "language invention was something of a seventeenth-century fad."[78] (26). In a 1629 letter to Father Marin Mersenne, for example, Descartes references a new language invented by a man named des Vallées. While Descartes appears sympathetic to the idea of developing a standardized and universal language, in this letter he also wonders about the pragmatics of learning a brand new language. *If* one could learn such a language, Descartes reasons, it would have to be based in the logic of mathematics because mathematics do not require us to learn every possible number, only to extrapolate clear relationships and sequences between numerical concepts.

> Now I believe that such a language is possible and that it is possible to discover the science upon which it must depend, a science through which peasants might judge the truth better than philosophers do today. Yet I do not expect ever to see it in use, for that would presuppose great changes in the present order of things; this world would have to become an earthly paradise, and that is something that only happens in the *Pays des Romans*.[79]

In a March, 1646 letter to Samuel Hartlib, Robert Boyle draws a similar comparison between real characters and mathematical symbols, writing that, "since our arithmetical Characters are understood by all Nations of *Europe* the same [...] I conceive no impossibility, that opposes the doing in words, that we see already done in numbers."[80] As Markley notes, such comparisons were commonplace among proponents of universal language schemes because they allowed reformers to capitalize on the supposedly "natural" (and thus transhistorical) qualities of mathematical semiotics.[81] One of the more memorable examples of such a mathematical approach to language invention can be found in George Dalgarno's *Ars signorum* (1661). A contemporary of Wilkins's, Dalgarno based his invented language on 935 "radicals" which he believed to be the most elemental and essential concepts for effective communication. Unlike other universal languages, however, Delgarno's was not organized into a hierarchical tree. Instead, he grouped his radicals into stanzas of seven lines each, believing that such an arrangement would allow them to be more easily memorized. Rather than require users to understand a complex categorical hierarchy, Delgarno's language asks users to master all of the radicals. This results in a kind of compound language system where concepts like "coal" are rendered as "mineral black fire" and "diamond" as "precious stone hard."[82]

While he admired Dalgarno's system, Wilkins felt that its conjunctive logic reflected nothing of the radicals' meaning, "just their arbitrary placement in a nonsense verse."[83] To Wilkins's mind, a new language system would have to be just that: systematic. In contrast to Dalgarno's attempts to simplify language in order to make it easier to memorize, Wilkins believed that natural languages at their core function according to complex patterns in which meaning obtains from a character's relation to other characters in the system and not according to its place in a contrived (although potentially memorable) framework like Dalgarno's stanzas. What ultimately distinguished Wilkins from the pack of language inventors was his ability to capture not only language's symbolic aspects but to incorporate language's relational dynamics into his system as well. Well before Saussure and the rise of structuralist linguistics, Wilkins understood that meaning in language emerges from relationships between concepts, and that these relationships are what enable ambiguities and indeterminacies to proliferate. Any universal language predicated upon the philosophy of the plain style, Wilkins believed, would need to find ways to approximate the relational dynamics of language while at the same time ensuring that the meanings produced through these relations are consistent (i.e., "universal") for all language users.

Wilkins's solution to this challenge was to organize concepts into various hierarchical structures. To help ease its acceptance among scholars and everyday language users, Wilkins based his taxonomies on Aristotle's system of classification, which many early modern scholars considered a universal way of organizing natural things into logical systems of relationality. For Wilkins, "[i]t was not enough simply to invent real characters for the new language; it was necessary also to develop a criterion that would govern the primitive features that would compose these characters."[84] In the *Posterior Analytics II*, Aristotle suggests that to define the essence of a thing we must identify attributes which, "although each of them has a wider extension than the subject, all together they have not."[85] In the middle ages, this logic was famously represented as Porphyry's Tree. In a Porphyrian Tree, each genus is divided by two differences that constitute a pair of opposites. With the addition of one of its differences, each genus produces an underlying species that is then defined by its genus and its constitutive difference. In the first half the *Essay*, Wilkins arranges his real characters in the form of a Porphyrian Tree. He constructs a table of 40 major genera, subdivided into 251 characteristic differences. From these, he derives 2,030 species, which ultimately appear in pairs. According to Wilkins, these tables represent the whole of the knowable universe (see Figure 3.1).[86] Like many language inventors of the time, Wilkins believed that the completeness of a language depended upon the completeness of the tables, "which were a mirror of the order of the real world."[87] However, Wilkins also recognized that tables alone were not sufficient to exhaust all of the complexities necessary for sustaining a practical language. And so he agrees early on to limit his tables to those things of "the simplest nature:"[88] those forty genera and their various subdivided species. After developing his classification schema over some thirty pages, Wilkins turns his attention to his philosophical grammar in order to establish morphemes and markers for derived terms that will allow him to generate primitives, conjugation, suffixes, and so on.[89] Wilkins's language of real characters is then split into two different languages: "(1) the first is an ideogrammatic form of writing, vaguely Chinese in aspect, destined to appear in print but never to be pronounced; (2) the second is expressed by alphabetic characters and is intended to be pronounced."[90]

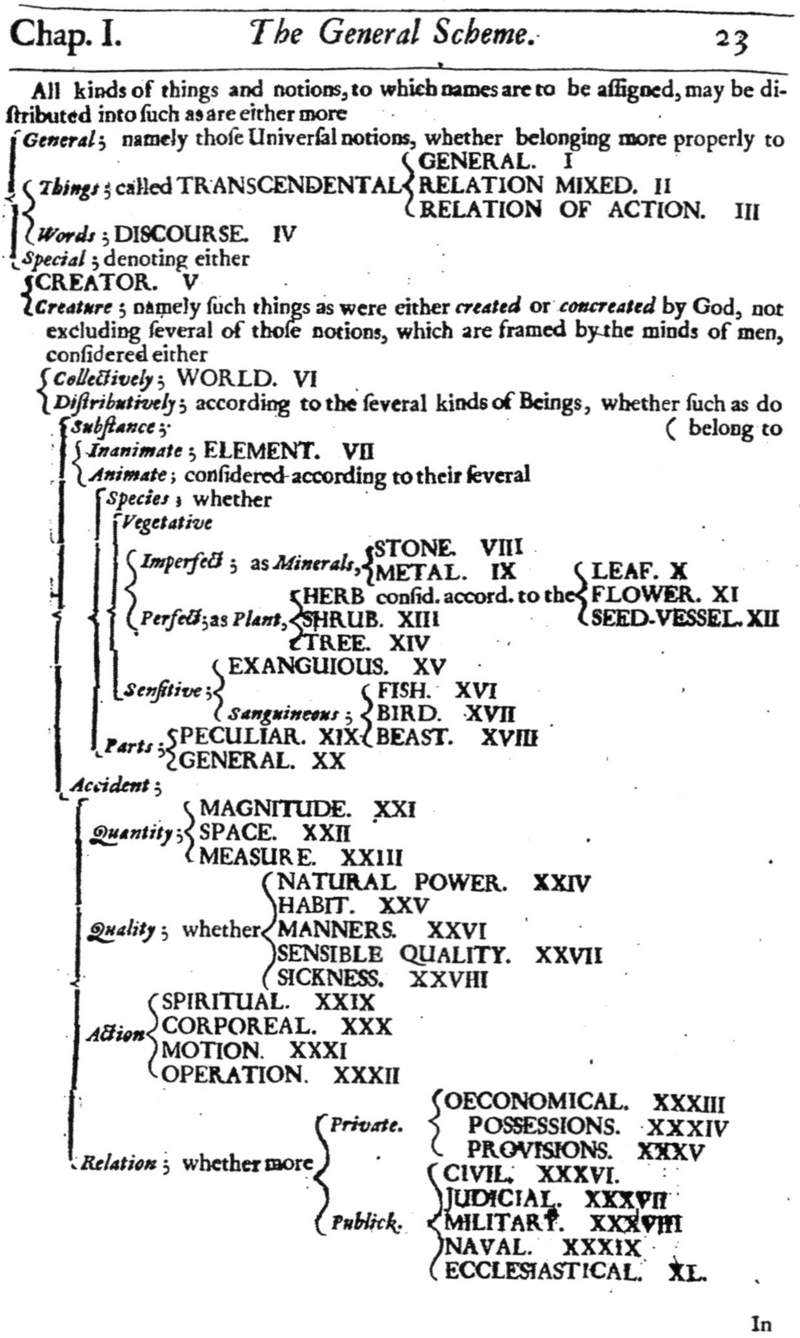

Chap. I.   *The General Scheme.*   23

All kinds of things and notions, to which names are to be assigned, may be distributed into such as are either more
- *General*; namely those Universal notions, whether belonging more properly to
  - *Things*; called TRANSCENDENTAL
    - GENERAL.   I
    - RELATION MIXED.   II
    - RELATION OF ACTION.   III
  - *Words*; DISCOURSE.   IV
- *Special*; denoting either
  - CREATOR.   V
  - *Creature*; namely such things as were either *created* or *concreated* by God, not excluding several of those notions, which are framed by the minds of men, considered either
    - *Collectively*; WORLD.   VI
    - *Distributively*; according to the several kinds of Beings, whether such as do belong to
      - *Substance*;
        - *Inanimate*; ELEMENT.   VII
        - *Animate*; considered according to their several
          - *Species*; whether
            - *Vegetative*
              - *Imperfect*; as *Minerals*,
                - STONE.   VIII
                - METAL.   IX
              - *Perfect*; as *Plant*, HERB confid. accord. to the
                - LEAF.   X
                - FLOWER.   XI
                - SEED-VESSEL.   XII
                - SHRUB.   XIII
                - TREE.   XIV
            - *Sensitive*;
              - EXANGUIOUS.   XV
              - *Sanguineous*;
                - FISH.   XVI
                - BIRD.   XVII
                - BEAST.   XVIII
          - *Parts*;
            - PECULIAR.   XIX
            - GENERAL.   XX
      - *Accident*;
        - *Quantity*;
          - MAGNITUDE.   XXI
          - SPACE.   XXII
          - MEASURE.   XXIII
        - *Quality*; whether
          - NATURAL POWER.   XXIV
          - HABIT.   XXV
          - MANNERS.   XXVI
          - SENSIBLE QUALITY.   XXVII
          - SICKNESS.   XXVIII
        - *Action*
          - SPIRITUAL.   XXIX
          - CORPOREAL.   XXX
          - MOTION.   XXXI
          - OPERATION.   XXXII
        - *Relation*; whether more
          - *Private*.
            - OECONOMICAL.   XXXIII
            - POSSESSIONS.   XXXIV
            - PROVISIONS.   XXXV
          - *Publick*.
            - CIVIL.   XXXVI.
            - JUDICIAL.   XXXVII
            - MILITARY.   XXXVIII
            - NAVAL.   XXXIX
            - ECCLESIASTICAL.   XL.

In

Figure 3.1 General Scheme, *An Essay Toward a Real Character and a Philosophical Language* by John Wilkins, public domain.

One of Wilkins's greatest fears was that he would not live long enough to complete his new language. Wilkins's concerns turned out to be prophetic, as he died leaving some of the latter portions of his language unfinished, most notably the phonetic aspects which he hoped would make his real character a spoken as well as a written language. Nonetheless, we can still learn much from the impressive amount of work Wilkins completed in his lifetime. From his existing taxonomies in particular we can begin to trace the realist assumptions that informed his real character and universal language. In Wilkins's trees, "the higher positions [...] are the most general categories, which are spit into subcategories on the basis of some distinguishing feature."[91] For example, at the top of his trees Wilkins juxtaposes two concepts, "general" and "special." Under "general," he first divides according to "things" and "words." "Things," he tells us, are "transcendental" whereas "words" refer to "Discourse." Under "special," Wilkins first divides according to "Creator" (which is not further divided) and "creature," which is subsequently divided into "collectively" and "distributively." Eventually, Wilkins's trees lead him to distinctions between "substance" and "accident," "quantity" and "quality," "inanimate" and "animate," "private" and "public," and "vegetative (which, oddly enough, contains divisions between "stone" and "metal") and "sensitive" (which includes most animal species). Altogether, Wilkins's tree of the universe breaks down into 40 numbered categories, each containing its own sprawling subcategories and sub-sub categories.[92]

Wilkins was not satisfied with simply offering another way to organize words into new configurations, however. He also maintained that a universal language would need to offer a sign system capable of representing the grammar and relations established therein. This new system would have to be comprised of new symbols and new diacritical markers that would identify the character's place in the overall regime of the established taxonomies. In keeping with his use of the Porphyrian Tree, Wilkins recommends new signs for each of the characters established as a result of his categorizations of things and concepts. His new sign system represents differences and species (the sign's place in the tree diagrams) with dashes (indicating a modification at its center to indicate genus) and little hooks and bars attached to the two extremities of the dash (see Figure 3.2).[93] For instance, if you wanted to know the real character for "dog" in Wilkins's language you would follow a line down from category XVIII (Beasts) to subcategory V (oblong-headed) and, finally, to sub-subcategory 1 (Bigger Kind). There, you would find the new symbol for dog, which consists of four discrete lines that vaguely approximate the image of a dog.[94] In contrast to other invented languages of the time, Wilkins's taxonomy did not only offer symbolic substitutions for existing words; much like our modern thesauruses, it also emphasized the meanings of concepts as they emerge relationally by way of contiguity and differentiation.

Chap. I.   *Concerning a Real Character.*   387

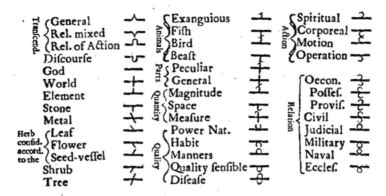

The Differences are to be affixed unto that end which is on the left side of the Character, according to this order;

1 2 3 4 5 6 7 8 9

The Species should be affixed at the other end of the Character according to the like order.

1 2 3 4 5 6 7 8 9

And whereas several of the Species of Vegetables and Animals, do according to this present constitution, amount to more than Nine, in such cases the number of them is to be distributed into two or three Nines, which may be distinguished from one another by doubling the stroke in some one or more parts of the Character; as suppose after this manner, ⌐ ⌐. If the first and most simple Character be made use of, the Species that are affixed to it, will belong to the first combination of *Nine*; if the other, they will belong according to the order of them, unto the second Combination.

Those Radicals which are paired to others uppon account of *Opposition*, may be expressed by a Loop, or (o) at the left end of the Character, after this manner, o—

Those that are paired upon the account of *Affinity*, are to be expressed by the like Mark at the other end of the Character, thus, —o

The double Opposites of *Excess* or *Defect*, are to be described by the Transcendental points, denoting *Excess* or *Defect*, to be placed over the Character, as shall be shewed after.

Ddd 2   *Adje-*

Figure 3.2 Of the Varieties of the Marks for Real Characters, *An Essay Toward a Real Character and a Philosophical Language* by John Wilkins, public domain.

Later in the *Essay*, Wilkins offers two examples of the written form of his real characters. His transcriptions of the Lord's Prayer and the Creed are presented to illustrate the simplicity of his new language because, as he notes, any characters worth their weight must be "simple and easie" as well as "graceful" in shape, "sufficiently distinguishable" from one another, and "methodical," having "some kind of sutableness and correspondence with one another" (see Figure 3.3).[95] Of course, the extent to which this script is as "simple and easie" (not to mention as "universal") as Wilkins claims is open for debate. Most likely, few average speakers or writers would have had the patience to learn this complex system in its entirety. Nonetheless, Wilkins's efforts to explain the grammar of the real character are genuine enough, and, as we saw above, were appreciated by many of his contemporaries.[96]

In addition to its overly complicated grammar, the main weakness of Wilkins's real character rests, oddly enough, in what it does not include in its six hundred or so pages. As Markley notes, Wilkins seems plagued throughout the *Essay* by the limitations of his ordering system: "Affinities [in his tables]," Wilkins confesses, "are sometimes less proper and more remote [than they should be], there being several things shifted into these places, because I knew not how to provide for them better."[97] At the end of the *Essay*, he offers a list of 15,000 English words that can be sufficiently expressed by the philosophical tables, thus suggesting that there is still work to be done by Society fellows and other interested scholars. For a language built on a presumably universal order of the world (reflected in Wilkins's adoption of the trees as coequal with Nature as the universal and transcendent order of things), such gaps can only serve to challenge the project's underlying methods and its aim of creating a real character capable of transcending time and place to become *the* language of the new sciences and economy.[98] Furthermore, as Eco notes, despite acknowledging lapses in his scheme, Wilkins presents his real character as a closed system, one that, once fully mapped, would no longer be able to accommodate names for yet unknown things. "Dominated by the notion of a definitely preestablished Great Chain of Being," Wilkins's language "cannot be creative," Eco concludes. "The language can name unknown things, but only within the framework of the system itself."[99] If there is one redeeming aspect of Wilkins's real character for Eco it lies in the language's enactments of relationality and referentiality. Wilkins's sense of relationality, Eco suggests, bears a striking similarity to a much more recent form of associative logic and aleatory invention: hypertext. Hypertext programs are built on logics of nodal connection in which internal references to other nodes in the program establish nonlinear pathways from one node to numerous other nodes.[100] Rather than organize things hierarchically, hypertext provides for lateral connections and references bisected by multiple pathways and multiple possible organizational schema. For Eco, establishing these kinds of pathways at a linguistic level seems to have been Wilkins's goal all along even as he allowed himself to become entangled in the Aristotelian system of hierarchical classification. If Wilkins had found a way to incorporate less rigid

CHAP. II.

Instances of this Real Character in the Lords Prayer and the Creed.

For the better explaining of what hath been before delivered concerning a Real Character, it will be necessary to give some Example and Instance of it, which I shall do in the *Lords Prayer* and the *Creed*: First setting each of them down after such a manner as they are ordinarily to be written. Then the Characters at a greater distance from one another, for the more convenient figuring and inter lining of them. And lastly, a Particular Explication of each Character out of the Philosphical Tables, with a Verbal Interpretation of them in the Margin.

The Lords Prayer.

[Real Character script]

1 2 3 4 5 6 7 8 9 10 11
Our Parent who art in Heaven, Thy Name be Hallowed, Thy

12 13 14 15 16 17 18 19 20 21 22 23 24 25 26
Kingdome come, Thy Will be done, so in Earth as in Heaven, Give

27 28 29 30 31 32 33 34 35 36 37 38 39 40 41 42 43
to us on this day our bread expedient and forgive us our trespasses as

44 45 46 47 48 49 50 51 52 53 54 55 56 57 58
we forgive them who trespass against us, and lead us not into

59 60 61 62 63 64 65 66 67 68 69 70
temptation, but deliver us from evil, for the Kingdome and the

71 72 73 74 75 76 77 78 79 80.
Power and the Glory is thine, for ever and ever, Amen. So be it.

relationships between characters, Eco thinks, "many of the system's contradictions would disappear, and Wilkins could be considered as a pioneer in the idea of a flexible and multiple organization of complex data."[101] As I elaborate upon in the next section, Eco's point says something as well about the realist logic underwriting Wilkins's real character and his philosophy of language. Rather than provide the essential natures of things through new concepts fashioned in accordance with their place in a Great Chain of Being, Wilkins's language models a relational theory of meaning whereby identities are established not on their own but through their (possible) connections to other things within the system. Unlike Saussure, for Wilkins this relational theory is not predicated upon the arbitrariness of signs but on the assumption that real characters correspond to actual things in the world. In order to construct his universal language, Wilkins needed to distinguish the essential natures of things—what things *are*—while at the same time situating these essences into a system that would allow for easier correspondence between sign and thing. In other words, he had to negotiate a pathway through the epistemological and ontological wings of rhetorical realism. The results are a complex and sometimes contradictory solution that sees language as both a thing in itself and a means for disseminating knowledge from one person to another.

Speaking with Things: Epistemological and Ontological Rhetorical Realisms

Understandably, modern rhetorical theorists and historians have not exactly known what to make of Wilkins's massive—and massively intricate—real character. On the one hand, readers continue to appreciate and admire the sheer scale and ambition of the project (sentiments most evident, perhaps, in works like Okrent's account of the history of invented languages). For rhetoricians, however, Wilkins's legacy has been more complicated given his prominent role in the Royal Society and his commitment to the plain style. For contemporary rhetorical theorists, the problem with Wilkins boils down to his characterizations of rhetoric and eloquence as obstacles standing in the way of truth and our ability to make knowledge commensurable through language. In terms of the plain style and Wilkins's real character, rhetoric can only appear synonymous with style and ornamentation, which unlike logic or grammar, serves to deflect and distort reality rather than helping to bring it more clearly into presence. However, as we saw above with respect to the Royal Society's advocacy of the plain style, this period in early modern British rhetoric may not have been as anti-rhetorical as some suggest. Throughout Bacon, Sprat, and Wilkins's writings we find innumerable metaphors and stylistic embellishments—sometimes in the same passages in which they impugn rhetoric. Whether or not these uses of rhetoric amount to hypocrisy or constitute a more nuanced attack against their rivals' uses of rhetoric, it is clear that Wilkins and his Society colleagues entertained a complicated and perhaps conflicted attitude toward rhetoric, one that saw rhetoric, at worst, as a problem to be solved, and, at best, as a potential ally in the construction of novel forms of discourse capable of meeting the demands of the new scientific sensibility. Hence, when rhetoric scholars such as Fish, Tillery, and Bizzell and Herzberg take issue with Wilkins for advocating a language "purged of ambiguity, redundancy, and indirection," they do so with an eye toward but one aspect of his complex understanding of rhetoric—in this case, toward his more inflammatory statements about rhetoric in works like *Ecclesiastes*. Another way to frame these critiques of Wilkins, then, is to see them as reactions to Wilkins's *realist* philosophy of the world—specifically, his *epistemological* realist view of things. While they do not always draw on the language of realism, historians of early modern rhetoric have tended to read Wilkins's view of rhetoric in terms of the correspondence theory of truth through which language functions as a medium for bringing mind and things into closer accord with one another. As I suggested in this chapter's introduction, however, epistemological realism is but one half of Wilkins's overall version of rhetorical realism. Alongside his assumptions about knowledge and correspondence, we find in the *Essay* a form of ontological realism as well that sees things as beings in their own rights irrespective of our knowledge or representations of them. This blending of the epistemological and ontological wings of realism, I want to submit, suggests a fuller and more nuanced view of early modern British rhetoric, one where assumptions about the accessibility of knowledge were supplemented with attunements to the ontological status of things in the world. As I suggest in this final section, the convergence of epistemological and ontological forms of realism in Wilkins's real character represents a critical moment in the development of rhetorical realism that continues to reverberate throughout modern rhetorical theory.

Broadly speaking, the difference between epistemological realism and ontological realism hinges on their respective assumptions about human being and the degree to which human beings are responsible for reality being what it is. Whereas epistemological realism claims that "our representations and language are accurate mirrors of the world as it actually is," ontological realism displaces the human's privileged status by refusing to "treat objects as constructions of humans."[102] According to Levi R. Bryant, ontological realism "thoroughly refutes epistemological realism or what ordinarily goes by the pejorative title of 'naïve realism.'"[103] Rather than treat objects as constructions of humans—or "being," for that matter, or "being *qua* language," or "being *qua* power," or "being *qua* history"[104]— ontological realism posits that objects, including human beings, "are not a pole opposing a subject, but exist in their own right, regardless of whether any other object or human relates to them."[105] By these accounts, Wilkins's real character clearly follows in the tradition of epistemological realism in attempting to streamline representations of reality and the dissemination of knowledge through language. Wilkins's tables, taxonomies, and script all reflect an effort to re-invent language by once and for all fulfilling language's promise to bring us closer to things in themselves. This is in good keeping with the major tenets of epistemological realism because, at its core, epistemological realism assumes a strong correlation between subject and object, one where the subject side of the relationship holds all or most of the cards in the "what is reality?" game. Whereas epistemological realists readily acknowledge the existence of mind-independent realities (more on this below), they insist as well that human beings have special abilities to access these realities—that, in effect, these realities exist (they *matter*) insofar as their discovery enhances our understanding of the world and things in the world. In this sense, epistemological realism constitutes a form of what speculative realists call "correlationism," or the belief that it is only possible to understand the correlations between mind and reality but never either term in itself. As we saw in Chapter 1, speculative realists see correlationism as *the* paradigmatic worldview of modern Western thought, following a line of thinkers as diverse as the Sophists, Kant, and more recent phenomenologists and deconstructionists. As what Graham Harman calls a "philosophy of access," correlationism privileges an anthropocentric view in which the human subject serves as the primary focal point or relay through which reality comes into presence and into meaning as such. Epistemological realism follows in this tradition when it essentializes correspondence—the adherence of objects to the cognitive and/or perceptual capacities of subjects—in an effort to render the world more accessible and knowable to human beings. This certainly seems to have been one of Wilkins's goals for his real character. For all of its complexity, Wilkins's language is first and foremost concerned with collapsing the distance between subject and object, symbol (character) and referent, so that language can finally serve as our mirror up to Nature.

As we also saw in the first chapter, one of the hallmarks of speculative realism is its opposition to various manifestations of correlationism. In order to understand the ontology of things, speculative realism suggests, we must first break the spell correlationism has held over us for the past several centuries. By uncritically accepting correlationism's philosophy of access, Harman and others argue that we have lost our ability to appreciate the depth, mystery, and plentitude of objects themselves—the ways objects exist and interact with other objects irrespective of our knowledge or perceptions of them.[106] Rather than see objects as agential and suasive beings in their own rights, correlationism reduces objects to their meaning and significance *for us*. Thus we find ourselves caught in what Quentin Meillassoux calls the "correlationist circle," "the argument according to which one cannot think the in-itself without entering into a viscous cycle, thereby immediately contradicting oneself."[107] From our vantage within the correlationist circle, "thought cannot get *outside itself* in order to compare the world as it is 'in itself' to the world as it is 'for us', and thereby distinguish what is a function of our relation to the world from what belongs to the world alone."[108] The goal of many of the new speculative realisms, then, is to loosen the grip correlationism has held over philosophy since at least the seventeenth century by asserting ontological considerations back into our discussions of objects and reality. In most cases, this has meant minimizing theories of language and signification, especially those that centralize language as our primary way of accessing objects in the world. As long as our understandings of language remain rooted in epistemology, speculative realism claims, we will continue to find ourselves trapped in the correlationist circle.

To be fair, many speculative realists recognize how challenging it will be to break free of correlationism. This is perhaps why Meillassoux resigns himself to working critically *within* the correlationist circle rather than attempting to find a clear pathway out of it. For all of his concerns about correlationism, Meillassoux himself is not especially interested in rejecting correlationism but in improving it so that it can accommodate (somewhat paradoxically) what it has been telling us for the past several centuries is impossible: "*to get out of ourselves*, to grasp the in-itself, to know what it is whether we are or not."[109] Meillassoux's equivocation on the issue of correlationism is instructive as we consider Wilkins's brand of rhetorical realism. On the one hand, as we have seen, it is easy to grasp (and subsequently dismiss, as Fish and others have done) the epistemological problems inherent in his real character. Truth does not inhere in things, and that is that, we could argue. However, as I have been suggesting, there is more to Wilkins's rhetorical realism than its adherence to R2 Correspondence suggests. While his new language certainly privileges correspondence between mind and world—in this sense, it constitutes a philosophy of access par excellence—at the same time it must also acknowledge the otherness and independence of objects *from* subjects in order for its case about correspondence to make sense in the first place. In other words, in order to legitimate his claims about R2 Correspondence, Wilkins must first suppose that there is *something* for truth to correspond *to*. This suggests a commitment to R1 Independence as well: the thesis that reality exists independent of the mind and thus of language's capacities to achieve correspondence between subject and object. While such a move back toward R1 Independence may seem contradictory, it is not uncommon when truth is defined as correspondence. As Braver notes, "If not mutually entailing metaphysical realism and correspondence truth naturally go together, which explains why the pair has been so common for much of the history of philosophy."[110] There are ways to get around this blending of ontological and epistemological realisms; some versions of idealism, for instance, attempt to locate the object of correspondence within the structures of the mind rather than in what Meillassoux calls "the Great Outdoors." But in Wilkins's case—and more famously in Kant's transcendental idealism, as we will see in the next chapter—we get a clear sense of objects existing outside of us and prior to our thoughts and beliefs about them. The correlation Wilkins is after, then, does not necessarily exclude the being of things from its orbit. In fact, it requires, as a condition of possibility, the existence of such things, an awareness that haunts almost every page of the *Essay*, making all the more urgent his efforts to invent a new language capable of getting us out of ourselves and closer to the things of the world.

While these ontological commitments are not always as explicitly rehearsed as Wilkins's epistemological goals, we can observe their traces in his tree diagrams, in particular in his adoption of the Aristotelian distinction between the general and the particular. In his introduction to his taxonomies, Wilkins suggests that creating a universal language requires a prerequisite understanding of the ontological status of things and concepts: what they *are* and, as importantly, how the differ from other things and concepts. While placing a great deal of emphasis on the correspondence between symbol and thing, Wilkins argues that any universal language worth its weight must also account for the being of things and concepts (and their relations to other things in the system) as well as their place within an overarching classificatory system. If his real character ever proves successful, Wilkins predicts, "we should, by learning the *Character* and *Names* of things, be instructed likewise in the *Natures*, the knowledge of both which ought to be conjoined."[111] In other words, by devising a real character based on scientific methods, Wilkins believes we will obtain greater understanding of the nature of things themselves—what makes a wolf a wolf, for example, and not a dog.[112] In describing his version of the Porphyrian Tree, Wilkins invokes the Aristotelian distinction between the "general" or "universal" and the "particular," writing, "The *particulars* are first in the order of *Being*, yet *Generals* are first in the order of *Knowing*, because by these, such things and notions as are less general, are to be distinguished and defined."[113] In the ontological terms of the previous chapter, the distinction here between particulars and the general is akin to the difference between *beings* and *being-as-such*. Much like Aristotle's discussion of general and particular justice in Book V of the *Nicomachean Ethics*, Wilkins's distinction conceives of particulars not simply as miniaturized expressions of the general but as more particularized beings nested and in dialogue with broader conditions of ontological possibility. In the *Ethics*, Aristotle equates general or universal justice with virtue (*aretē*). When we speak of virtuous acts as "just," he says, we are emphasizing a particular aspect of these acts, such as when justice is administered in civil cases or in the allocation of public lands to the needy. Justice in the general sense, then, serves as a kind of template for the everyday enactments of justice in particular settings. By understanding these particular expressions of justice, Aristotle says, we come to understand the nature of justice as a universal virtue: "With regard to justice and injustice we must consider (1) what kind of actions they are concerned with, (2) what sort of mean justice is, and (3) between what extremes the just act is intermediate."[114] The same logic holds for Wilkins and his taxonomies. The problem Wilkins runs into, however, is that metaphysics has not yet "enumerated and explained" all of these more general terms. If metaphysicians had succeeded in defining generals as plainly as possible, Wilkins observes, it would not have been necessary for him to recreate them by way of an elaborate new classificatory system. With Aristotle, Wilkins believes he must find new ways of approaching the general, in his case deriving understanding of the general from both its everyday meaning and, more importantly, from its manifestations in particular things "plain enough of themselves."[115]

For Wilkins, such "plain" things stem from nature and are therefore fixed and stable enough to ground his real character. Wilkins's critique of "natural" language and language evolution follows from this basic insight—that language, at its best, should enable us to speak confidently about the world by bringing the things of world into presence through speaking or writing. This insight sees language as more than a tool for representing reality; it sees it as an ontological condition of possibility, a way of being-in-the-world through discoursing or talking. Writing more than two centuries after Wilkins, Heidegger offers an ontological view of language not unlike Wilkins's, one that sees language as the way in which the world itself is revealed to *Dasein* as something we are concerned about and attend to in our everyday dealings with things and others in the world. In *Being and Time*, Heidegger characterizes language as an intentional activity as well as a way of revealing world *as world*: "Discoursing or talking is the way in which we articulate 'significantly' the intelligibility of Being-in-the-world."[116] As Rickert explains in his extensive reading of Heidegger's writings on language, passages such as this suggest that for Heidegger "language emerges from a background of holistic meanings and tacit coping" (rather than from an autonomous and individual speaker or writer) and, further, "that meaning already permeates the world around us, even if it is not yet linguistic meaning."[117] For Heidegger, language precedes us. Thus, language is already infused with meaning and possibility that is not necessarily the result of human action in the world. Language is our means of engaging the world, including others in the world, but prior to these activities language opens us to the world as an "a priori relationship and exposure to world."[118] Heidegger's best known, if least understood, statement on language—"Language is the house of Being"[119]—describes the ontological conditions that enable *Dasein* to come into relation with Being as such. As Rickert points out, contemporary readers sometimes view this statement as anticipating more recent constructionist claims about language in which language serves as a constitutive force in the production of social realities. Rickert argues against such interpretations, rightly insisting that Heidegger's statement must be understood within the scope of his overall thought, which resists idealism in favor of a more holistic—that is to say, ontological—conception of Being:

> Language does not grant things their being. Rather, language stems from world, understood as a composite of meaning and matter. On this account, the world comes to speaking in language and gives

bearings to being, human beings included, but cannot be understood to issue solely from human being; the world is the largely assumed and relied-on background stitchwork of relations emergent with our everyday doing and making.[120]

Heidegger's ontology of language gives a great deal of agency back over to language. "It is *language* that speaks," Heidegger proclaims. We not only give voice to language, he continues, "we speak *from out of* it. We are capable of doing so only because in each case we have already listened to language. What do we hear there? We hear language speaking."[121] Not simply the property right of human beings, language for Heidegger is what speaks by saying (*die Sage*), that is, by showing. Out of unspokeness or the unsaid (what has not yet been shown) emerges the possibility of a kind of saying that precedes signs and that puts us on the way to speech and that lets what is coming to presence shine forth.[122] This is *language*, and language is what "delivers us human beings over to releasement toward unconstrained hearing."[123]

Like other forms of ontological realism, Heidegger's ontology of language sees language as a suasive and irreducible thing of this world. And like all things of the world, Heidegger's conception of language cannot be easily reduced to human commands or interventions—it is what speaks when we are speaking; it is what disposes us to the world as world, as beings-in-the-world. It would be a mistake to graft Heidegger's ontological and phenomenological concepts onto Wilkins. That being said, I nevertheless want to suggest that what Wilkins was trying to invent—the kind of language to which he wanted to return—was a language that could similarly speak, to speak the world that is speaking us. While Fish was too hasty in dismissing Wilkins's real character, in my view he was correct in surmising that what Wilkins was after in the end was a way to "speak with things." But speaking with things, for Wilkins, did not necessarily mean returning to an Edenic state "in which every word perfectly expressed its referent." Nor did it mean living in "a world without rhetoric, a world where people would speak of things as they really were, without the colorings of style, in plain language as clear as glass—so many words for so many things," as Bizzell and Herzberg suggest. As we saw in his writings on preaching, Wilkins was hardly opposed to rhetoric or rhetorical figures. Even in the *Essay*, which feels like his least rhetorical work, Wilkins leaves plenty of room for rhetoric, most notably in his acknowledgement of the project's gaps and limitations and his hope that his Society colleagues will carry on his work.[124] Indeed, the gaps in Wilkins's system may prove to be as important as what he says over the course of the *Essay* itself because it is in the moments when the "elaborate fiction of objective and universal coding breaks down that we can glimpse underlying Wilkins's and his contemporaries' theorizing an associative logic that has less to do with a 'scientific' impulse than with the 'traces,' in Derrida's sense, of occult presuppositions that haunt their construction of the 'real.'"[125] This rhetorical sensibility carries over to Wilkins's real character and its ontological approach to language. For Wilkins, "speaking with things" is not only the (epistemological) dream of a common language, where the word perfectly expresses its referent, but an ontological attunement to the world speaking as such. The former takes its lead from the correspondence theory of truth, where truth and knowledge emerge from a correlation between thought and world. The latter sees subjects as fundamentally entwined with objects in ways that make it difficult to discern where one begins and the other ends. To speak with things in an ontological sense is to speak things as they are speaking you, not with the aim of representing the world accurately but in the everyday sense of being-in-the-world as being-with-others-in-the-world.

Perhaps the most lasting lesson we can take away from Wilkins's strange project is that epistemological realism and ontological realism need not always be at odds with one another—that neither of these realisms is "more rhetorical" than the other. As I have argued, Wilkins's attempt to create a universal language illustrates some of the ways epistemological and ontological rhetorical realisms overlap and mutually inform one another. While it arguably falls short on the basis of epistemology, from an ontological perspective Wilkins may have been on to something. He recognizes, for one, that language is not only an instrument for representing concepts in the world but has a material weight of its own that precedes understanding and that establishes the conditions of possibility for rhetorical action. Where Wilkins potentially falls short in his ontology is in presuming that one can master and control language; this, in the end, is his dream of a common language—that *we* can engineer a system that will reveal the world as such to us. Language, however, cannot be so easily reduced to human intentions or interventions. As anyone who has struggled to find the right words can attest, language resists us at times, it withdraws from our grasp, and it sometimes acts in ways we cannot always predict or control. These are not imperfections to be corrected or avoided but are what characterize language as such and that shape our relationship to language as beings in the world. Nonetheless, despite overlooking some of these ontological implications, Wilkins and his Society colleagues represent one of the first noteworthy attempts to bring the epistemological and ontological wings of rhetorical realism (back) together (again). As I argue in the next chapter, it is Immanuel Kant, the great German philosopher credited with cementing correlationism's legacy, who, somewhat surprisingly, offers the next step in bringing epistemology and ontology together again. With respect to seventeenth-century rhetoric, however, there is still much we can learn about rhetoric, realism, and language. A multi-faceted realist approach to rhetoric such as the one we find in the works of language inventors like John Wilkins may help further attune us to the rhetoricity at work in language and the world, so long as we are willing to listen to what language—to what rhetoric—is saying to us.

Notes

1. In the *Encomium of Helen* and *A Defense of Behalf of Palamedes*, Gorgias forwards a conception of *logos* that is at once constitutive and restrictive. While *logos* has the power to seduce auditors and change their views of the world, it also reveals the limits of language to bring things and knowledge into precise accord with one another. For Gorgias, the tension between the world-forming power of *logos* and the limits of *logos* to make worlds expressible is what ultimately makes the human condition a tragic one. As I suggest in Chapter 4 in terms of Kant, the sense of loss we find in Gorgias's works—that we are missing out on something by not being able to know it—indicates that we have at least tacit awareness of the existence of mind-independent realities. In the case of Gorgias, the specter of such a reality leads to a tragic view of *logos* in which reason and truth are no longer capable of adjudicating arguments (*Palamedes*) or resolving disputes (*Helen*). Similar representational accounts of language have been enormously influential in many postmodern and poststructuralist theories of language.
2. Bruno Latour, *We Have Never Been Modern*, trans. Catherine Porter (Cambridge: Harvard University Press, 1993), 89.
3. Ibid.
4. H. Lewis Ulman, *Things, Thoughts, Words, and Actions: The Problem of Language in Late Eighteenth-Century British Rhetorical Theory* (Carbondale: Southern Illinois University Press, 1994), 47.
5. Bizzell, Patricia and Bruce Herzberg, ed., *The Rhetorical Tradition: Readings from Classical Times to the Present*, 2nd Edition (Boston: Bedford/St. Martin's, 2001), 795.
6. John Wilkins, John, *An Essay Toward a Real Character and a Philosophical Language* (1668) (Menston, UK: Scolar, 1968), 13.
7. Wilbur Samuel Howell, *Logic and Rhetoric in England, 1500–1700* (Princeton: Princeton University Press, 1956), 448.
8. Ibid., 450.
9. Ibid.; see also Vickers, Brian and Nancy S. Struever, *Rhetoric and the Pursuit of Truth: Language Change in the Seventeenth and Eighteenth Centuries* (Los Angeles: William Andrews Clark Memorial Library, 1986), 15–16.
10. Thomas Sprat, *History of the Royal Society*, ed. Jackson I. Cope and Harold Whitmore Jones (St. Louis: Washington University Press, 1958), 112.
11. Francis Bacon, *The Advancement of Learning. Francis Bacon: The Major Works*, ed. Brian Vickers (Oxford: Oxford University Press, 2002), 226.
12. Peter Ramus, *Arguments in Rhetoric Against Quintilian*, trans. Carole Newlands (Carbondale: Southern Illinois University Press, 2010), 86.
13. Ibid.
14. Walter J. Ong, *Ramus, Method, and the Decay of Dialogue* (Chicago: University of Chicago Press, 2004), 284.
15. Bacon, *The Advancement of Learning*, 233.
16. Ibid., 235.
17. Howell, 375.
18. Bacon, *The Advancement of Learning*, 222–223.
19. Ibid.
20. Ibid., 238.
21. Ong, 302–303.

22. Francis Bacon, *The New Organon. The Works of Francis Bacon*, ed. James Spedding, Robert Ellis, and Douglas Heath (New York: Garrett, 1968), 48.
23. Paolo Rossi, *Logic and the Art of Memory: The Quest for a Universal Language*, trans. Stephen Clucas (Chicago: University of Chicago Press, 2000), 147.
24. Bacon, *The New Organon*, 48–49.
25. Ibid., 49.
26. Bacon, *The Advancement of Learning*, 228.
27. In both the *Advancement* and *Nova organum*, Bacon concedes that, while language dissembles, it is also the only means we have for discoursing our observations and understandings of the world. As he states in the *Advancement*, it is "not possible to divorce ourselves from these fallacies and false appearances, because they are inseparable from our nature and condition of life"; Bacon, *The Advancement of Learning*, 228.
28. While many Society fellows advocated some version of the plain style, this style was by no means universal in England, nor was it entirely uncontroversial at the time. Several recent studies have highlighted how contemporary natural philosophers such as Margaret Cavandish challenged the plain style, in particular for its presumption of a certain gendered relationship to objects of analysis. For more on Cavendish's contributions to rhetorical theory in the seventeenth century, see Ryan J. Stark, "Margaret Cavendish and Composition Style," *Rhetoric Review* 17, no.1 (1999): 264–281; and, Denise Tillery, "'English Them in the Easiest Manner You Can': Margaret Cavendish on the Discourse and Practice of Natural Philosophy," *Rhetoric Review* 26, no.3 (2007): 268–285.
29. Vickers and Struever, 4. Most students of rhetoric today have encountered Sprat's attack on rhetoric and eloquence (among other places, it is cited in Bizzell and Herzberg's introduction to their section on "Renaissance Rhetoric"). However, Vickers notes that Sprat's famous account of the Society's preferred style is virtually nonexistent in accounts of early modern rhetoric until well into the twentieth century. Indeed, even contemporary seventeenth-century references to these passages are "negligible." The relative dearth of historical attention to Sprat and the Royal Society's style is perhaps one reason why these passages are often read at face value with little or no contextualizing of them within the Society's complex political and rhetorical situations.
30. Sprat, 111.
31. Ibid., 112.
32. Ibid.
33. Ibid., 113.
34. Thomas Conley cites an example of scientific prose from Sir Thomas Browne that typified the kind of unclear and overblown writing against which Baconians and advocates of the plain style railed: "For if Crystal be a stone (as in the number thereof it is confessedly receiv'd) it is not immediately concreted by the efficacy of cold, but rather by a Mineral spirit, and lapifidical principles of its own, and therefore while it lay *in solutis pinciplis*, and remained in a fluid Body, it was a subject very unapt for proper conglaciation."; Sir Thomas Browne, quoted in Thomas M. Conley, *Rhetoric in the European Tradition* (Chicago: University of Chicago Press, 1990), 168.
35. Vickers and Struever, 42–43.
36. Ryan J. Stark, *Rhetoric, Science, and Magic in Seventeenth-Century England* (Washington, DC: Catholic University Press, 2009), 2.

37. Vickers and Struever, 7.
38. Arika Okrent, *In the Land of Invented Languages* (New York: Spiegel and Grau, 2010), 23.
39. John Wilkins, *A Discourse Concerning a New World and Another Planet in 2 Books* (1640), quoted in Howell, 448.
40. Stanley Fish, "Rhetoric," in *Doing What Comes Naturally: Change, Rhetoric, and the Practice of Theory in Literary and Legal Studies*, by Fish (Durham: Duke University Press, 1989), 474.
41. Ibid., 477.
42. Tillery, 271.
43. Jonathan Swift, *Gulliver's Travels into Several Nations of the World. With a Memoir of the Author* (New York: Oxford University Press, 2006), 214.
44. Ibid.
45. Ibid., 215.
46. Ibid.
47. Ibid.
48. Wilkins states on the first page of his Dedicatory Epistle, "I now at length present to your Lordship those papers I had drawn up concerning a Real Character and a Philosophical Language, which by several Orders of the Society have been required of Me."
49. Robert Markley, *Fallen Languages: Crises of Representation in Newtonian England, 1660–1740* (Ithaca: Cornell University Press, 1993), 84.
50. Quoted in Markley, 84.
51. Wilkins, *An Essay Toward a Real Character and a Philosophical Language*, biv.
52. Quoted in Markley, 85.
53. According to Howell, by 1693 (47 years after its initial publication), *Ecclesiastes* had already amassed a total of seven editions. The work continued to be in vogue, despite some publishing interruptions, for the next hundred and fifty years.; Howell, 451, n451.
54. Howell, 451.
55. Ibid., 458.
56. Ibid.
57. Ibid., 454.
58. Ibid.
59. John Wilkins, *Ecclesiastes or, A Discourse Concerning the Gift of Preaching as it Fals Under the Rules of Art* (1646) (Gale ECCO, 2010), 128.
60. Ibid.
61. Wilkins, *An Essay Toward a Real Character and a Philosophical Language*, iv.
62. Umberto Eco, *The Search for the Perfect Language*, trans. James Fentress (Malden: Blackwell, 1997), 209.
63. Ibid.
64. Ibid.
65. Wilkins, *An Essay Toward a Real Character and a Philosophical Language*, 5.
66. Ibid., 8.
67. Ibid.
68. Ibid., 4.
69. Ibid., 1.
70. Ibid., 2.
71. Bacon, *The Advancement of Learning*, 231.

138 *Speaking with Things*

72. Ibid., 230–231. See also, Rossi, 145.
73. Bacon, *The Advancement of Learning*, 231.
74. Eco, 213.
75. Rossi, 145–146.
76. Wilkins, *An Essay Toward a Real Character and a Philosophical Language*, 12–13.
77. Ibid., 21.
78. Okrent, 26. The most notable examples of this "fad" include: Francis Lodowick's *The Groundwork of Foundation Laid (or so Intended) for the Framing of a Perfect Language* (1652); Thomas Urquhart's *Logopandecteision, or an Introduction to the Universal Language* (1653); Cave Beck's *The Universal Character by Which all Nations may Understand One Another's Conceptions* (1657); Dalgarno's *Ars Signorum* (1661); and Wilkins's *Essay Towards a Real Character and a Philosophical Language* (1668).
79. Quoted in Eco, 218.
80. Quoted in Markley, 66.
81. Markley, 67.
82. Okrent, 49.
83. Ibid.
84. Eco, 221.
85. Aristotle, *Posterior Analytics*, trans. Jonathan Barnes, in *The Complete Works of Aristotle, Vol. 1*, ed. Barnes (Princeton: Princeton University Press, 1984), 96a35.
86. Wilkins, *An Essay Toward a Real Character and a Philosophical Language*, 445. See also Eco, 239.
87. Rossi, 161.
88. Ibid.
89. Eco, 242.
90. Ibid.
91. Okrent, 39.
92. Ibid., 39–44.
93. Eco, 243.
94. Okrent, 51–52.
95. Wilkins, *An Essay Toward a Real Character and a Philosophical Language*, 386.
96. Markley, 84–85; 93.
97. Wilkins, *An Essay Toward a Real Character and a Philosophical Language*, 22.
98. Markley, 79.
99. Eco, 250.
100. Ibid., 259.
101. Ibid.
102. Levi R. Bryant, *The Democracy of Objects* (Ann Arbor: Open Humanities Press, 2011), 18.
103. Ibid., 18–19.
104. Ibid., 39.
105. Ibid., 249.
106. See Graham Harman, *Prince of Networks: Bruno Latour and Metaphysics* (Melbourne: re.press, 2009), 156.
107. Quentin Meillassoux, *After Finitude: An Essay on the Necessity of Contingency*, trans. Ray Brassier (London: Continuum, 2008), 5.
108. Ibid., 3.

109. Ibid., 27.
110. Lee Braver, *A Thing of This World: A History of Continental Anti-Realism* (Evanston: Northwestern University Press, 2007), 17.
111. Wilkins, *An Essay Toward a Real Character and a Philosophical Language*, 21.
112. Eco is not convinced by Wilkins's claim that taxonomizing things instructs us as to their essences. At best, Eco argues, what Wilkins's tables teach us is a thing's place within the overall classification system, not what distinguishes one thing from another.; Eco, 254–255. I have no reason to question Eco's conclusion. My purpose in invoking Wilkins's belief on this point is simply to show how he is attempting to intertwine ontological and epistemological approaches to reality.
113. Ibid., 24.
114. Aristotle, *Nicomachean Ethics*, trans. David Ross (New York: Oxford University Press, 1998), 1129a3–6.
115. Wilkins, *An Essay Toward a Real Character and a Philosophical Language*, 24.
116. Martin Heidegger, *Being and Time*, trans. John Macquarrie and Edward Robinson (New York: Harper and Row, 1962), 204.
117. Thomas Rickert, *Ambient Rhetoric: The Attunements of Rhetorical Being* (Pittsburgh: University of Pittsburgh Press, 2013), 171.
118. Ibid., 163.
119. Martin Heidegger, "Letter on Humanism," in *Basic Writings*, ed. David Farrell Krell (New York: HarperCollins, 1993), 217.
120. Rickert, 102.
121. Martin Heidegger, "The Way to Language," in *Basic Writings*, ed. David Farrell Krell (New York: HarperCollins, 1993), 411.
122. Heidegger, "The Way to Language," 411; 413.
123. Ibid., 419.
124. According to Eco, the simplest way for readers to build on Wilkins's trees would be to locate synonyms for his primitives and/or extending the meaning of the characters to which the primitives are linked. For example, if we needed a word not translated in the *Essay* such as "result" we would need to locate primitive terms such as Event, Summe, or Illation and then build from there.; Eco, 245. While such "rhetorical solutions," as Eco calls them, may end up reproducing the same ambiguities and imprecisions Wilkins was hoping to correct, it nevertheless remains the case that Wilkins leaves considerable room for rhetoric to contribute to the future development of his perfected language.
125. Markley, 88.

Bibliography

Aristotle. *Nicomachean Ethics*. Translated by David Ross. New York: Oxford University Press, 1998.
Bacon, Francis. *The Advancement of Learning. Francis Bacon: The Major Works*, edited by Brian Vickers. Oxford: Oxford University Press, 2002.
———. *The New Organon. The Works of Francis Bacon*, edited by James Spedding, Robert Ellis, and Douglas Heath. New York: Garrett, 1968.
Bizzell, Patricia and Bruce Herzberg, ed. *The Rhetorical Tradition: Readings from Classical Times to the Present, 2nd Edition*. Boston: Bedford/St. Martin's, 2001.
Braver, Lee. *A Thing of This World: A History of Continental Anti-Realism*. Evanston: Northwestern University Press, 2007.

Bryant, Levi R. *The Democracy of Objects*. Ann Arbor: Open Humanities Press, 2011.
Conley, Thomas M. *Rhetoric in the European Tradition*. Chicago: University of Chicago Press, 1990.
Eco, Umberto. *The Search for the Perfect Language*. Translated by James Fentress. Malden: Blackwell, 1997.
Fish, Stanley. "Rhetoric." In *Doing What Comes Naturally: Change, Rhetoric, and the Practice of Theory in Literary and Legal Studies*, by Fish, 471–502. Durham: Duke University Press, 1989.
Harman, Graham. *Prince of Networks: Bruno Latour and Metaphysics*. Melbourne: re.press, 2009.
Heidegger, Martin. *Being and Time*. Translated by John Macquarrie and Edward Robinson. New York: Harper and Row, 1962.
———. "Letter on Humanism." In *Basic Writings*, edited by David Farrell Krell, 217–265. New York: HarperCollins, 1993.
———. "The Way to Language." In *Basic Writings*, edited by David Farrell Krell, 397–426. New York: HarperCollins, 1993.
Howell, Wilbur Samuel. *Logic and Rhetoric in England, 1500–1700*. Princeton: Princeton University Press, 1956.
Latour, Bruno. *We Have Never Been Modern*. Translated by Catherine Porter. Cambridge: Harvard University Press, 1993.
Markley, Robert. *Fallen Languages: Crises of Representation in Newtonian England, 1660–1740*. Ithaca: Cornell University Press, 1993.
Meillassoux, Quentin. *After Finitude: An Essay on the Necessity of Contingency*. Translated by Ray Brassier. London: Continuum, 2008.
Okrent, Arika. *In the Land of Invented Languages*. New York: Spiegel and Grau, 2010.
Ong, Walter J. *Ramus, Method, and the Decay of Dialogue*. Chicago: University of Chicago Press, 2004.
Ramus, Peter. *Arguments in Rhetoric Against Quintilian*. Translated by Carole Newlands. Carbondale: Southern Illinois University Press, 2010.
Rickert, Thomas. *Ambient Rhetoric: The Attunements of Rhetorical Being*. Pittsburgh: University of Pittsburgh Press, 2013.
Rossi, Paolo. *Logic and the Art of Memory: The Quest for a Universal Language*. Translated by Stephen Clucas. Chicago: University of Chicago Press, 2000.
Sprat, Thomas. *History of the Royal Society*, edited by Jackson I. Cope and Harold Whitmore Jones. St. Louis: Washington University Press, 1958.
Stark, Ryan J. "Margaret Cavendish and Composition Style." *Rhetoric Review* 17, no.1 (1999): 264–281.
———. *Rhetoric, Science, and Magic in Seventeenth-Century England*. Washington, DC: Catholic University Press, 2009.
Swift, Jonathan. *Gulliver's Travels into Several Nations of the World. With a Memoir of the Author*. New York: Oxford University Press, 2006.
Tillery, Denise. "'English Them in the Easiest Manner You Can': Margaret Cavendish on the Discourse and Practice of Natural Philosophy." *Rhetoric Review* 26, no.3 (2007): 268–285.
Ulman, H. Lewis. *Things, Thoughts, Words, and Actions: The Problem of Language in Late Eighteenth-Century British Rhetorical Theory*. Carbondale: Southern Illinois University Press, 1994.

Vickers, Brian and Nancy S. Struever. *Rhetoric and the Pursuit of Truth: Language Change in the Seventeenth and Eighteenth Centuries.* Los Angeles: William Andrews Clark Memorial Library, 1986.

Wilkins, John. *An Essay Toward a Real Character and a Philosophical Language* (1668). Menston, UK: Scolar, 1968.

———. *Ecclesiastes or, A Discourse Concerning the Gift of Preaching as it Fals Under the Rules of Art* (1646). Gale ECCO, 2010.

4 The Question Concerning Reality
Post-Kantian Rhetorical Realism

> I was often unable to think of external things as having external existence, and I communed with all that I saw as something not apart from, but inherent in, my own immaterial nature. Many times while going to school have I grasped at a wall or tree to recall myself from this abyss of idealism to the reality.
> —William Wordsworth, "Ode: Imitations of Immortality"

In the opening pages of his book *Pandora's Hope*, Bruno Latour tells the story of a conversation he had once with a respected psychologist. This conversation occurred while Latour was attending a cross-disciplinary conference in Brazil which aimed to promote more productive interactions between scientists and science studies scholars. As Latour recounts, the psychologist approached him one evening, nervously clutching "a crumbled piece of paper on which he had scribbled a few key words."[1] Taking a deep breath, the psychologist asked just a single question of Latour, whose name he had no doubt recognized—or *misrecognized*, as the case may be—as belonging to a school of thought which argues that scientific knowledge is socially constructed and thus contingent upon a range of human-produced variables including vocabularies, technical instruments, epistemologies, and the like. To this perceived representative of the postmodern turn—in his mind perhaps, to the living embodiment of postmodern theorizing about knowledge—the psychologist asked, "Do you believe in reality?"[2]

Latour admits to finding the question "bizarre" and "strange"—indeed, his reply attempts to turn the psychologist's question on its ear, proclaiming in return, "But of course! [...] What a question! Is reality something we have to believe in?"[3] Nonetheless, Latour actually takes the question quite seriously, treating it in *Pandora's Hope* as an exigency for that book's examination of the role reality plays in science studies and social inquiry generally. What interests Latour most about the question, "Do you believe in reality?", however, is not just that it memorably captures a confusion shared by many of his readers who sometimes interpret his actor-network theory as just another version of social constructionism or postmodern language games. Rather, what interests Latour most about the psychologist's question is the *fear* it embodies, a fear that was lit centuries ago in Plato's cave and that has been stoked ever since by figures such as Descartes, Kant, and many of our modern rhetoricians, philosophers, and social theorists. That we moderns tend to worry as much as we do about losing touch with reality is, for Latour, a weird consequence of our ways of thinking about the world and ourselves in the world. In the modern epoch—within which Latour situates postmodernism as "a symptom, not a fresh solution," and thus not the alternative we need to make visible modernity's efforts to purify distinctions between humans and nonhuman[4]—the human-world correlate comes to define a relationship in which human being and reality occupy separate and distinct ontological zones. Alluding to the Cartesian mind-in-a-vat, which brackets the human mind from its enmeshment in the world outside of thought, Latour concludes that, "Only a mind put in the strangest position, looking at a world *from the inside out* and linked to the outside by nothing but the tenuous connection of the *gaze*, will throb in constant fear of losing reality."[5]

I begin this chapter with Latour's story about his alleged disbelief in reality because I think it parallels a comparable dilemma at the heart of modern rhetorical theory, one that finds rhetoricians seeing the world "from the inside out" while at the same time grasping, in Wordsworth's terms, "at a wall or tree to recall [themselves] from this abyss of idealism to the reality." Indeed, one of the defining features of modern rhetorical theory is its ability to define rhetoric's scope and jurisdiction in strikingly contrary ways: on the one hand, as a symbolic and discursive art practiced exclusively by human speakers and writers, and on the other as a more expansive force involving a wide array of beings, including objects, animals, environments, and technologies. How modern rhetoric came to this point, and how nonhuman rhetorics in particular have found increasing purchase within a discipline historically committed to human forms of symbolic action, is a story much like the one Latour tells about the weird relationship moderns have with reality. Comparable to concerns raised in the social sciences and science studies, the fear that rhetoricians will lose reality, that by descending deeper and deeper into the darkest corners of the cave they will somehow lose their connection to the world outside of thought and language, is one that continues to haunt rhetoric as a discipline and an object of inquiry. This was the fear that spurred Plato's critiques of rhetoric and the Sophists and it has persisted in various forms ever since, from the Renaissance and early modern language inventors, as we saw in Chapter 3, to the most recent revival of rhetoric as an epistemic art in the wake of the linguistic and social turns of the late nineteenth and early-mid twentieth centuries. On their surface, of course, epistemic theories of rhetoric could hardly seem less concerned about losing touch with reality. If anything, epistemic rhetorics seem more interested in *multiplying* our points of contact with reality (assuming, that is, we understand reality as what follows from rhetorical and symbolic action in the world and not reality "in itself"). As Barry Brummett suggests, rhetoric from an epistemic perspective "is in the deepest and most fundamental sense the *advocacy of realities*."[6] From this perspective, reality is not an objective state or entity, but is what people themselves *make*. "To say that people participate in making reality," Brummett explains, "is to say that reality, or what is observed, will be partially determined by the way in which people observe, which is a form of participation."[7] In the modern epistemic paradigm, in other words, it is the mind and intersubjective communication that imbue reality with meaning, not the other way around. Brummett is quick to point out, however, that adopting the epistemic position does not require one to accept the idea that "reality is subjective" or that we can dream up whatever reality we wish.[8] Retaining something like mind-independence, I will argue, is one of the ways modern rhetoricians have attempted to alleviate their own fears of losing reality, i.e., of lapsing into full-blown idealism or anti-realism to such an extent that reality only matters in terms of the meanings we ourselves project onto it. In what I will describe as modern rhetoric's Kantian Compromise, epistemic rhetoricians safeguard reality from the excesses of absolute idealism by positing the existence of something outside of the structures of human consciousness and cognition. Much like Kant's transcendental idealism, modern epistemic theories of rhetoric are not the full-blown idealisms they sometimes claim—or hope—to be.

As I argue in this chapter, the structure of modern rhetoric is Kantian in nature insofar as it prioritizes human experience and cognition even as it acknowledges that certain things exist independent of human understanding and therefore cannot be known as such. Short of positing a solipsistic view of reality, Kantianism depends upon a blending of realism and idealism, with each constituting the other's condition of possibility. The complexities of this arrangement are many, as I discuss in this chapter. But at its core, Kant's theory of knowledge foregrounds the figure of the active knower as the proper subject for inquiry while at the same time limiting the cognitive capacities of that subject. One of clearest examples of Kant's entwining of realism and idealism can be found in his distinction between the phenomenal (the realm of appearances) and the noumenal or the thing-in-itself (*ding an sich*). As I elaborate upon below, contemporary philosophers and rhetoricians sometimes view this distinction as problematic and perhaps even unnecessary given Kant's so-called Copernican Revolution and its attempt to install the active knower at the center of inquiry. However, these critiques of Kantianism often overlook not only the importance the thing-in-itself has in Kant's thought, but also Kant's own statements on why he insists on retaining the noumenon despite its fundamental unknowability. In a critical passage in the *Critique of Pure Reason*, which I take up in more detail later in the chapter, Kant states that the noumenon constitutes a "boundary concept" that helps "limit the pretension of sensibility."[9] Much more than a theoretical blindness or holdover from prior versions of metaphysics, Kant's insistence on the existence and unknowability of the thing-in-itself makes clear something that may well be true of all epistemologies—that theories of knowledge, even the most staunchly anti-realist, depend upon some realist commitments about the world.

This is true of rhetoric as well. While understandably weary of Kant's infamous critique of rhetoric as "the machinery of persuasion," modern rhetoricians have nonetheless tended to follow the overall structure of his transcendental idealism by emplacing the human agent at the center of things such that objects conform to human cognitions rather than the other way around. At the same time, modern rhetoricians also follow Kant's lead in acknowledging the existence of certain things that exceed or lie beyond the realms of appearance and knowledge. Such things are especially pronounced in rhetorics of religion, where the divine is often figured as existent but beyond our capacities to see or know it as such. But noumenal things also appear in more secular rhetorics such as Diane Davis's recent work on alterity in which the Levinasian Other is understood as real but nonetheless fundamentally unknowable and inassimilable to myself (ideas I take up in the next chapter).[10] In inquiring about rhetoric and its relationship to reality and knowledge, modern rhetoricians, like Kant before them, find themselves having to contend with what I call *the question concerning reality*—with the specter of things-in-themselves which exceed the limits of human knowledge and experience. Short of permitting rhetoric and reality to go their separate ways, the Kantian compromises we find in rhetoric's epistemic and postmodern traditions suggest a more complicated relationship between rhetoric and reality at play within modern rhetorical theory. In contrast to claims made about rhetoric in the wake of the linguistic turn, the recurrent specter of the thing-in-itself suggests that modern rhetoric retains within itself a significant connection to reality—to things existing outside of thought, language, and appearance—and that this attunement to a vibrant but otherwise irreducible ontology of things marks both the limit and the condition of possibility for rhetoric as a critical and ethical praxis.

To explore these tensions and possibilities, I turn to a specific moment in modern rhetorical history, the debates surrounding rhetoric's status as an epistemic or knowledge-making art, which began with Robert L. Scott's 1967 declaration and continued off and on in the literature throughout the 1970s and 1980s. I am interested in this admittedly dated debate for several reasons. First, because it explicitly foregrounds the question concerning reality, the epistemic rhetoric debate allows us to see quite clearly the Kantian roots of modern rhetorical theory and the extent to which this inheritance continues to inform rhetoricians' thinking about the world and rhetoric's place in the world. Second, despite its appearing to have run its course as a topic of debate and discussion, the central insights of epistemic rhetoric continue to inform our thinking about rhetoric. While the term itself may have fallen out of favor, the notion that rhetoric shapes our understandings of reality has evolved into something like the first law of modern rhetorical theory. In addition to contributing to our understandings of modern rhetoric, then, revisiting the debates surrounding epistemic rhetoric also sheds light on the challenges facing object-oriented rhetoric and its aim to involve things and nonhumans in rhetorical theory and practice. Finally, returning to epistemic rhetoric helps us understand why it is possible for rhetorical theorists to propose such wildly different relationships between rhetoric and reality. A few notable exceptions notwithstanding, the bulk of the literature in epistemic rhetoric reads as a passionate defense of idealism and social constructionism. However, even as they argue for discursive conceptions of truth and knowledge, proponents of epistemic rhetoric nonetheless rely consistently—and necessarily, I will argue—upon realist assumptions about the world.

The inability to banish realism from rhetorical theory and reduce the thing-in-itself to merely what it can be *for us* demonstrates that within the structures of modern rhetoric lies the makings of a complex rhetorical realism, one that is capable of accounting for things that have a mind-independent reality but that have all too often been overlooked or brushed aside in favor of more human-centered views of rhetoric. While rhetoricians may not exactly share Dr. Johnson's realist skepticism, we nevertheless find ourselves from time to time kicking the same stones and grasping the same trees, if for no other reason than to recall ourselves from the abyss of idealism to the reality of rhetoric's place in the world.

The Structures of Modern Rhetoric

The story of rhetoric's rehabilitation in the twentieth century is a familiar one, or so it seems. Whether told in terms of pedagogy or theoretical realignments within English and Communication studies, the revival of rhetoric in the past century is often associated with (and often credited to) specific developments in the history of higher education, such as the growth in college composition programs or the rise of antifoundationalist theories of language and knowledge in the humanities. Certainly, these institutional developments contributed greatly to rhetoric's recent revival as a methodological approach to discourse and a modern course of study. However, the intellectual origins of modern rhetoric can, and should, be traced much farther back. Almost a century and a half before its resurgence in American English and Communications departments, rhetoric won a silent but crucial victory from perhaps the unlikeliest rhetorician of all: Immanuel Kant. While Kant is perhaps best known among rhetoricians for his criticisms and dismissals of rhetoric, it was his widely influential Copernican Revolution and its blending of realism and idealism that eventually enabled twentieth-century rhetoricians such as Robert L. Scott, Barry Brummett, James Berlin, and others to (re)assert rhetoric's epistemic status and in so doing rehabilitate rhetoric as a "master discipline" at the heart of modern humanistic inquiry.

Before exploring this last point at more length, it is worthwhile to revisit a few of the dominant narratives that have shaped understandings of rhetoric's return in the past century and its reimagining as more than a mere handmaiden to philosophy or supplement to truth and knowledge.[11] In the second of his two-part history of writing instruction in American colleges, Berlin discusses how rhetoric's revival in the 1950s as "a discipline of profound historical importance and of considerable contemporary relevance" helped establish deeper historical and theoretical groundings for the study and teaching of writing. Whereas the current-traditional models of the nineteenth and twentieth centuries tended to reduce writing to a series of generic school-based themes, the new rhetorical approaches of the 1950s sought to redefine writing in the context of "Aristotelian humanism" and its emphases on argument and invention.[12] In addition to enabling writing teachers to develop new methods for "discovering content" in the first-year writing course, the revival of rhetoric in 1950s English departments also helped spur new research on writing and education, including historical and theoretical studies of classical rhetorical models of invention as foundations for contemporary writing theory and instruction. As Berlin's essential histories of the field suggest, the rehabilitation of rhetorical theory in the twentieth century followed largely from the practical and professional needs of college composition and communication instructors.

In his posthumously published work *Rhetorics, Poetics, and Cultures*, however, Berlin complicates this narrative, suggesting that rhetoric's revival as a modern course of study should also be understood within the intellectual context of modern theories of language and knowledge. "The influence of structuralist and poststructuralist theories in the humanities, social sciences, and even the sciences—what Jameson has called the linguistic turn," Berlin writes, "can be seen as an effort to recover the tools of rhetoric in discussing the material effects of language in the conducts of human affairs [...] The structuralist and poststructuralist influence can thus be seen as an effort to recover the view from rhetoric, the perspective that reveals language to be a set of terministic screens, to recall Kenneth Burke, that constructs rather than records the signified."[13] In his introduction to *The Rhetorical Turn: Invention and Persuasion in the Conduct of Inquiry*, Herbert W. Simons offers a similar assessment of rhetoric's modern rehabilitation. In Simons's account, as inquiry in the humanities and social sciences turned increasingly toward the influence discursive forms have on thought and expression as a way to critique "the dominant objectivist presuppositions of our age," rhetoric reemerged as a valuable means of accounting for realities now construed as contingent, historically situated, and symbolically constructed.[14] As Simons puts it, "It is within our own century that the intellectual climate for a new rhetoric of inquiry seems to have proven most hospitable."[15] This intellectual climate has been noted as well by Alan G. Gross, Terry Eagleton, and Stanley Fish, all of whom acknowledge the extent to which new developments in contemporary philosophy and literary theory contributed to rhetoric's return while at the same time helping blur age-old distinctions between rhetoric, philosophy, and science. In Gross's narrative, over the last half of the twentieth century, rhetoric effectively "colonized" other disciplines in large part because "a new climate of opinion emerged, signaled by the linguistic turn in philosophy" and exemplified by theorists such as Ludwig Wittgenstein, John Austin, and Richard Rorty.[16] In Fish's case, the antifoundational fervor of the last century made possible not only the rehabilitation of rhetoric but a theoretical program for rhetoric going forward as well. "As I write, the fortunes of rhetorical man are on the upswing," Fish announces, "as in discipline after discipline there is evidence of what has been called the interpretative turn, the realization (at least for those it seizes) that the givens of any field of activity—including the facts it commands, the procedures it trusts in, and the values it expresses and extends—are socially and politically constructed, are fashioned by man rather than delivered by God or Nature."[17]

Whether understood as responding to various turns in the human sciences, be they linguistic, rhetorical, or interpretative, each of these accounts points to dramatic changes in our understandings of knowledge, language, and the human subject as precipitating new developments in rhetorical theory and epistemology. In lieu of following the naïve realist claim that truth inheres in things and that knowledge therefore implies a correspondence between thought and thing, the majority of modern rhetoricians, philosophers, and linguists argue that truth emerges out of social and discursive practices and in turn constitutes the reality of things by endowing it with saliency and significance. "It is this way with all of us concerning language," Nietzsche writes at the dawn of the linguistic turn. "We believe that we know something about the things themselves when we speak of trees, colors, snow, and flowers; and yet we possess nothing but metaphors for things—metaphors which correspond in no way to the original entities."[18] Given these shifts away from naïve realism toward more inter/subjective understandings of reality produced rhetorically through metaphors, vocabularies, and ideologies, it is no surprise that theorists eventually returned to the rhetorical tradition for assistance in bolstering such views. Perhaps more than anyone else, rhetoricians have long been attuned to the contingencies of meaning and the constructedness of knowledge through language and other symbol systems.

And so while the rise of rhetoric as a discipline certainly contributed to rhetoric's rehabilitation in the past century, larger shifts in the intellectual climate shared by rhetoric, composition, philosophy, and linguistics were at play as well. Specifically, for these historically associated, although sometimes antagonistic, disciplines to come into such agreement with one another, there needed to be a significant change in the one thing about which philosophers and rhetoricians have consistently quarreled: *truth*, and more precisely the question of where truth resides and what responsibilities the subject has vis-à-vis truth. If truth inheres in objects rather than in the social forces that frame understandings of reality, then rhetoric by implication can only serve to communicate truth after it has already been discovered through some other means (typically, *apodeixis*, dialectic, or other philosophical methods). When we imagine truth as transcendental rather than immanent and constructed, when we imagine it as *substance* rather than *process*, in other words, rhetoric almost always comes up on the short end of the epistemology debate, often getting reduced, as in the Platonist and Ramist traditions, to the stylistic embellishments of thought rather than the substance of thought itself.

In the wake of the linguistic turn in the human sciences, however, it became increasingly difficult to ignore the constructionist view of truth in which language plays a central role in constituting social realities. Thus, in philosophy alone, we find a number of thinkers over the last century whose work not only touches on the rhetorical tradition but substantially engages it as well, from Nietzsche's work on the Sophists and pre-Socratics to Derrida's explorations of writing and speech in the *Phaedrus*. This renewed interest in rhetoric among continental philosophers was no accident; nor was it simply the product of one or two rhetorically minded thinkers. As I have been suggesting, the focus on language in the late-nineteenth and twentieth centuries helped prepare the way for the rhetorical turn in the humanities and social sciences. But language alone was not enough to spark the rehabilitation of rhetoric as a discipline, let alone as the master discipline some have taken it to be. In addition to language, epistemology itself had to change for rhetoric's return to make sense and gain traction among related fields of study. Eventually, of course, it would, shifting from realist epistemologies, predicated on a correspondence theory of truth, toward anti-realist theories of knowledge in which speculation on the intrinsic natures of things is replaced by observation of the cognitive and communicative capacities of human beings. Distinctly rhetorical and rhetorically advantageous at the same time, the dramatic transformation in epistemology witnessed over the last century is what ultimately enabled and gave credence to a new era of rhetorical theory.

Rehabilitating Rhetoric as Epistemic: The Question Concerning "Reality"

By the time Robert L. Scott published his foundational article "On Viewing Rhetoric as Epistemic" in 1967, the concept of truth had already undergone something of a rhetorical turn, thus leaving Scott in hindsight with the enviable challenge of making this connection visible and asserting its implications for rhetoric as both a critical and ethical practice. In any event, these efforts by Scott and subsequent proponents of epistemic rhetoric proved fruitful to say the least; within a remarkably short period of time, epistemic rhetoricians effectively established what would become the defining characteristic of rhetoric in the late twentieth century. No longer the handmaiden of philosophy nor the stylistic dressing of thought, rhetoric in the latter half of the last century came instead to designate a distinct "way of knowing,"[19] one attuned to the contingencies and uncertainties that result from and motivate human communication. As Scott eloquently puts it, "Man must consider truth not as something fixed and final but as something to be created moment by moment in the circumstances in which he finds himself and with which he must cope."[20] According to epistemic rhetoric, rhetoric not only creates truth, it also creates "reality," with both terms designating distinct *processes* taking place within communities.

The anti-realist bent of epistemic rhetoric is perhaps most pronounced in its proponents' tendency to place the word "reality" under erasure as a way of signifying a distrust of realism's commitment to mind-independent reality (R1). Here, for instance, is Berlin's description of language in *Rhetorics, Poetics, and Cultures*:

> language never acts as a simple referent to an external, extralinguistically verifiable thing-in-itself. It instead serves as a terministic screen, to use Burke's phrase, that forms and shapes experience [...] Thus, language practices engender a set of ideological prescriptions regarding the nature of "reality": economic "realities" and the distribution of wealth; social and political "realities" regarding class, race, age, ethnicity, sexual orientation, and gender and their relations to power; and cultural "realities" regarding the nature of representation and symbolic form in art, play, and other cultural experiences.[21]

Berlin's account of rhetoric hews closely to poststructuralist theories of language as well as critical theories of culture and ideology. Stylistically, however, what is notable about this passage is Berlin's repeated use of quotation marks or scare quotes around the word "reality" to indicate the word's so-called ability to signify a world outside of language or socially constituted realities.

This stylistic device can be seen in a number of works in modern rhetorical theory. In his essay on the "Definition of Man," for example, Kenneth Burke asks the following:

> can we bring ourselves to realize just how overwhelmingly much of what we mean by "reality" has been built up for us through nothing but our symbol systems [...] To meditate on this fact until one sees its full implications is much like peering over the edge of things into an ultimate abyss. And doubtless that's one reason why, though man is typically the symbol-using animal, he clings to a kind of naïve verbal realism that refuses to let him realize the full extent of the role played by symbolicity in his notions of reality.[22]

The tendency Burke identifies to "cling to a kind of naïve verbal realism" surfaces as well in Brummett's essay on "Process" and "Intersubjectivity" in which he claims, "If objective reality exists people will never know it. Thus, the only reality ever to be encountered is what is observed. The implication of that conclusion is that 'reality' will be different with different ways of observing it."[23] (27). Finally, Ernest Bormann similarly invokes the specter of "reality" as he attempts to forge a clear distinction between rhetoric, or what he calls "the word," and the "things of reality:"

> When there is a discrepancy between the word and the thing the most important cultural artifact for understanding the events may not be things of "reality" but the words or the symbols. Indeed, in many vital instances the words, that is, the rhetoric, are the social reality and to try to distinguish one symbolic reality from another is a fallacy widespread in historical and sociological scholarship which the rhetorical critic can do much to dispel.[24]

While "things of 'reality'" may well exist, for Bormann this possibility is ultimately beside the point; because we are only capable of accessing and making sense of the world through words and symbols, the only reality that matters for the rhetorician is "social reality," the reality we constitute ourselves through our discursive actions in the world. Much like Kant and his notion of the thing-in-itself, for many of these rhetoricians "reality" designates a probable realm about which we can speculate but can never perceive, relate to, or know in any meaningful way. Hence, the question concerning "reality" rarely constitutes a question concerning reality as such. Rather, in most anti-realist epistemologies such as those we find in the epistemic rhetoric literature, the question concerning "reality" almost always reverts back to the more familiar terrain of human subjectivity and to the nature and limits of human understanding.

And yet, the act of invoking "reality," however dismissively, may also serve to reinscribe the very notion of mind-independent reality Scott and others are attempting to leave behind. Similar to the *sous rature* (placing under erasure) device developed by Heidegger and used extensively by Derrida, the typographical rendering of reality as "reality" suggests that the word is both *inadequate* and *necessary*. When Heidegger places the word Being under erasure by crossing it out but permitting the deleted word to remain, he does so in order to highlight the contested meaning of the word as well as its (for now) necessary existence. "Since the word is inaccurate, it is crossed out. Because it is necessary, it remains legible," Gayatri Spivak explains in her preface to Derrida's *Of Grammatology*.[25] Rhetorically, *sous rature* works by marking the impossibility of presence—of meaning standing completely in the open or clearing, as Heidegger will suggest. Even as it attempts to call into question the metaphysics of presence, however, erasure does not claim to be working outside of the structures of presence and absence that are so very close to the heart of the Western metaphysical tradition. Although utterly insufficient, Heidegger and Derrida acknowledge that words such as Being, Thing, and Reality continue to exert a certain hold over us, invoking multiple meanings, but also signifying the impossibility of our ever being able to transcend them and all of their metaphysical baggage. So, when epistemic rhetoricians place "reality" under erasure, they do so to mark the unreliability and naïveté of the word. And yet, like Heidegger's Being and Derrida's trace, "reality" is also "the mark of the absence of a presence, an always already absent present, of the lack of the origin that is the condition of thought and experience."[26] And as a condition of possibility, "reality" remains present to a degree even when placed under erasure. "Reality," then, remains meaningful precisely because the erasure itself repeats the contrast between realist and anti-realist conceptions of reality. While it can be tempting to read epistemic rhetoricians as idealists, Rickert has suggested that "the presence of distancing quotation marks [in Burke and epistemic rhetoricians] perhaps suggests some reservations on his part, some sense that there is material he has not quite adequately covered."[27] To raise the question concerning "reality" may therefore already commit oneself, however implicitly, to certain realist precepts as a condition of possibility, a point I will return to later by way of Kant's transcendental idealism.

Furthermore, and in keeping with the epistemological transformations in the humanities discussed above, proponents of epistemic rhetoric also tend to accept the anti-realist critique of truth as an objective force separate from the realms of knowledge and experience. Indeed, the realist thesis most frequently targeted by epistemic rhetoricians is Braver's R2 Correspondence thesis which defines truth as a correspondence between thoughts, ideas, and sentences on the one hand and things, objects, or external states of affairs on the other.[28] To offer one example, in elaborating his theory of intersubjectivity, Brummett calls out the correspondence thesis for "collaps[ing] metaphysics and epistemology into one mode of inquiry."[29] In Brummett's view, truth is not "out there" waiting to be verified. When we imagine truth in this way, we ignore the social and rhetorical activities that frame and make possible such discoveries, if they are indeed "discoveries" at all. At the same time, when we accept the correspondence theory of truth we remove a vital aspect of rhetoric from epistemology, namely, ethics, and in particular our ability to accept responsibility for the realities we create as individuals and as a society. If "reality" is as objective and stable as realists would have us believe, then our abilities to apply ethical reasoning to states of affairs are significantly weakened if not entirely beside the point. If, however, we understand ourselves as being responsible for reality, then suddenly ethics and rhetoric not only matter again but assume even more central roles in our dealings with things. Thus, epistemic rhetoric's foregrounding of contingency tends to assume a strong ethical dynamic that puts greater responsibility on the rhetor whose actions are as much world-forming as they are persuasive. While the rhetor may still have the responsibility to "discover" his/her truth, the "rhetor also has the responsibility to recognize that this truth is his/her responsibility, for he/she is part of the context that determines in part how others will view reality."[30] According to Scott and Brummett's versions of epistemic rhetoric, for ethics to remain a part of rhetoric, realist assumptions about reality must give way to process-oriented understandings that place the utmost agency and responsibility in human beings rather than in things-in-themselves. It is worth noting, however, that Brummett's notion of intersubjective truth "is still a correspondence of ideas to reality," but with the caveat that "reality is now an intersubjective one,"[31] a shifting target, as it were, that changes based on context and social consensus. While firmly committed to an anti-realist epistemology, Brummett's passing remark reminds us how difficult it can be to fully eliminate realist assumptions such as correspondence from our thinking about rhetoric.

My focus thus far has been on the proponents of epistemic rhetoric; however, it is important to remember that the idea of epistemic rhetoric inspired a number of critics as well. For many of these critics, most notably Richard Cherwitz, James Hikins, and Earl Croasmun, the problem with Scott and others' versions of epistemic rhetoric is that they tend to conflate epistemology and ontology, particularly in their assumption that the meanings we attach to objects define or otherwise change the ontological character of those objects. I will take up some of these counter-conceptions of epistemic rhetoric later in the chapter. In terms of the narrative I am developing here, however, what is most remarkable about the emergence of realist responses to epistemic rhetoric is not the responses per se but the backlash to them and eventual consensus that took hold despite many of the sophisticated arguments levied against relativism and social constructionism in the 1980s. In his *Sourcebook on Rhetoric*, for example, James Jasinski begins his lengthy entry on epistemic rhetoric by citing the historical precedents for epistemic rhetoric and its critics, which he identifies as the sophistic tradition for epistemic rhetoric and the philosophical tradition of "objectivism" for its realist critics. According to Jasinski's narrative, objectivism has long been a thorn in rhetoric's side and has only recently been subjected to criticism from "relativists" and "social constructionists." Quoting the philosopher Richard J. Bernstein, Jasinski defines objectivism as "the basic conviction that there is or must be some permanent, ahistorical matrix or framework to which we can ultimately appeal in determining the nature of rationality, knowledge, truth, reality, goodness, or rightness."[32] In contrast to sophistic and contemporary forms of relativism, objectivism assumes and searches after certainty, some ground "that will *guarantee* knowledge."[33] According to Jasinski, realist versions of epistemic rhetoric presume comparable grounding for knowledge. This is particularly evident in realists' assertions of "an equivalence" between two objectivist theses: 1) objects in the world are presented *directly* to consciousness; and 2) reality exists independent of consciousness.[34] The problem here, as Jasinski sees it, is that of direct correspondence between reality and consciousness. It is safe to assume that most rhetoricians today accept the idea that things exist independently of consciousness. However, in granting such a point, it does not follow that one must also accept the notion that things present themselves *directly* to consciousness.[35] Citing rebuttals to realist epistemology from Brummett and political theorists Ernesto Laclau and Chantel Mouffe, Jasinski summarizes (and not-so subtly endorses) the relativist position that withstood and ultimately emerged out of the spirited debates over epistemic rhetoric:

> The point can be summarized as follows: Objects external to the individual and community exist, and they impose *constraints* to a greater or lesser degree on human action and decision making, but such objects enter consciousness—the individual's as well as that inchoate idea of the public consciousness—through discourse, language and rhetorical practice.[36]

Again, the emphasis here is on the constructedness of knowledge through language, rhetoric, and other symbolic practices. And yet, despite their clear desire to privilege relativism over objectivism, arguments such of Jasinksi's continue to allow for the existence of mind-independent realities, and even more remarkably, they attribute to them limiting if not agential powers that serve to constrain the possibilities of human rhetorical action. Much like Rorty when he disassociates language from the external realities of things, arguments like this equivocate on the mind-world dualism in such a way that the relation between subject and object remains at least partly in place. While they may not enter consciousness directly, objects nonetheless exist and impinge themselves upon us in ways that affect (narrow, expand, constrain, etc.) the available means of persuasion. As Jasinski's summary demonstrates, it can be tempting to frame epistemic rhetoric as postmodern, that is, as a theoretical disposition uniquely attuned to the social, cultural, and technological challenges characterizing rhetorical life today. However, as we will soon see, epistemic rhetoric is more accurately understood as an extension of Kant's transcendental idealism, which grants the existence of things-in-themselves but maintains that we can never know such things. For all of its contemporaneity, postmodern relativism embodies and carries forth Kant's decision over two centuries ago to install mind-independent reality at the heart of an otherwise idealist philosophy of knowledge.

Although they were ultimately unable to fully shake off the realist theses they seek to overturn, rhetorical theorists in the last century nonetheless succeeded in shifting the scope of rhetoric toward epistemology and rehabilitating its reputation within the human sciences. In sum, as epistemology in the modern era moved away from realist understandings of the world toward more anti-realist approaches, the prospects of rhetoric began to improve. With classical distinctions between *epistēmē* and *doxa* proving increasingly arbitrary and unstable, rhetoricians and philosophers (for once!) found themselves confronting a similar foe: naïve realists committed to the existence and preservation of external (mind-independent) standards for adjudicating truth claims and governing ethical behavior. Whereas realists see the world as populated, in Aristotle's terms, with "things that are eternal [and] ungenerated and imperishable,"[37] anti-realists see things as circumscribed by our capacities to know, meaning that truth inheres not in objects as such but in the complex social and rhetorical environs within which knowing takes place. The consequences of this reversal have been quite profound, of course. As Stephen Toulmin has argued, even "facts" such as the laws of nature do not exist entirely apart from our methods of observing them. Rather, the "laws of nature" are simply ways we have devised for *representing* what is observed: "they are principles for drawing inferences and are constraints upon the observer, not upon reality."[38] One way to understand the emergence of epistemic rhetoric in the late 1960s, therefore, is to see it as a gathering of efforts among rhetoricians to rethink rhetoric's scope and meaning in light of broader intellectual transformations taking place across the human and social sciences.

Like many intellectual movements, however, interest in epistemic rhetoric eventually waned, so much so, in fact, that in 1990 Brummett is able to confidently proclaim the death of epistemic rhetoric as an active research area.[39] Despite how generative the epistemological turn may have proven for rhetoric, Brummett laments how the philosophical tenor that characterized many of the discussions around epistemic rhetoric ultimately led to its demise. "In sum," he reflects, "we have been doing philosophy, we have been doing critical theory, we have been doing anything but *studying communication*."[40] In order to study communication, Brummett suggests, one must have "grounding" in the world, and this is presumably what "philosophizing about rhetoric" avoids or lacks altogether. As my interest in the Kantian roots of epistemic rhetoric no doubt reveals, I strongly disagree with Brummett on this point. Rhetoric is and always has been "grounded" in one way or another, which is another way of saying that rhetoric has always been a realist art attuned to the existence and vibrancy of things in the world. Moreover, even historically, Brummett is on shaky ground in proclaiming the death (or exhaustion, more generously) of epistemic rhetoric. While it is true that the debates themselves have cooled and mostly disappeared, the central insights of epistemic rhetoric are still alive and well in the field. One need only open any journal or book today to see that rhetoricians' present understandings of truth and knowledge bare more than passing resemblance to the one Scott and other proponents of epistemic rhetoric advanced almost a half century ago. While we may no longer advocate passionately on behalf of epistemic rhetoric, our lack of interest in epistemic rhetoric is, ultimately, moot; the case, as it were, was won decades ago. In accordance with epistemological shifts in the humanities and social sciences, consensus among contemporary rhetorical theorists is that rhetoric and realism should go their separate ways and that rhetoric as a result should stake its future on an anti-realist platform. Thus was born the latest renaissance in rhetorical theory: in staunch opposition to realism as an epistemology and condition of possibility.

Anti-Realist Epistemology: Kant's Rhetoric Against Rhetoric

My account of rhetoric's rehabilitation in the modern era has thus far focused on the ways rhetorical theorists such as Robert Scott, Barry Brummett, and James Berlin were able to identify synergies between the rhetorical tradition and the anti-realist epistemologies that emerged in the wake of the linguistic turn of the nineteenth and twentieth centuries. As mentioned above, Berlin in particular ties the reemergence of rhetoric in the twentieth century to the renewed sense in the humanities of language as a "set of terministic screens [...] that constructs rather than records the signified."[41] In *Rhetorics, Poetics, and Cultures*, Berlin further suggests that the linguistic turn's attunement to the material effects of language functioned as both a response to and corrective for the Enlightenment view of language and rhetoric that denies "the inevitable role of signification in affecting communication, insisting instead that signs can and must become neutral transmitters of externally verifiable truth—truths, that is, existing separate from language."[42] As we saw in the previous chapter, however, early modern views of language are exceptionally more complex than such characterizations would have us believe. While it is true that many thinkers of the time held realist views of language, this framework did not always lead to language being viewed as a "neutral transmitter" of external truth. Bishop John Wilkins, in particular, understood and embraced the "thingness" of language, and it was his attunement to the material effects of language—that language represents things but is also a thing itself in the world—that spurred his efforts to construct a universal language system. Leaving these issues aside, however, Berlin's narrative suggests that modern rhetoric stands fundamentally apart from Enlightenment conceptions of truth and reality. Indeed, it is easy to read Berlin's narrative as a story of progress and maturation: Where, in the past, realism and objectivism limited understandings of rhetoric, today rhetoric thrives for the simple reason that rhetoricians have been able to distance themselves from the naïve worldviews of the past. While persuasive to the extent that they position rhetoric at the heart of heroic struggle between a conservative past and an enlightened present/future, narratives such as this too hastily encourage us to locate the origins of modern rhetoric in the nineteenth century and its linguistic turn when questions about language's mediational and epistemological capacities became something of a first philosophy for many thinkers.

Certainly, the linguistic turn played an important role in rhetoric's modern revival and its epistemic turn. But, as I have suggested already, the seeds for rhetoric's flourishing in the past century were actually planted many years before the linguistic turn, specifically in Kant's transcendental idealism, which established the intellectual framework for what would eventually become phenomenology, social constructionism, and other anti-realisms of the nineteenth and twentieth centuries. By shifting the focus of philosophical inquiry from our abilities to conform our thoughts to objects to how objects instead conform to the structures of human understanding, Kant literally changed the subject of philosophy. In place of natural and objective truths intrinsic to the world outside of thought, Kant argued that philosophy should only be concerned with the conditions of human sensation and understanding, because these are the only things we can know and about which we can reasonably speculate. In his study of anti-realism in the history of continental philosophy, Braver argues that modern continental philosophy's aversion to realism—in particular to the realist thesis that beings are "unaffected by the facts that and what we are, think, or say"—follows directly from Kant's groundbreaking transcendental idealism.[43] Indeed, it is Kant, Braver argues, "who forms the great fault line for realism. Although other philosophers had challenged individual tenets of realism, Kant was the first to undermine it radically and offer a coherent, powerful alternative account of reality, subjectivity, and knowledge."[44] It is through Kant, in other words, that modern realism finds its first substantial objector. Rather than proceed under the assumption that objects themselves can be known *a priori*, Kant's epistemology assumes a wholly different approach to knowledge and experience—that "we can know *a priori* of things only what we ourselves put into them."[45] While it is ultimately unable to fully resist the lure of realism, a problem I will take up a bit later, Kant's transcendental idealism nonetheless succeeded in establishing the basic framework of modern anti-realism, which, as Braver demonstrates, follows a line of thought from Kant and Hegel to Foucault and Derrida. It is this Kantian paradigm, I am suggesting, that helped transform the intellectual environment in the humanities and that in turn made possible the epistemic turn in rhetoric during the past century.

For his part, however, Kant appears to want little to do with rhetoric. Much like Rousseau and Hobbes before him, Kant holds a typically Enlightenment view of rhetoric, one that equates rhetoric with deception and manipulation. Of course, like many of rhetoric's most passionate critics, there is a rich irony in Kant's critiques of rhetoric. While it rails against rhetoric, Kant's critique is ultimately a highly *rhetorical* defense of his *anti-rhetorical* epistemology. In his marvelous book *Saving Persuasion: A Defense of Rhetoric and Judgment*, Bryan Garsten argues that Enlightenment thinkers such as Kant often engaged in this kind of "rhetoric against rhetoric." This rhetoric sought to immunize citizens against revolutionary democratic rhetorics by alienating "their capacity for private judgment to a sovereign public authority."[46] Rather than entrust the demos with the power to cultivate and exercise its own judgment, thinkers such as Rousseau and Hobbes instead sought to isolate judgment into a single political body or idea: in the externalized representative of the Leviathan or in the internalized sovereignty of public conscience. In Kant's case, sovereignty took the form of "critical reason" rooted in a particular understanding of "freedom." As Garsten explains, "to think for oneself was first and foremost to reject the authority of other people, of tradition, and of prejudice;"[47] for Kant, this is what "enlightenment" truly means. Rhetoric, therefore, "posed a threat to free thought in Kant because it challenged the authority of the critique of reason. In Kant as in Hobbes, rhetoric was dangerous because it threatened to insubordinate the sovereign."[48]

Kant's rhetoric against rhetoric appears most explicitly in the *Critique of Judgment*. In the section of Part 1 on "Comparison of the Aesthetic Value of the Fine Arts," Kant proposes what can only be described as a hierarchy of the arts, with poetry holding the "highest rank" over all other arts, including music and persuasion. According to Kant, poetry "fortifies the mind: for it lets the mind feel its ability—free, spontaneous, and independent of natural determination—to contemplate and judge phenomenal nature as having aspects that nature does not on its own offer in experience either to sense or to the understanding."[49] Poetry, in this sense, offers a means to exercise one's freedom "without intending to deceive or manipulate its audience."[50] In contrast to the kind of freedom offered through poetry, rhetoric constitutes merely "the art of engaging in a task of the understanding as if it were a free play of the imagination."[51] Akin to Plato's critique of rhetoric as a "sham art" of flattery, Kant's understanding of rhetoric suggests only the illusion of free play of the imagination, not enlightenment as such:

> Oratory, in so far as this is taken to mean the art of persuasion (*ars oratoria*), i.e. of deceiving by a beautiful illusion, rather than mere excellence of speech (eloquence and style), is a dialectic that borrows from poetry only as much as the speaker needs in order to win over people's minds for his own advantage before they judge for themselves, and so make their judgment unfree. Hence it cannot be recommended either for the bar or for the pulpit.[52]

In a revealing footnote to this section, Kant intensifies his attack on rhetoric, this time in reference to some "disagreeable feelings" he experienced while reading "the best speech of a Roman public orator":

> an insidious art that knows how, in important matters, to move people like machines to a judgment that must lose all its weight with them when they meditate about it calmly. Rhetorical power and excellence of speech (which together constitute rhetoric) belong to fine art; but oratory (*ars oratoria*), the art of using people's weaknesses for one's own aims (no matter how good these may be in intention or even in fact), is unworthy of any *respect* whatsoever.[53]

Kant's remarks on rhetoric are not extraneous to the rest of his philosophy, even if, as I am arguing, the overall logic of his philosophy proves much friendlier to rhetorical theory than one might expect. According to Samuel Ijsseling, Kant's dismissal of rhetoric in the third Critique "fits well into the context of his thought" and follows closely from his understanding of enlightenment as discussed in his 1784 essay "What is Enlightenment?"[54] In this short but important work, Kant proclaims that enlightenment is "man's emergence from his self-imposed immaturity." He continues:

> This immaturity is the inability to use one's understanding without guidance from another. This immaturity is self-imposed when its cause lies not in lack of understanding, but in lack of resolve and courage to use it without guidance from another. *Sapere Aude*! [dare to know] "Have courage to use your own understanding"—that is the motto of enlightenment.[55]

For Kant, enlightenment is the emancipation from the conflict between immaturity and guidance out of which one emerges released from both immaturity and the desire for external guidance.[56] In enlightenment, in other words, one is fundamentally *free* (that is to say, autonomous) to "openly make use of one's own understanding and to reflect for oneself"[57] absent the influence or persuasive force of other people. If immaturity is characterized by laziness and cowardice, and guidance implies the presence of a guardian (i.e., governor, teacher, politician, rhetorician, even philosopher) who thinks and speaks on our behalf, then enlightenment, for Kant, is when both of these crutches fall away and we are finally free to accept our capacity to judge and decide for ourselves. Such a view, of course, poses problems for rhetoric and the rhetorician, whose duties typically revolve around educating and persuading others toward some notion of the true or the good.[58] According to Kant's view of enlightenment, the rhetor would appear to deprive "man of [his] freedom, setting himself up as a guardian to think and speak on behalf of others and determining how others should think and speak."[59] In "moving people like machines" and endeavoring to "win over people's minds [...] before they judge for themselves," rhetors deny people the freedom and autonomy to utilize their own capacities to reason and make judgments on important matters of public concern.

What, then, are we to make of Kant's rejection of rhetoric in favor of reason, autonomy, and freedom? Is his resistance to rhetoric enough to persuade us that Kant is simply *too* anti-rhetorical and thus better left to the dustbin of rhetorical history? The evidence at first glance certainly appears overwhelming. In Kant's infamous terms, rhetoric is nothing more than "the machinery of persuasion," sufficient enough to influence human minds but hardly commendable as a vocation or subject of study. From the rhetorician's perspective, Kant's devaluation of rhetoric can also be seen as following a long and troubling line of critique from antiquity to modernity that laments our capacities to deceive one another (and be deceived ourselves) by a beautiful illusion. Like many classical and early-modern critiques of rhetoric, Kant's rhetoric against rhetoric presumes close affinities between rhetoric and force; *If* there is anything positive about rhetoric, it is in its affinities with style, which enable us to communicate ideas and persuade others on matters of public (and philosophic) concern.[60] As Robert J. Dostal argues, this familiar reduction of rhetoric to style means, ultimately, "that one needs no rhetorical skill—one needs only to speak the truth."[61] Such an assumption would appear to put Kant fundamentally at odds with one of the central theses of epistemic rhetoric: that truth does not precede experience but is rather "created moment by moment in the circumstances in which [the rhetor] finds himself and with which he must cope."[62] As we will soon see, however, Kant's epistemology is not nearly as a fixed and stable as his devaluation of rhetoric would have us believe. Indeed, as Pat J. Gerhrke has argued, even Kant's discussions of freedom and autonomy suggest interesting rhetorical implications, particularly when read in terms of ethics and the obligations rational beings have to community as a result of autonomy and freedom. In his recent book *Kant and the Problem of Rhetoric*, Scott R. Stroud offers a similar reassessment of Kant's rhetoric against rhetoric in terms of autonomy and self-determination. "It is not disingenuous to say that one needs a certain amount of faith to find a sense of rhetoric in Kant," Stroud admits.[63] For Scott, Kant's problem is not with rhetoric per se, but with manipulative rhetorics that deliberately hide "some important features of the situation from listeners that such auditors would want to know."[64] While Kant is undeniably suspicious of rhetorics that force rational persons to make decisions they would not otherwise make on their own, there is room in his thought, Stroud argues, for other forms of communication that are nonmanipulative and "aimed toward persuasion and audience change that are animated by valuing autonomy."[65] Manifesting in Kant's writings on education and other topics, this other rhetoric "is nonmanipulative insofar as it does not compromise an auditor's autonomy, and it is truly educative in that it cultivates the power of autonomy in line with the ideal of the kingdom of ends."[66] As Gerhrke and Stroud each make clear, Kant's hostility toward rhetoric may not have been as universal as it appears; similar to Sprat and other Royal Society fellows, his objections to rhetoric may have been targeted more toward the abuses of specific persuasive techniques than toward the art as a whole. That being said, even by the standards of rhetoric's "long and conflicted relationship" with philosophy, Kant's rhetoric against rhetoric cannot (and should not) be easily ignored or brushed aside. As Don Paul Abbott rightly remarks, the brevity and intensity of Kant's hostility toward rhetoric is "extraordinary," and has probably managed to discourage many rhetoricians from lingering too long in his thought.[67]

While we need not condone or excuse Kant's devaluation of rhetoric, the fact that an Enlightenment philosopher would target rhetoric in these ways should not surprise us; nor should it dissuade us from considering what Kant's transcendental idealism in the broader sense might have contributed to modern rhetorical theory (perhaps against the best intentions of its author). After all, it is not as though rhetoricians have never had to reconcile a philosopher's disparaging statements about rhetoric with his/her influence on rhetorical theory (Plato and Ramus immediately come to mind). And much like Plato and Ramus, Kant has played a vital if under-appreciated role in the development of modern rhetorical theory. With respect to epistemological approaches to rhetoric in particular, the influence of Kant's transcendental idealism cannot be overstated. In Daniel J. Royer's estimation, our modern understanding of rhetoric as a knowledge-making art "is the culmination of many influences that ultimately sink their roots in the philosophies of [Ernst] Cassirer and Kant."[68] While there are significant differences between Kant's transcendental idealism and more recent epistemic rhetorics, Royer's sense of Kant's importance to the rhetorical tradition suggests the merit of further exploring rhetoric's Kantian roots, particularly in light of Kant's alleged anti-realism, which has itself proven to be highly influential within the modern rhetorical tradition.

While Kant's writings themselves may no longer be as popular as they once were, the impact of his transcendental idealism can still be felt across the humanities and in rhetoric in particular. "In fact, we can almost say of Kant what Nietzsche says of God," Braver observes, "that he 'is dead; but given the way of men, there may still be caves for thousands of years in which his shadow will be shown.—And we—we still have to vanquish his shadow.'"[69] If what Braver and Nietzsche suggest is true, then the prospect of stepping outside of the Kantian Revolution so as to overturn it may no longer be available to us. Rather than attempt such a feat, I believe the better way to proceed is through Kantianism itself, to inhabit it critically and imaginatively in order to explore both its problems and its opportunities.

Flipping the Realist Script: The Copernican Revolution

As we have seen, Kantianism seeks to reverse the traditional tenets of realism, most notably the realist belief in the "passive knower" who is able to obtain knowledge of reality as it is in itself, sans mediation, obfuscation, or partiality.[70] Indeed, Kant fancies himself as not only correcting some longstanding confusion in philosophy's understanding of metaphysics, but as reimagining philosophy from the ground up, complete with a brand new set of first principles and a new outlook on reality. As he boasts in the *Prolegomena to Any Future Metaphysics*, his is a "perfectly new science, of which no one has ever even thought, the very idea of which was unknown, and for which nothing hitherto accomplished can be of the smallest use."[71] In order for the realist philosophies of his time to make sense, Kant believed they must assume *a priori* that the world is "out there" and that it is therefore independent of our experience. To be a realist, in Kant's view, is thus to accept as given a separation between *thought* and *being*, a separation Kant will eventually insist is impossible to maintain either empirically or transcendentally. Rather than perpetuate the realist ideal of the passive knower, Kant proposes instead a more radical solution: "Philosophy must start over with a new understanding of the relationship between subject and world or thought and being that actually establishes the connection rather than simply assuming it."[72] For Kant, what he calls transcendental idealism captures precisely these kinds of connections. By focusing attention on the *appearances* (*Erscheinungen*) and *presentations* (*Vortstellungen*) of things, transcendental idealism establishes a doctrine in which "all objects of experience possible for us are nothing but appearances, i.e., they are mere presentations that—in the way in which they are presented, viz., as extended beings, or as series of changes—have no existence with an intrinsic basis, i.e., outside our thoughts."[73] As an epistemic doctrine, transcendental idealism emplaces understanding squarely within the limits of human cognition. Although Kant repeatedly insists that some things exist independent of the structures of human cognition, his transcendental idealism insists as well that, by definition, such things can never count as objects *for us* because knowledge is necessarily tied to appearances and "mere representations" rather than things-in-themselves.[74] Often translated as "representation," *Vortestellugen* is more accurately rendered as "presentation," as this shifts emphasis away from ideas "standing in" for objects, a notion Kant does not endorse, toward objects of our direct awareness such as sensations, intuitions, perceptions, concepts, cognitions, ideas, and schemata. As presentations, such objects do not exist outside of thought (as most versions of representation suggest) but firmly within the structures and limits of sensibility and understanding, that is to say, within the subject herself. Most importantly for Kant, and what makes this version of idealism transcendental, knowledge itself is conditioned by categories of understanding that are common to all human beings. Categories such as quantity, quality, and causality, he will argue, are not learned empirically but "are part of every experience—the very conditions on which experience is possible for human beings, and hence transcendental."[75] The doctrine of transcendental idealism thus builds from the idea of *the transcendental subject*, a subject that, while actively involved in the production of knowledge, is structured *a priori* to sense and understand the world in specific and predetermined ways.

Kant's best-known articulation of the doctrine of transcendental idealism appears in the preface to the second edition of the *Critique of Pure Reason*. In this revised and updated introduction, Kant proposes the now famous analogy between his transcendental idealism and Copernicus's heliocentric view of the universe. In Kant's estimation, the Copernican Revolution[76] he seeks to incite promises nothing less than a complete transformation in our thinking about the world and ourselves in the world. It is worth listening to him at some length, particularly given how prescient his writing reads today in the wake of the linguistic and epistemic turns in nineteenth and twentieth-century rhetorical theory:

> Thus far it has been assumed that all our cognition must conform to objects. On that presupposition, however, all our attempts to establish something about them a priori, by means of concepts through which our cognition would be expanded, have come to nothing. Let us, therefore, try to find out by experiment whether we shall not make better

> progress in the problems of metaphysics if we assume that objects must conform to our cognition.—This assumption already agrees better with the demanded possibility of an a priori cognition of objects—i.e., a cognition that is to ascertain something about them before they are given to us. The situation here is the same as was that of *Copernicus* when he first thought of explaining the motions of celestial bodies. Having found it difficult to make progress there when he assumed that the entire host of stars revolved around the spectator, he tried to find out by experiment whether he might not be more successful if he had the spectator revolve and stars remain at rest.[77]

Leaving aside the appropriateness of the Copernicus analogy, which has generated considerable debate among commentators,[78] we can begin to understand the exigency for Kant's revolution by seeing it as a response to the perceived failures of realism to explain how the mind can anticipate any of the properties of objects presented to it.[79] If cognition truly conforms to objects, as some realists claim, then it follows that we can only know objects to the extent that our thoughts conform to their real nature. This would effectively make all knowledge *a posteriori* and, as a consequence, render cognition passive and finite. In the first version of the Fourth Paralogism, Kant names this form of realism *transcendental realism* and contrasts it with his own transcendental idealism. As Henry Allison explains, transcendental realism for Kant represents a confusion of appearances with things-in-themselves.[80] In Kant's terms, "the transcendental realist conceives outer appearances (if their actuality is granted) as things in themselves that exist independently of us and of our sensibility, and that would therefore be *outside* us even according to pure concepts of understanding."[81] The problem with transcendental realism, as Kant sees it, is that it assumes that objects themselves are what appear to us, thus giving fuel to the assumption that we are merely "passively recording the intrinsic structure of the world" rather than actively participating in the production and interpretation of phenomena or appearances.[82] While Kant is not at all prepared to jettison the idea of things-in-themselves from his transcendental idealism, he nevertheless wants to distance himself (and philosophy writ large) from the tendency to define them exclusively in terms of appearances, which only exist and have meaning within the structures of thought itself. The Copernican Revolution thus insists upon a necessary distinction between appearances and things-in-themselves, of which only the former resonate explicitly with our *a priori* conditions of cognition. As Deleuze puts it, "the first thing that the Copernican Revolution teaches us is that it is we who are giving the orders [...] we are the legislators of Nature."[83]

In spite of Kant's notorious rhetoric against rhetoric, many modern rhetoricians nonetheless find themselves channeling and repeating his famous revolution. This is particularly true for epistemic rhetoricians who, similar to Kant, are interested in turning rhetoric's focus away from objective notions of truth and language to the only being about which we can reasonable speculate: us. In the conclusion to "On Viewing Rhetoric as Epistemic," for example, Scott characterizes epistemic rhetoric as a turn away from objective notions of truth toward more relative and rhetorical understandings of reality that effectively emplace human beings as "the legislators of Nature." He does this by way of a familiar astronomical metaphor:

> Man must consider truth not as something fixed and final but as something to be created moment by moment in the circumstances in which he finds himself and with which he must cope. Man may plot his course by fixed stars but he does not possess those stars; he only proceeds, more or less effectively, on his course. Furthermore, man has learned that his stars are fixed only in a relative sense.[84]

While Kant's name is not mentioned here, nor does it appear anywhere else in this essay, it is impossible not to hear Kant's famous analogy in a statement such as this. Kant himself would probably not consider himself a relativist when it comes to truth. However, the logic of his revolution is nevertheless firmly on display here. Much like Kant's understanding of cognition as active rather than passive, Scott's notion of truth is one in which thinking and communication frame and give substance to the world, not the other way around. Furthermore, for both Kant and Scott, truths are not fixed in things themselves; rather it is we who are in motion, with objects appearing to us only in a relative sense.[85]

In his essay revisiting epistemic rhetoric ten years after his 1967 essay, Scott extends this line of thinking by suggesting a shift in terminology for epistemic rhetoric from "knowing" to "understanding." While Scott's original essay explicitly defines rhetoric as a way of knowing, in the later essay he questions whether his decision to use the word "knowing" might have unwittingly confused matters for some readers. In particular, he worries that the term "knowing" stresses "a sense from-the-outside-in, taking knowledge as an external anchor point that may bring one into a consistent relationship with the world."[86] By contrast, the term "Understanding," he proposes, stresses "the sense of from-the-inside-out, taking understanding as a human and personal capacity to embrace what is outside the self, creating rather than finding meaning in the world."[87] Here, again, Scott's argument echoes Kant and the Copernican Revolution in that it shifts the origin of understanding from the world outside of the subject to the structures of subjectivity itself. At the same time, his proposed shift in terminology, from knowing to understanding, suggests additional Kantian roots for his version of epistemic rhetoric. As one of Kant's key philosophical terms, "understanding" holds a critical place in his transcendental idealism as that which provides the forms that structure our cognition of the sensible world. Insofar as experience is itself a way of cognizing, it requires the understanding. "Understanding has its rule," Kant says, "a rule that I must presuppose a priori;

and that rule is expressed in a priori concepts. Hence all objects of experience must necessarily conform to these concepts and agree with them."[88] If "understanding" highlights our abilities to actively create meaning in the world rather than to discover or receive them passively, as Scott suggests, then perhaps rhetoric is not nearly so anathema to Kant's transcendental idealism as it sometimes seems.

Of course, for all of its prescience and influence, Kant's Copernican Revolution did not invent anti-realism; nor was it the first model to propose something like a constructionist understanding of truth and knowledge. In a response to Royer's argument that epistemic rhetoric is the culmination of influences that began with Cassirer and Kant, Bruce McComiskey raises the important and perhaps obvious historical question: Couldn't one just as easily say that epistemic rhetoric's source of inspiration lies as much with the older Sophists as with Kant's transcendental idealism? In the argument that follows, McComiskey counters Royer's Kantian hypothesis by tracing a number of sophistic references and allusions in the epistemic rhetoric literature. In addition to his extensive reliance on Toulmin, for example, McComiskey notes that Scott draws implicitly on arguments from Gorgias and Protagoras as well, in particular their belief in "the historical and empirical contingency of truth."[89] Similar sophistic allusions can be found in Michael Leff's "In Search of Ariadne's Thread" and Burke's "Definition of Man" and "Terministic Screens." Given the affinities that exist between sophistic notions of truth and modern epistemic rhetorics, McComiskey understandably concludes that epistemic rhetoric "has its deepest and most significant roots in the rhetorical theories of the ancient Sophists," not, as Royer proposes, in the modern epistemologies of Cassirer and Kant.

What McComiskey fails to consider, however, is the extent to which the revival of sophistic rhetoric in the late twentieth century, and its appropriation by neo-sophistic rhetorical theorists, may itself have been enabled by the same Copernican Revolution he sees as a mere extension of ancient sophistic doctrine. Put differently, although McComiskey is clearly committed to (and clearly able to) trace the lineage of epistemic rhetoric back to the Sophists, it is likely this historical insight would not have been possible, or even thinkable, were it not for the epistemological transformations in the human sciences that began with Kant and that continued well into the twentieth century. Epistemic rhetoric may indeed resonate well with sophistic theories of truth and contingency, as McComiskey suggests, but our abilities to see and appreciate these resonances have been never guaranteed and are anything but inevitable, as the long history of forgetting and disparaging the Sophists attests.

The implications of this tension for histories of rhetoric, and for epistemic historiography in particular, are significant. In his insightful reading of the sophistic precedents for epistemic rhetoric, McComiskey reminds historians of rhetoric of the importance of paying close attention to the texts themselves: to the what they are saying, of course, but also to what may be lurking "between the lines and on the margins of every page."[90] This, of course, is essential advice for any exploration of Kant's contributions to modern rhetorical theory. At the same time, I would argue that historiography must also find ways to account for context, for the intellectual environments within which versions of epistemology emerge and become meaningful. At its best, therefore, historiography demands a style of reading that is sensitive to both texts *and* contexts. When we take seriously the potential meaning and legacy of Kant's Copernican Revolution for modern histories of rhetoric, we are bringing texts and contexts together to explore how texts perform contexts and how contexts in turn are constituted through texts.

What the Copernican Revolution provided rhetoric, then, is an environment within which rhetorical understandings of truth and knowledge could once again resonate—not just as counterpoints for philosophical realists, but as valuable contributions in their own rights to philosophical conceptions of truth and knowledge. From Hegel and the British empiricists to phenomenology and deconstruction, the legacy of continental anti-realism that began with Kant has indeed proven quite conducive for rhetorical thinking and rhetorical approaches to epistemology in particular. And yet, for all of his contributions to anti-realism, Kant himself struggles to resist many of the realist assumptions he clearly hopes to move beyond. As mentioned in Chapter 1, Kant's transcendental idealism presupposes the existence of a transcendental subject, one capable of providing the consistent grounding needed for a "critique of pure reason" to get going in the first place. This version of the subject, Braver notes, serves as a condition of possibility for Kant's idealism by ensuring that all subjects remain the same at all times. In other words, the persistence of the transcendental subject effectively re-inscribes "a realism of the subject" back into Kant's philosophy. Kant's transcendental idealism, it turns out, could not have gotten off the ground were it not for his willingness to retain certain realist foundations for knowledge, both within the subject and, as we will see below, outside of the subject in the form of the noumenon or thing-in-itself.

And yet, as Braver argues as well, these vestiges of realism, despite being apparently contradictory with his otherwise idealist argument, are ultimately essential for Kant, who on the one hand wishes to affirm the anti-realist thesis of the active knower while, on the other, retain the idea that universal knowledge of the phenomenal world is indeed possible.[91] Insofar as it encompasses the *a priori* conditions of cognition, the transcendental subject provides Kant the grounding he needs to announce his Copernican Revolution while at the same time safeguarding idealism from outright relativism in which anything goes vis-à-vis knowledge and reality. But in order to fulfill these two goals, Kant must equivocate on the anti-realist arguments underlying his transcendental idealism. For instance, if time, space, and causation constitute *a priori* categories of understanding rather than objective realities observable in the world, it stands to reason they must still come to us from somewhere; moreover, they must be shared by all (or most) human beings, and they must function analytically rather than synthetically. Taking all of this into account, Kant concludes that because our understandings of space, time, and causation do not depend on sensory experience, they must therefore be transcendental *and* mind-independent. As Braver summarizes, the transcendental subject "is the unconstituted constitutor, the mind on which all mind-dependent things depend."[92] This is the *Kantian Compromise*, the necessary equivocation on the validity of realism that makes possible his and subsequent anti-realist epistemologies. In the case of transcendental idealism, the transcendental subject constitutes the realist presupposition—the mind-independent reality—that makes possible anti-realist theses about knowledge, truth, and understanding. More than a philosophical blindness, the persistence of realism in Kant's work reminds us just how difficult it can be to fully eliminate realist assumptions from our thinking about the world. Kant's Copernican Revolution may have founded many modern forms of anti-realism, and in turn made possible the revival of rhetoric in the past century; however, it did so largely in spite of itself. For all of its arguments to the contrary, Kantianism remains "conceived strictly along the lines of a realist metaphysics."[93]

My point here is not to poke holes in Kant's purported idealism. While I do want to argue that idealism (and rhetoric, ultimately) requires as a condition of possibility some realist commitments, I want to emphasize here that the lessons to be learned from Kant go much farther than any simple debunking of idealism. Indeed, I would say, it is Kant's willingness to compromise on the question of realism, and in so doing allow realism a vital place in his view of things, that makes him a particularly compelling figure for rhetorical theorists today. The question we need to consider, then, is whether similar kernels of realism persist in post-Kantian rhetorical theory, and if so, what these realist commitments suggest about modern rhetorical realism in the epistemic tradition.

Realism Revisited: The Thing-in-Itself

For good reason, the idea of the transcendental subject has largely fallen out of favor over the course of the past century. Among rhetorical theorists in particular, the prospect of some essential and universal state of being that would determine the foundations for knowledge and communication has almost unanimously given way to more constitutive understandings of identity and subjectivity. Faced with something like the transcendental subject, rhetoricians today are apt to wonder, if there are shared and universal categories of understanding, then how is it that we continue to disagree about the nature of reality? Moreover, if we take Aristotle to heart—that we only deliberate over matters that might be other than they are—then would not the existence of the transcendental subject render moot many of these kinds of debates? Couldn't we simply appeal to our mutual understandings of space, time, and causation, and be on our way? For all of its importance to Kant's idealism, the transcendental subject is, finally, too far afield from the concerns of rhetoric to merit much significant attention today. In acknowledging this, however, I do not mean to suggest that as goes the transcendental subject so goes Kant's rhetorical realism. Quite the contrary, in fact. Although rhetorical theorists today resist the notion of the transcendental subject, as I argue in this section epistemic theorists in particular continue to follow Kant's lead by incorporating realist objects of concern into their theories of knowledge. But rather than look *within us*, the transcendental subject, for such backing, modern rhetoricians instead follow another line out of Kantian epistemology, one that recognizes the *externality* of some mind-independent objects as 1) an inaccessible, although *affecting*, reality in its own right, and 2) a means of reminding ourselves that our perceptions and knowledge of the world are inherently limited by all that we cannot see and all that we cannot know.

For Kant, it is thing-in-itself that serves the function of limiting cognition's range and reminding us that there is always something "behind the appearance"—something that, while having an effect on thought, remains inaccessible to knowledge by virtue of its essence.[94] While Kant can be frustratingly inconsistent in his use of terms, many commentators accept at least some degree of synonymy between the thing-in-itself and Kant's notion of the noumenon, a concept that derives its meaning largely in contrast to his understanding of phenomena or appearances.[95] In Kant's idiom, phenomena refer to objects of the understanding, intuition, and sensibility, while noumena refer to objects (or aspects of the same object, as I discuss below) that resist knowing altogether and therefore cannot be known through categories or brought under any concept. Whereas phenomena are given to us through experience, and thus avail themselves to our *a priori* categories of understanding, noumena or things-in-themselves "signif[y] only the thinking of something as such—something in which I abstract from all form of sensible intuition."[96] Because we cannot know the thing-in-itself—"No object can be given to us in any other manner than through sensibility"[97]—the only thing we can ascertain about it is its existence as such. The noumenon, therefore, appears to us as a kind of placeholder, a gap or abyss (or X, as Kant sometimes renders it) in our subjective experience alerting us to the reality of something beyond the phenomenal, something real but otherwise inaccessible to our sensibility or understanding. And because we cannot know anything for certain about things-in-themselves, Kant insists we bracket the possibility of knowing such things and focus instead on the being about which we can reason *a priori*—i.e., the thinking or transcendental subject:

> External things, namely matter, are [...] nothing but mere appearances, that is, representations in us, of whose reality we are directly conscious [...] Objects [...] in themselves remains unknown to us [...] If I remove the thinking subject, the whole corporeal world must vanish.[98]

The Question Concerning Reality 169

Things-in-themselves exist—this much we can say for certain. However, because appearances or representations (*Vortestellugen*) are the only things about which we are directly conscious, phenomena alone must constitute the whole of our worldly knowledge and experience. "What may be the case regarding objects in themselves and apart from all this receptivity of our sensibility remains to use entirely unknown. All we know [*kennen*] is the way in which we perceive them."[99] So tightly bound are appearances to the thinking subject (indeed, Kant will argue that phenomena are not things external to the subject but are what appears *in* the subject) that if we remove the thinking subject the whole of the phenomenal world would cease to exist. For all of its obvious idealism, however, the distinction between appearances and things-in-themselves is exceedingly complex and often contradictory. Kant himself seems uncertain at times about how to accommodate the thing-in-itself into his transcendental idealism. As I hope to show, these uncertainties on Kant's part are not entirely unjustified as the thing-in-itself does indeed pose substantial challenges to transcendental idealism and anti-realism in general. Kant's sometimes confusing equivocation on this question, what I have called the Kantian Compromise, allows us to see just how difficult it can be to eliminate realism entirely from our thinking about the world.

Given his transcendental idealism, it is reasonable to wonder why Kant insists on the distinction between phenomena and noumena in the first place. If the goal in the first Critique is to put the spectator in motion in order to examine her means of understanding the world, then why not simply do away with the thing-in-itself altogether? Why retain the notion of something outside of knowledge and experience when it is human subjectivity that limits what we can know about things in the world? This is an issue that has long perplexed readers of Kant, including those whose work builds directly on the Kantian tradition. For example, despite his many affinities with Kant, Hegel fails to understand why Kant persists in championing a chasm between thinking and being, which for Hegel only serves to separate the knowing subject from the subject of experience.[100] In the *Science of Logic*, Hegel declares things-in-themselves "mere abstractions, void of truth and content." In Hegel's assessment, Kant errs when he assumes that there are two kinds of objects, phenomenal objects (those that can be known) and things-in-themselves (those that cannot be known), rather than a singular perceptual field comprised of appearances, all of which are real and potentially knowable to us. To address this problem, Hegel, like many post-Kantian idealists, suggests doing away with the noumenon altogether, or at least collapsing the distinction between the phenomenal and the noumenal so that in the end they become effectively identical. As Braver puts it, "Hegel's task is to be the Kant that Kant should have been were he sufficiently free of predispositions to follow his own insights to their proper conclusions."[101]

To his credit, Kant seems to have anticipated objections such as Hegel's. In the chapter "On the Basis of the Distinction of all Objects as Such into Phenomena and Noumena," he insists that the concept of a noumenon, "i.e., of a thing that is not to be thought at all as an object of the senses but is to be thought [...] as a thing in itself," is "not at all contradictory."[102] In fact, the noumenon offers a valuable and necessary supplement to the phenomenal that helps keep its boundaries and pretensions in check:

> Moreover, the concept of a noumenon is necessary in order not to extend sensible intuition even over things in themselves, and hence in order to limit the objective validity of sensible cognition [...] The concept of a noumenon is, therefore, only a *boundary concept* serving to limit the pretension of sensibility, and hence is only of negative use But it is nonetheless not arbitrarily invented; rather, it coheres with the limitation of sensibility, yet without being able to posit anything positive outside sensibility's range.[103]

As a placeholder and boundary concept, the thing-in-itself ensures there are limits to sensibility, even if the exact nature of those limits remains unknown to us. For Kant, placeholders such as this are important to the extent that they alert us to the finite shape and reach of the understanding. This, in turn, helps keep the sensible coherent enough for us to examine it as a fixed (i.e., transcendental) field. If there were no limits to sensibility, Kant surmises, if the world only exists insofar as it appears to us, there would be no limits to what transcendental idealism would need to explain. In an interesting parallel to rhetoric, Kant seems to want to caution against his own version of "Big Rhetoric," with everything under (and behind) the sun falling problematically under the jurisdiction of his new transcendental idealism.

As a critical device, then, the thing-in-itself serves an important function in helping corral the phenomenal into a domain fixed and stable enough for analysis. Echoing the first Critique's mention of the thing-in-itself as a boundary concept, Kant further suggests in the *Prolegomena*, "Our critical deduction by no means excludes things of that sort (noumena), but rather limits the principles of the Aesthetic in such a way that they shall not extend to all things (as everything would then be turned into mere appearance) but that they shall hold good only of objects of possible experience."[104] The thing-in-itself draws attention to important limits for what is otherwise an idealist approach to epistemology. As previously suggested, some readers of Kant remain unconvinced and unsatisfied by such statements, believing them unnecessary and, in the worst cases, relics of the old naïve realism Kant ultimately failed to recognize in his own thinking. Kant himself, however, appears to take them quite seriously. Indeed, many of his discussions of noumena imply that we are both ignorant of things-in-themselves and that we are "missing out on something in not knowing things as they are in themselves."[105] As Rae Langton notes in her compelling study of things-in-themselves in Kant's thought, Kant frequently "speaks of our yearning for something more, he speaks of doomed aspiration, he speaks of 'our inextinguishable desire to find firm footing somewhere beyond the bounds of experience.'"[106] In ways that anticipate more recent work in phenomenology, most notably Heidegger's fundamental ontology, Kant wants us to know that there are aspects of our world that remain hidden or withdrawn from us, aspects that do not appear to us as such and that cannot be easily accessed, represented, or drawn under the regime of concepts. The "sense of loss" we have about our ignorance of things-in-themselves constitutes, in Langton's terms, Kant's "epistemic humility." Although the tendency for many commentators today is to apologize for or explain away things-in-themselves, Langton argues for taking them seriously as necessary aspects of Kant's epistemology. "When Kant tells us that we have no knowledge of things in themselves, he thinks he is telling us something new and important," she says.[107]

But what are things-in-themselves? Following Hegel's critique, many readers assume that things-in-themselves refer to discrete objects in the world, objects wholly separate from phenomena or the objects of appearances. Such an arrangement, sometimes referred to as the "two-world" problem, poses a number of problems for Kant's transcendental idealism, as we have seen. Specifically, it invites the kinds of questions critics such as Hegel have asked: Why, if he is such an idealist, does Kant insist upon two kinds of objects, one knowable and the other unknowable? While there is ample evidence in the *Prolegomena* and first Critique to support the two-world thesis (again, like many thinkers who revised their ideas over several decades, Kant is inconsistent in his discussions of many of his key concepts, including things-in-themselves), there is evidence as well to suggest that Kant may not have intended to carve the world up in this way, and that, in fact, things-in-themselves (with all of their realist baggage and implications) are actually quite consonant with his doctrine of transcendental idealism. As Langton argues, it is possible, and perhaps more logical, to read Kant as positing *one world* rather than two:

> The explanation I would like to suggest draws on what Kant says elsewhere [...] There is one world; there are simply, as Kant says with appropriate vagueness, objects, or things. But there are two, non-overlapping sets of properties. Kant speaks in this passage of the nature that things have in themselves, as he speaks elsewhere of the 'distinctive and inner predicates' of things (A565/B593). The nature things have in themselves is different from what we encounter when we intuit them: the inner or *intrinsic* predicates are different from the predicates encountered by us.[108]

Langton's reading of Kant hinges on the old philosophical distinction between substances and their properties. More important for us, however, is her suggestion that appearances and things-in-themselves are not separate entities at all but rather "oppositional" properties within every single object. "The labels 'phenomena' and 'noumena' seem to label different entities," she goes on to suggest, "but really they label different classes of properties of the same set of entities."[109] In other words, the same object can be described both as phenomenon and thing-in-itself because each object has relations with other objects and also has an intrinsic (and inexhaustible) nature of its own.[110] In his 1927/1928 lecture course on Kant's first Critique, Heidegger argues for a similar reading of things-in-themselves. He cites the *Opus Postumum* in which Kant claims that the thing-in-itself is not a being different from its appearance: "the difference between the concept of a thing in itself and the appearance is not objective but merely subjective. The thing in itself is not another Object, but is rather an other aspect (*respectus*) of the presentation of *the same Object*."[111] Here, again, there are not two worlds for Kant, but one: "What is 'behind appearance' is the same being as the appearance."[112]

Finally, Allison notes how various iterations of the term "thing-in-itself" in Kant's writing, particularly in the original German, suggest the possibility of objects having both intrinsic and relational qualities. Even as he remains skeptical of Langton's one world reading, Allison's etymology allows us to appreciate the ambiguous forms this much-debated concept take in Kant's work. Allison notes, for example, how the short form *ding an sich* implies that the referent is to a discrete thing with its own mode of existence. Although Kant rarely uses this locution, it has nevertheless become the preferred one in the literature, and thus may be responsible for much of the confusion that has surrounded the idea of the thing-in-itself. By far, however, Kant's preferred way of representing the idea of the thing-in-itself is *ding an sich selbst*. This longer form places greater emphasis on the idea of a thing as it is in itself, a seemingly subtle shift that suggests a bit more vibrancy, and perhaps even a degree of self-determination, on the part of object. Regardless, Allison argues that both short and long forms constitute truncated forms of the canonical "thing considered as it is in itself" (*ding an sich selbst betrachtet*), where "the *an sich selbst* functions adverbially to characterize *how* a thing is being considered rather than the kind of thing it is or the way in which it exists."[113] Even at the level of language, then, Kant seems to suggest that things-in-themselves do not constitute separate objects but refer instead to the intrinsic properties within objects themselves. Herein lies the seed of his epistemic humility: a persistent kernel of realism which finds within objects a subterranean surplus of possibility that is never fully revealed and never fully exhausted through one's relations to that object.

Of course, the notion that things are not exactly what they seem has a long history in rhetoric as well, particularly in the modern era as attention turned increasingly to issues of epistemology and relativist theories of truth. At its core, relativism is itself a doctrine of limits, albeit one that locates limits within language and the finite faculties of human perception rather than in the "real" world outside of thought or language (consider, for example, Kenneth Burke's terministic screens or Paul de Man's "insights and blindnesses"). If the relativist version of epistemic rhetoric were to have a slogan, then, it could do worse than Protagoras's famous dictum that "of all things the measure is man."[114] And yet, even as they endow the human being with world-forming power, epistemic rhetoricians hew closely to the Kantian Compromise by blending realist and anti-realist theses into complex rhetorical understandings of reality. For example, in his 1982 response to Richard Cherwitz and Earl Croasmun, Brummett sets out to formalize and defend epistemic rhetoric or, as he calls it here, "consensus theory." According to Brummett, there are three major claims that are at the heart of consensus theory: (1) "reality is rhetorically created, (2) it *has* been carefully argued and not just assumed by consensus theorists, and (3) it means that at the heart of the controversy concerning epistemic rhetoric is ontology, or the issue of *what it means to be real.*"[115] I will take up the third of Brummett's claims a bit later. For now, let us consider Brummett's first two points, both of which speak to a prevailing argument within modern rhetorical studies that rhetoric constitutes reality and that debates about rhetoric mostly concern questions about how we understand and construct reality. Certainly, Brummett is not saying that physical objects do not exist, or that the experience of getting knocked on the head by a hammer is merely a rhetorical event constructed out of individual or shared meanings about head injuries, hammers, and the like. And yet, Brummett is also clearly not a realist as evidenced by his claim a bit later in the essay that "objects come into existence for humans through the same rhetorical process by which they are known."[116] Like many post-Kantian rhetoricians who believe that objects conform to thought but who fear at the same time the prospect of losing mind-independent reality as a limit case or point of reference, Brummett finds himself having to negotiate a difficult balancing act between realism on the one hand and anti-realism on the other, wherein things such as "the sun, the earth, rocks and trees" have existence outside of the mind but are nevertheless only ever "what we *mean* them to be."[117]

What Brummett fails to notice in his efforts to articulate a vision of rhetoric as epistemic is the extent to which he grants certain things presence and being while at the same time denying other things their being altogether. In Brummett's conflicted terms, "we know that people are persuaded all the time by appeals to values, biases, and meanings that are not *things*, that have no physical referents."[118] Brummett's point here is that values, biases, and meanings are not "real things" in any physical sense of the term, but are intangible ideas constituting the sum total of reality as we are capable of knowing and accessing it. In order to make this claim, however, Brummett first has to position values, biases, and meanings in a precarious place between autonomy and intentionality, much as Kant conceives of space, time, and causation in transcendental terms preceding and constituting the structures of sensation and understanding. Only by so doing is he then able to claim, on the one hand, that values actively persuade us and help constitute us as subjects whether we are aware of them or not, while on the other that values and the like remain solely the responsibility of human rhetors who alone have the power to revise or reshape such things according to their needs and desires. While values may not constitute "real things" having real physical referents for Brummett, they nonetheless assume an important realist responsibility in the making of rhetorical relativism, most notably establishing the existence of a semi-autonomous realm that precedes and exceeds the subject's knowledge while at the same time serving as its condition of possibility.[119]

Brummett's anti-realism is at best an ideal, one that attempts to distance rhetoric once and for all from the specter of naïve realism.[120] The reality of Brummett's anti-realism, however, is that it remains committed to, even dependent upon, realist assumptions about the world, a point he acknowledges in reference to Burke's idea of "recalcitrance" or the rhetorical factors "that substantiate a statement, the factors that incite a statement, and the factors that correct a statement."[121] "We simply cannot talk rocks and trees into existence," Brummett concedes. "For that reason," he concludes, "consensus theorists *postulate* that reality = meaning + something else that causes recalcitrance."[122] The need for Brummett to retain "something else that causes recalcitrance," something lying outside of language that can serve to incite language and meaning-making, embodies the peculiar tension at the heart of the Kantian Compromise. Although knowledge originates in human beings, and not in the world outside of thought, knowledge is always bumping against the limits of its own explanatory power, which is nothing less than the limits—the recalcitrance—of things-in-themselves.

Perhaps the most promising take on the Kantian Compromise in the epistemic rhetoric debates can be found in the under-appreciated work of Richard Cherwitz and James Hikins. In unapologetically realist terms, they define the "first postulate" of their realist theory of rhetorical perspectivism as "the independence of reality [...] In experience, there is presented to us, directly, a world of phenomena largely independent of our attitudes, beliefs and values."[123] According to Cherwitz and Hikins, if the world exists independent of discourse and subjective interests, this means we cannot simply will or wish the world away.[124] With respect to rhetoric, they argue it is therefore not enough to assume that reality begins and ends with the social because commonsense tells us that there are always limits to what change discourse can enact in the world. Rather than accept the idea that rhetoric provides the sole means by which the world appears to us and comes into meaning, Cherwitz and Hikins propose a realist view of rhetoric which sees rhetoric as functioning as a kind of mediator helping us uncover and coordinate differing perspectives of reality. Although we frequently disagree about our perceptions of a given object or event, we are, they conclude, still debating "aspects of the same object."[125]

Even as they champion the realist thesis of mind-independent reality, Cherwitz and Hikins insist that perception, ambiguity, and partiality continue to play crucial roles in shaping understandings of reality. In their theory, objects are not merely uniform lumps of matter. They are assemblages of innumerable qualities that collectively define the object as a singular idea or concept. And it is these qualities that we encounter in our dealings with things, and that withdraw to remain inaccessible and (at least for now) unknowable. In the spirit of Berkeleyan idealism, Cherwitz and Hikins conceive of objects as "bundles of qualities" or *relata* that collectively make up the whole of a thing. To borrow one of their examples, we can read Richard Nixon's presidency as both the product of multiple (and obviously competing) perceptions and as a multitudinous object in its own right, one that gathers a wide range of materialities, from language and politics to war machines and national infrastructure. According to the authors, when disagreements emerge over the thing in question—"Nixon was a good president" versus "Nixon was a bad president"—they do so as a result of the rhetor's abilities to appeal to specific aspects "within the collection of particulars comprising the Nixon presidency."[126] While the qualities evoked by critics and supporters of Nixon's presidency vary greatly, Cherwitz and Hikins insist that these qualities are nonetheless aspects of the same thing; they simply "*appear* to be different because of the differing *perspectives* in which each arguer stands."[127] Contradictory arguments, therefore, "are really not contradictory at all," because "they are *judgments about different aspects of the same object.*"[128] Rhetorical perspectivism, then, seeks to ground knowledge in response to real objects understood as assemblages of multiple, and oftentimes competing, profiles and qualities. While there may be a correspondence theory of truth here, just as there is in Brummett's conception of intersubjective truth, it is not the usual thesis presuming an open circuit between a singular unified object and a passive subject. Of course, the subject-object dichotomy is still very much in place here. However, these are not the active, all-knowing subjects or the mute and passive objects we typically associate with humanist versions of the subject-object dichotomy. The objects here are multiple and unbounded. Likewise, insofar as any subject (a la Nixon) may himself become an object of inquiry, subjects too can be understood within Cherwitz and Hikins's framework as similarly fractured and inexhaustible. If not the intertwining of subject and object, where it is impossible to discern where one begins and the other ends, rhetorical perspectivism at least suggests that all parties in a rhetorical event are composed of innumerable qualities or properties, some relational and others intrinsic.

Rhetorical perspectivism thus recognizes that knowledge is necessarily determined by our perceptions of reality. At the same time, it suggests that our perceptions never fully capture or exhaust the totality of reality. As a form of rhetorical realism, perspectivism does not ask us to abandon constructionism; nor does it compel us to accept a two-world thesis in which there are things we can know and things we cannot know. All objects, it turns out, are both present and absent, which is another of saying they are simultaneously phenomenal and noumenal, appearances and things-in-themselves. Direct inheritors of Kant's transcendental idealism, Cherwitz and Hikins carry forth the realist notion of properties and relations lurking behind Kant's understandings of the world and objects in the world. This is true for most of the theorists associated with epistemic rhetoric. Despite their differences with one another on issues of epistemology and the nature of reality, Scott, Brummett, Berlin, and Cherwitz and Hikins each situate their versions of epistemic rhetoric roughly within the same Kantian framework. That these versions of epistemic rhetoric often seem contradictory to their proponents is simply a consequence of the compromise Kant had to make in order to keep his theory of knowledge grounded in reality and constrained by the recalcitrance of things in the world. In both the relativist and realist versions of epistemic rhetoric, we find traces of this compromise and with it a shared distrust of any epistemology claiming to grasp and understand the whole of reality.[129] At its core, modern rhetorical realism is characterized by an ambiguous tension between idealism on the one hand and realism on the other. If there is one theme uniting all of the theorists who participated in the epistemic debates in the mid-late twentieth century, it is epistemic humility: the recognition that our perceptions, cognitions, and symbol systems are necessarily partial and interested—that they simultaneously representations *and* deflections of reality, in Burke's terms.

Toward an Ethics of Care

Although it has its roots in epistemology, epistemic humility offers more than just a doctrine of knowledge. As I suggested in the introduction and first chapter of this book, realist commitments have as much to say about ethics as they do the limits of knowledge and understanding. This insight was certainly not lost on epistemic rhetoricians such as Scott and Brummett who saw epistemic rhetoric as recuperating a strong sense of ethical responsibility for rhetoric in the wake of rhetoric's diminution to style in the post-Ramist tradition. If rhetoric is the construction and advocacy of realities rather than their discovery through other means, then the question of responsibility must be front and center in our understandings of rhetoric. In contrast to epistemologies that situate action in relation to already existing principles "for which the individual is simply the instrument," epistemic rhetoric maintains that "one who acts without certainty must embrace the responsibility for making his acts the best possible. He must recognize the conflicts of the circumstances he is in, maximizing the potential good and accepting responsibility for the inevitable harm."[130] As Brummett adds, "the rhetor also has the responsibility to recognize that this truth is his/her responsibility, and its actualization and consequences are his/her responsibility, for he/she is part of the context that determines in part how other will view reality."[131] If we understand ethics as moral codes rooted in absolute and universal standards of truth, then epistemic rhetorics may seem, if not unethical, at least outside of the purview of traditional understandings of ethics. For Scott and Brummett, however, it is actually the relativist theory of truth and knowledge, rather than the realist worldview, that makes ethics necessary and relevant for rhetoric in the first place. If absolute standards of truth existed, one would not have to accept any responsibility for her actions as long as those actions were directed in the service of fulfilling such universal standards. It is only when we acknowledge that truths are produced through human rhetorical action, they argue, that ethical responsibility comes to matter at all.

In saying that rhetors are responsible for (and to) the realities they construct, Brummett and Scott recognize that reality is always a shared experience, even if this experience is multiple and relative to the differing perspectives we bring to them. At the same time, they recognize that realities themselves hold sway—that they have material effects on a wide range of actors, from rhetors and audiences to epistemologies and ways of being. This is in keeping with the rhetorical realism at the heart of epistemic rhetoric: Knowledge originates in human beings and communities, and thus conditions what we come to know about the world and ourselves in the world; however, objects also never fully reveal the innermost depths of their being. With regard to ethics, this suggests that the rhetor is not just responsible for the realities she constructs; she is also responsible to the community of others whose reality is potentially affected by her actions. The emphasis on responsibility we find in Scott and Brummett is compelling for how it ties issues of epistemology to the more mundane concerns of everyday rhetorical action. In this sense, epistemic rhetoric may not have been nearly as "philosophical" as Brummett feared, but in excellent keeping with rhetoric's long history of casting its eyes toward the earth rather than upward toward the heavens.

But it is necessary to push this idea further, as I suggest in the next chapter. Much like the objects of knowledge that exceed our grasp and understanding, the others who share community with us similarly reveal and conceal essential qualities of themselves. While I may experience and gain some understanding of the shifting profiles of the other, I can never fully know the Other as such. Like the thing-in-itself, the Other is always something more than what I encounter in my dealings with her. Thus, my sense of responsibility is more originally directed toward that which it cannot fully see, know, or appropriate, and not just toward abstract truths or objects of knowledge. This sense of uncertainty in the face of the other—this epistemic and ontological humility—is what characterizes and makes possible our being-with one another in an increasingly entangled world of humans and nonhumans, a prospect I explore in more detail in the next chapter.

Notes

1. Bruno Latour, *Pandora's Hope: Essays on the Reality of Science Studies* (Cambridge: Harvard University Press, 1999), 1.
2. Ibid.
3. Ibid.

178 *The Question Concerning Reality*

4. Bruno Latour, *We Have Never Been Modern*, trans. Catherine Porter (Cambridge: Harvard University Press, 1993), 46.
5. Ibid., 4.
6. Barry Brummett, "Some Implications of 'Process' and 'Intersubjectivity': Postmodern Rhetoric," *Philosophy and Rhetoric* 9 (1976): 31.
7. Ibid., 28.
8. Ibid.
9. Immanuel Kant, *Critique of Pure Reason* (Unified Edition), trans. Werner S. Pluhar (Indianapolis: Hackett, 1996), B311.
10. While Levinas's ethical writings clearly have their roots in religious doctrine (as we will see in the next chapter), Davis's engagements with Levinas do not emphasize these aspects of his philosophy, thus, my decision to frame her reading as "secular."
11. See, Dilip Parameshwar Gaonkar, "Rhetoric and Its Double: Reflections of the Rhetorical Turn in the Human Sciences," in *The Rhetorical Turn: Invention and Persuasion in the Conduct of Inquiry*, ed. Herbert W. Simons, 341–366 (Chicago: University of Chicago Press, 1990).
12. Berlin, *Rhetoric and Reality*, 115.
13. James Berlin, *Rhetorics, Poetics, and Cultures: Refiguring College English Studies* (Urbana: NCTE, 1996), xvii–xviii.
14. Hebert W. Simons, introduction to *The Rhetorical Turn: Invention and Persuasion in the Conduct of Inquiry*, ed. Simons (Chicago: University of Chicago Press, 1990), 2.
15. Ibid., 7.
16. Alan G. Gross, *Starring the Text: The Place of Rhetoric in Science Studies* (Carbondale: Southern Illinois University Press, 2006), 9.
17. Stanley Fish, "Rhetoric," in *Doing What Comes Naturally: Change, Rhetoric, and the Practice of Theory in Literary and Legal Studies*, by Fish (Durham: Duke University Press, 1989), 485.
18. Friedrich Nietzsche, "On Truth and Lies in a Nonmoral Sense," in *The Nietzsche Reader*, edited by Keith Ansell Pearson and Duncan Large (Malden: Blackwell, 2006), 116.
19. Robert L. Scott, "On Viewing Rhetoric as Epistemic," *Central States Speech Journal* 18 (1967): 17.
20. Ibid.
21. Berlin, *Rhetorics, Poetics, and Cultures*, 92–93.
22. Kenneth Burke, "The Definition of Man," in *Language as Symbolic Action: Essays on Life, Literature, and Method* (Berkeley: University of California Press, 1966), 5.
23. Brummett, "Some Implications of 'Process' and 'Intersubjectivity': Postmodern Rhetoric," 27.
24. Ernest G. Bormann, "Fantasy and Rhetorical Vision: The Rhetorical Criticism of Social Reality," *Quarterly Journal of Speech* 58 (1972): 400–401.
25. Gayatri Chakravorty Spivak, introduction to *Of Grammatology*, by Jacques Derrida (Baltimore: Johns Hopkins University Press, 1997), xiv.
26. Ibid., xvii.
27. Thomas Rickert, *Ambient Rhetoric: The Attunements of Rhetorical Being* (Pittsburgh: University of Pittsburgh Press, 2013), 169.
28. Lee Braver, *A Thing of This World: A History of Continental Anti-Realism* (Evanston: Northwestern University Press, 2007), 15.

29. Brummett, "Some Implications of 'Process' and 'Intersubjectivity': Postmodern Rhetoric," 33.
30. Ibid., 39.
31. Ibid., 33.
32. Richard J. Bernstein, *Beyond Objectivism and Relativism: Sciences, Hermeneutics, and Praxis* (Philadelphia: University of Pennsylvania Press, 1983), 8, quoted in James Jasinski, *Sourcebook on Rhetoric: Key Concepts in Contemporary Rhetorical Studies* (Thousand Oaks: Sage, 2001), 220.
33. Jasinski, 220.
34. Ibid., 222–223.
35. Ibid., 223.
36. Ibid.
37. Aristotle, *Nicomachean Ethics*, trans. David Ross (New York: Oxford University Press, 1998), 1139b20–21.
38. Brummett, "Some Implications of 'Process' and 'Intersubjectivity': Postmodern Rhetoric," 25.
39. Barry Brummett, "A Eulogy for Epistemic Rhetoric," *Quarterly Journal of Speech* 76 (1990): 69–72.
40. Brummett, "A Eulogy for Epistemic Rhetoric," 71.
41. Berlin, *Rhetorics, Poetics, and Cultures*, xviii.
42. Ibid., xvii.
43. Braver, 15.
44. Ibid., 33.
45. Kant, *Critique of Pure Reason*, Bxviii.
46. Bryan Garsten, *Saving Persuasion: A Defense of Rhetoric and Judgment* (Cambridge: Harvard University Press, 2006), 10.
47. Ibid., 89.
48. Ibid., 91.
49. Immanuel Kant, *Critique of Judgment*, trans. Werner S. Pluhar (Indianapolis: Hackett, 1987), 53: 326.
50. Ibid.
51. Ibid., 51: 321.
52. Ibid., 53: 327.
53. Ibid., 53: 328.
54. Samuel Ijsseling, *Rhetoric and Philosophy in Conflict: An Historical Survey*, trans. Paul Dunphy (The Hague: Martinus Nijhoff, 1976), 86.
55. Immanuel Kant, "An Answer to the Question: What is Enlightenment?" in *Immanuel Kant: Practical Philosophy*, trans. Mary J. Gregor (Cambridge: Cambridge University Press, 1996), 17.
56. Ijsseling, 87.
57. Ibid.
58. Despite his anti-rhetorical conception of enlightenment, Kant nevertheless retains an important role for education in bringing about enlightenment. In contrast to rhetorical education, however, Kant's idea of education is one in which individuals are educated into freedom. Teachers who confront their students with authority ("Do not argue, obey!") instead of teaching them to think and judge for themselves as rational beings, are merely "orators" and not teachers as such.; Ijsseling, 88. For more on Kant and education, see Scott R. Stroud, "Kant on Education and the Rhetorical Force of the Example," *Rhetoric Society Quarterly* 41, no. 5 (2011): 416–438.

59. Ibid., 88.
60. Robert J. Dostal, "Kant and Rhetoric," *Philosophy and Rhetoric* 13 (1980): 225–226.
61. Ibid., 225.
62. Scott, "On Viewing Rhetoric as Epistemic," 17.
63. Scott R. Stroud, *Kant and the Promise of Rhetoric* (University Park: Pennsylvania State University Press, 2014), 138.
64. Ibid., 101.
65. Ibid.
66. Ibid., 105.
67. Don Paul Abbott, "Kant, Theremin, and the Morality of Rhetoric," *Philosophy and Rhetoric* 40, no. 3 (2007): 274. A notable exception can be found in recent work on Kant's moral philosophy, particularly among rhetoricians in communications interested in questions of community and obligation. See, Pat J. Gehrke, "Turning Kant Against the Priority of Autonomy: Communication Ethics and the Duty of Community," *Philosophy and Rhetoric* 35, no. 1 (2002): 1–21; Samuel McCormick, "The Artistry of Obedience: From Kant to Kingship," *Philosophy and Rhetoric* 38, no. 4 (2005): 302–327; and, Stroud, "Kant on Education and the Rhetorical Force of the Example."
68. Daniel J. Royer, "New Challenges to Epistemic Rhetoric," *Rhetoric Review* 9, no. 2 (1991): 287.
69. Braver, 10.
70. See Braver, 21–22.
71. Immanuel Kant, *Prolegomena to Any Future Metaphysics*, trans. James W. Ellington (Indianapolis: Hackett, 1977), 262.
72. Braver, 34.
73. Kant, *Critique of Pure Reason*, A491/B519.
74. Henry E. Allison, *Kant's Transcendental Idealism: An Interpretation and Defense* (New Haven: Yale University Press, 2004), 12.
75. John Lyne, "Idealism as a Rhetorical Stance," in *Rhetoric and Philosophy*, ed. Richard A. Cherwitz (New York: Routledge, 1990), 156.
76. Although the idea of a "Copernican Revolution" is widely attributed to Kant, the phrase itself never appears in his writings.
77. Kant, *Critique of Pure Reason*, Bxvi–xvii.
78. For more on Kant's Copernican analogy, see S. Morris Engel, "Kant's Copernican Analogy: A Re-Examination," *Kant Studies* 54 (1963): 243–251; and Norwood Russell Hanson, "Copernicus' Role in Kant's Revolution," *Journal of the History of Ideas* 20 (1956): 274–281.
79. Allison, 37.
80. Ibid., 22.
81. Kant, *Critique of Pure Reason*, A369.
82. Braver, 37. Interestingly, this problem is shared as well by empirical idealists such as Descartes and Locke, who also adhere to the realist presupposition that "outer appearances" are things in themselves. As Allison explains, the Cartesian-Lockean theory of ideas posits that "the mind can have immediate access only to its own ideas or representations." If outer appearances constitute things in themselves, then empirical idealists such as Descartes and Locke are "forced to concede that the existence of such objects is problematic, since the mind has no immediate access to them."; Allison, 21.

83. Gilles Deleuze. *Kant's Critical Philosophy: The Doctrine of the Faculties*, trans. Hugh Tomlinson and Barbara Habberjam (Minneapolis: University of Minnesota Press, 1985), 14.
84. Scott, "On Viewing Rhetoric as Epistemic," 17.
85. Although objects still exist (are still real) in Kant's revamped metaphysics, there is a significant problem in our presuming that truth or experience originate in external objects rather than in the structures of human experience and consciousness. For example, if what we perceive as space or time actually belong to objects intrinsically rather than to our cognition of objects, then it is unclear, Kant will later argue, how we could ever have arrived at any reasonable understanding of these ideas, because both space and time seem to require a priori intuitions about internal/external and simultaneity/succession in order for any subsequent understanding of space and time to take place.
86. Robert L. Scott, "On Viewing Rhetoric as Epistemic: Ten Years Later," *Central States Speech Journal* 27 (1976): 262.
87. Ibid.
88. Kant, *Critique of Pure Reason*, Bxviii.
89. Bruce McComiskey, "Neo-Sophistic Rhetorical Theory: Sophistic Precedents for Contemporary Epistemic Rhetoric," *Rhetoric Society Quarterly* 24, no. 3/4 (1994): 16.
90. Ibid., 22.
91. Braver, 49.
92. Ibid., 56.
93. Ibid.
94. Martin Heidegger, *Kant and the Problem of Metaphysics*, trans. Richard Taft (Bloomington: Indiana University Press, 1997), 23.
95. There is considerable debate about whether these two terms are indeed synonymous for Kant. At times, such as in the first Critique, Kant seems to differentiate the noumenon from the thing-in-itself. In the *Prolegomena*, however, he repeatedly equates noumena with things in themselves (see in particular 315). For the purposes of this chapter, I am following Langton and others who see Kant's use of the terms as more or less synonymous.
96. Kant, *Critique of Pure Reason*, A252.
97. Ibid., A19/B33.
98. Ibid., A371–2; A379; A383.
99. Ibid., A42/B59.
100. Braver, 60–61.
101. Ibid., 60.
102. Kant, *Critique of Pure Reason*, A254/B310.
103. Ibid., A254/B 310; A255/B311.
104. Kant, *Prolegomena to Any Future Metaphysics*, 315.
105. Rae Langton, *Kantian Humility: Our Ignorance of Things in Themselves* (Oxford: Oxford University Press, 1998), 10.
106. Ibid.; see also, Kant, *Critique of Pure Reason*, A796/B824.
107. Langton, 10.
108. Langton, 12.
109. Ibid., 13.
110. Ibid., 19.
111. Heidegger, 23.

112. Ibid.
113. Allison, 52.
114. Sextus, *Against the Schoolmasters*, in *The Older Sophists*, ed. Rosamond Kent Sprague (Indianapolis: Hackett, 2001), 19.
115. Barry Brummett, Thomas B. Farrell, Joseph Cappella, John R. Greene, and Susan B. Shimanoff, "The Forum," *Quarterly Journal of Speech* 68, no. 4 (1982): 426.
116. Ibid., 428.
117. Ibid., 426.
118. Ibid., 429.
119. For more on Brummett's realism, as well as Burke's realist notion of recalcitrance, see Lawrence J. Prelli, Floyd D. Anderson, and Matthew T. Althouse, "Kenneth Burke on Recalcitrance," *Rhetoric Society Quarterly* 41, no. 2 (2011): 97–124.
120. In Brummett's terms, naïve realism "always creates the scientific temptation to claim that one either *has* by way of an ingenious method found the Truth about Absolute Reality, or that one has come *closer* to the Grail than has anyone else."; Brummett, Farrell, Cappella, Greene, and Shimanoff, 430.
121. Kenneth Burke, *Attitudes Toward History* (Berkeley: University of California Press, 1984), 60n, quoted in Prelli et al., "Kenneth Burke on Recalcitrance," 97.
122. Brummett, Farrell, Cappella, Greene, and Shimanoff, 425.
123. Richard A. Cherwitz and James W. Hikins, "Rhetorical Perspectivism," *Quarterly Journal of Speech* 69, no. 3 (1983): 251.
124. Ibid., 253.
125. Ibid., 264.
126. Ibid.
127. Ibid.
128. Ibid.
129. In one of the last essays on epistemic rhetoric, Jeffrey L. Bineham characterizes Cherwitz and Hikins not as Kantians but as modern-day Cartesians. Their objectivist view of knowledge, he argues, presumes "correspondence with reality (truth), and the subject's rational certainty of that correspondence (belief and justification)" (46). The method Cherwitz and Hikins develop over their several essays parallels Descartes, Bineham claims, insofar as it grounds knowledge in the properties of the subject's mind while at the same time defining reality as external to the subject and therefore dualistically opposed to the subject (46–47). Such a dualist structure results in what Bineham, after Bernstein, calls "Cartesian Anxiety," or the "assumption that only two options are available for those who inquire into matters of knowledge and action: either some ultimate ground for knowledge and action exists, some objective and ahistorical foundation against which claims to know can be measured and the utility of actions ascertained, or we are beset by relativistic skepticism and are unable to speak of knowledge or 'justified' action in any meaningful sense" (44). While Descartes's influence can certainly be felt in the epistemic rhetoric debates, I would argue the anxiety Bineham diagnoses owes more to Kant's extensions of Cartesianism, which solidified the idea of the transcendental subject while at the same endowing that subject with certain epistemological limits or incapacities. In other words, it is not so much Cartesian Anxiety as "epistemic humility" that defines modern epistemology that in turn ensures the persistence of

realism in post-Kantian rhetorical theory.; Jeffrey L. Bineham, "The Cartesian Anxiety in Epistemic Rhetoric: An Assessment of the Literature," *Philosophy and Rhetoric* 23, no. 1 (1990): 43–62.
130. Scott, "On Viewing Rhetoric as Epistemic," 16–17.
131. Brummett, "Some Implications of 'Process' and 'Intersubjectivity': Postmodern Rhetoric," 39.

Bibliography

Abbott, Don Paul. "Kant, Theremin, and the Morality of Rhetoric." *Philosophy and Rhetoric* 40, no. 3 (2007): 274–292.
Allison, Henry E. *Kant's Transcendental Idealism: An Interpretation and Defense.* New Haven: Yale University Press, 2004.
Aristotle. *Nicomachean Ethics.* Translated by David Ross. New York: Oxford University Press, 1998.
Berlin, James. *Rhetoric and Reality: Writing Instruction in American Colleges, 1900–1985.* Carbondale: Southern Illinois University Press, 1987.
———. *Rhetorics, Poetics, and Cultures: Refiguring College English Studies.* Urbana: NCTE, 1996.
Bineham, Jeffrey L. "The Cartesian Anxiety in Epistemic Rhetoric: An Assessment of the Literature." *Philosophy and Rhetoric* 23, no. 1 (1990): 43–62.
Bormann, Ernest G. "Fantasy and Rhetorical Vision: The Rhetorical Criticism of Social Reality." *Quarterly Journal of Speech* 58 (1972): 396–407.
Braver, Lee. *A Thing of This World: A History of Continental Anti-Realism.* Evanston: Northwestern University Press, 2007.
Brummett, Barry. "A Eulogy for Epistemic Rhetoric." *Quarterly Journal of Speech* 76 (1990): 69–72.
———. "Some Implications of 'Process' and 'Intersubjectivity': Postmodern Rhetoric." *Philosophy and Rhetoric* 9 (1976): 21–51.
Brummett, Barry, Thomas B. Farrell, Joseph Cappella, John R. Greene, and Susan B. Shimanoff. "The Forum." *Quarterly Journal of Speech* 68, no. 4 (1982): 425–437.
Burke, Kenneth. "The Definition of Man." In *Language as Symbolic Action: Essays on Life, Literature, and Method*, 3–24. Berkeley: University of California Press, 1966.
Cherwitz, Richard A., and James W. Hikins. "Rhetorical Perspectivism." *Quarterly Journal of Speech* 69, no. 3 (1983): 249–266.
Deleuze, Gilles. *Kant's Critical Philosophy: The Doctrine of the Faculties.* Translated by Hugh Tomlinson and Barbara Habberjam. Minneapolis: University of Minnesota Press, 1985.
Dostal, Robert J. "Kant and Rhetoric." *Philosophy and Rhetoric* 13 (1980): 223–244.
Engel, S. Morris. "Kant's Copernican Analogy: A Re-Examination." *Kant Studies* 54 (1963):243–251.
Fish, Stanley. "Rhetoric." In *Doing What Comes Naturally: Change, Rhetoric, and the Practice of Theory in Literary and Legal Studies*, by Fish, 471–502. Durham: Duke University Press, 1989.
Gaonkar, Dilip Parameshwar. "Rhetoric and Its Double: Reflections of the Rhetorical Turn in the Human Sciences." In *The Rhetorical Turn: Invention and Persuasion*

in the Conduct of Inquiry. Edited by Herbert W. Simons, 341–366. Chicago: University of Chicago Press, 1990.

Garsten, Bryan. *Saving Persuasion: A Defense of Rhetoric and Judgment.* Cambridge: Harvard University Press, 2006.

Gehrke, Pat J. "Turning Kant Against the Priority of Autonomy: Communication Ethics and the Duty of Community." *Philosophy and Rhetoric* 35, no. 1 (2002): 1–21.

Gross, Alan G. *Starring the Text: The Place of Rhetoric in Science Studies.* Carbondale: Southern Illinois University Press, 2006.

Hanson, Norwood Russell. "Copernicus' Role in Kant's Revolution." *Journal of the History of Ideas* 20 (1956): 274–281.

Heidegger, Martin. *Kant and the Problem of Metaphysics.* Translated by Richard Taft. Bloomington: Indiana University Press, 1997.

Ijsseling, Samuel. *Rhetoric and Philosophy in Conflict: An Historical Survey.* Translated by Paul Dunphy. The Hague: Martinus Nijhoff, 1976.

Jasinski, James. *Sourcebook on Rhetoric: Key Concepts in Contemporary Rhetorical Studies.* Thousand Oaks: Sage, 2001.

Kant, Immanuel. *Critique of Pure Reason* (Unified Edition). Translated by Werner S. Pluhar. Indianapolis: Hackett, 1996.

———. *Critique of Judgment.* Translated by Werner S. Pluhar. Indianapolis: Hackett, 1987.

———. *Groundwork for the Metaphysics of Morals.* Translated by Allen W. Wood. New Haven: Yale University Press, 2002.

———. *Prolegomena to Any Future Metaphysics.* Translated by James W. Ellington. Indianapolis: Hackett, 1977.

———. "An Answer to the Question: What is Enlightenment?" In *Immanuel Kant: Practical Philosophy.* Translated by Mary J. Gregor. Cambridge: Cambridge University Press, 1996.

Langton, Rae. *Kantian Humility: Our Ignorance of Things in Themselves.* New York: Oxford University Press, 1998.

Lanham, Richard A. *The Motives of Eloquence: Literary Rhetoric in the Renaissance.* Eugene: Wipf and Stock, 1976.

Latour, Bruno. *Pandora's Hope: Essays on the Reality of Science Studies.* Cambridge: Harvard University Press, 1999.

———. *We Have Never Been Modern.* Translated by Catherine Porter. Cambridge: Harvard University Press, 1993.

———. "Where are the Missing Masses? The Sociology of a Few Mundane Artifacts." In *Shaping Technology/Building Society: Studies in Sociotechnical Change,* edited by Weibe E. Bijker and John Law, 225–258. Cambridge: Massachusetts Institute of Technology Press, 1992.

Lyne, John. "Idealism as a Rhetorical Stance." In *Rhetoric and Philosophy,* edited by Richard A. Cherwitz, 149–186. New York: Routledge, 1990.

McComiskey, Bruce. "Neo-Sophistic Rhetorical Theory: Sophistic Precedents for Contemporary Epistemic Rhetoric." *Rhetoric Society Quarterly* 24, no. 3/4 (1994): 16–24.

McCormick, Samuel. "The Artistry of Obedience: From Kant to Kingship." *Philosophy and Rhetoric* 38, no. 4 (2005): 302–327.

Nietzsche, Friedrich. "On Truth and Lies in a Nonmoral Sense." In *The Nietzsche Reader*, edited by Keith Ansell Pearson and Duncan Large, 115–123. Malden: Blackwell, 2006.

Prelli, Lawrence J., Floyd D. Anderson, and Matthew T. Althouse. "Kenneth Burke on Recalcitrance." *Rhetoric Society Quarterly* 41, no. 2 (2011): 97–124.

Rickert, Thomas. *Ambient Rhetoric: The Attunements of Rhetorical Being*. Pittsburgh: University of Pittsburgh Press, 2013.

Royer, Daniel J. "New Challenges to Epistemic Rhetoric." *Rhetoric Review* 9, no. 2 (1991): 282–297.

Scott, Robert L. "On Viewing Rhetoric as Epistemic." *Central States Speech Journal* 18 (1967): 9–17.

———. "On Viewing Rhetoric as Epistemic: Ten Years Later." *Central States Speech Journal* 27 (1976): 258–266.

Sextus. *Against the Schoolmasters*. In *The Older Sophists*, edited by Rosamond Kent Sprague, 18–19. Indianapolis: Hackett, 2001.

Simons, Herbert W. Introduction to *The Rhetorical Turn: Invention and Persuasion in the Conduct of Inquiry*, edited by Simons. Chicago: University of Chicago Press, 1990.

Spivak, Gayatri Chakravorty. Introduction to *Of Grammatology*, by Jacques Derrida. Baltimore: Johns Hopkins University Press, 1997.

Stroud, Scott R. "Kant on Education and the Rhetorical Force of the Example." *Rhetoric Society Quarterly* 41, no. 5 (2011): 416–438.

———. *Kant and the Promise of* Rhetoric. University Park: Pennsylvania State University Press, 2014.

5 Care for Things
Ethics and Responsibility in the World of Things

If rhetorical inquiry moves us to consider how responsibility is threaded through rhetorical situations, then rhetoric at its core is an ethical art, one deeply concerned with the power discourse—and rhetors, by extension— hold in shaping understandings of reality. As we saw in the previous chapter, this was the conclusion reached by Robert L. Scott and Barry Brummett in their respective accounts of epistemic rhetoric: If we understand rhetoric as a knowledge-making art, as a key factor in determining how we understand ourselves vis-à-vis social reality, then the question of responsibility (who is responsible for the world being what it is?) needs to factor into our considerations of public discourse. One of the reasons why responsibility emerges as a central concern for Scott and Brummett is because their epistemic theory places so much emphasis on human rhetors as the primary sources and recipients of rhetorical knowledge. Given what we have learned over the course this book about rhetorical realism and its ability to accommodate epistemological and ontological approaches to reality, however, such a fixation on the human subject is, if anything, an outlier in the history of Western rhetoric, a point perhaps not lost on Scott and Brummett who, I argued, can also be read as attempting to accommodate realist theses with their otherwise anti-realist conception of epistemic rhetoric. Yet for all of epistemic rhetoric's limitations, I believe it is worthwhile to take its sense of responsibility's centrality to rhetoric seriously, particularly in the context of rhetorical realism which directs our attentions to the limits of knowledge and the natures of rhetorical being-in-the-world. If rhetoric constitutes more than an art of human persuasion or expression—if, indeed, it is defined by the entanglements of beings and relations, as I have argued—then it is reasonable to ask what the ethical implications are for this conception of rhetoric. Indeed, one often hears questions of this kind when the topics of object-oriented ontology and speculative realism come up. Why should we care so much about nonhumans, one is sometimes asked, particularly when there is so much human suffering and injustice happening in the world all around us? With all of the challenges and tragedies that plague human existence, why should we turn our attentions to things? I hope the preceding chapters offer something of an answer to this question. In a word, however, I would say that my answer to questions of this kind is *ethics*. Specifically, I would say that attending to the vibrancy and otherness of things is not only a speculative endeavor, it is an ethical project of the highest order, one that, as Adorno suggests, is in good keeping with concerns about alterity and responsibility that have characterized so much of the work on ethics in the postwar period. As I hope to demonstrate over the course of this final chapter, care, tenderness, and attention are not finite resources; it is possible—and desirable, I argue—to do two (and more) things at once.

Implicit throughout this book, then, has been the belief that attending to the rhetoricity of things constitutes an ethical as much as a historiographical project. While the bulk of our focus thus far has been on historical formulations of realism in rhetoric, we have seen as well how bringing the perspective of rhetorical realism to bear on rhetoric's history offers more than an enriched understanding of how a particular age went about inventing rhetoric's place alongside things in the world. In addition to these insights, rhetorical realism offered us the opportunity to cultivate attunements to things, to the ways things exert force in rhetorical situations and histories of rhetoric—indeed, constitute the very conditions for rhetoric as such—while also withdrawing from relations with us and other things. As I tried to illustrate in the previous chapters, speculative readings of rhetorical history have the potential to enrich understandings of rhetoric in part because they invite rhetoricians to approach "the history of rhetoric" from a counter-revolutionary perspective rather than from a more familiar perspective rooted in assumptions about the inevitability of historical progress and the increasing purification of subjects and objects over time. When we adopt a counter-revolutionary historiography, we gain valuable insight into the strange existences of things that have intrigued and exasperated rhetoricians from antiquity to the present. "Things themselves have a history," Bruno Latour has said, and this is no less true in rhetoric as it is in Latour's field of science studies. Things have a history in rhetoric that we can explore by bringing different sensibilities to bear on rhetoric's past and on how rhetoricians over time have endeavored to bring rhetoric into accord with their own understandings of reality.

Such engagements with rhetoric's things and the thingness of rhetoric are attunements of a kind: They are moods or states-of-mind that orient us in particular ways to things as beings in the world. Throughout his work, Heidegger argues for a disposition toward beings he calls *Gelassenheit* ("releasement" or "letting-be"). When we let a being be, Heidegger says, we "let the entity which has this Being be encountered."[1] Where we run into trouble, according to Heidegger, is when we try to calculate beings or theorize their significance in excess of our everyday, practical experiences as beings in the world. In the context of Heidegger's ontology, all of us already have a sense of the answer to the most fundamental question at the heart of Western philosophy—"what does it mean *to be*?"—for no other reason than our existence (our "ownmost potentiality for being," in Heidegger's terms) is always already attuned to the structures of Being as such. Being reveals itself to us every day, but never entirely or all at once. This is why the question of Being is both the simplest and most confounding one we can ask. How we understand Being is by "letting-be," by allowing Being to show itself to us, even just as a sliver or echo of Being as such. Letting-be for Heidegger is thus a kind of attunement that disposes us toward Being while at the same time preserving some of its inherent mystery and concealedness. As Heidegger suggests in "On the Essence of Truth," "What conserves letting-be in this relatedness to concealing? Nothing less than the concealing of what is concealed as a whole, of beings as such, i.e., the mystery; not a particular mystery regarding this or that, but rather the one mystery—that, in general, mystery (the concealing of what is concealed) as such holds sway throughout man's Da-sein."[2] The word *mystery*, as Heidegger is no doubt aware, comes from the Greek *muein*, meaning "to close." What we conserve in letting rhetoric's things be, then, is the mystery (*muein*) that makes rhetoric possible, the closed off, secret, and unspeakable alterities of things that entreat us to "let-be," to "let the other be" in his, her, or its being. Through such a disposition we move closer toward what Heidegger calls a *"releasement toward things,"* an attunement to things not in terms of their instrumentality (their means to an end) but in terms of the beingness as such.[3] As Heidegger suggests, "Releasement toward things and openness to the mystery belong together. They grant us the possibility of dwelling in the world in a totally different way. They promise us a new ground and foundation upon which we can stand and endure in the world of technology without being imperiled by it."[4]

If there is one consistent lesson we can draw from the versions of rhetorical realism explored in the previous chapters, it is that things are deeper, more elusive, and more mysterious than we sometimes give them credit for. Whether we are talking about Aristotle's wooden bedsteads, Wilkins's real character, or Kant's thing-in-itself, things occupy an unusual place in rhetorical theory: framing rhetoric's scope and meaning while at the same time exceeding our knowledge and understanding of them. Even as they approach things with different assumptions about what things are and why they matter for rhetoric, each of the thinkers we examined comes to things from a decidedly humble position, one characterized by an overwhelming sense of wonder about the world and a desire to think *with* things as well as *about* things. This attunement is what allows them—and us, perhaps—to *let things be*, not in the sense of passivity, apathy, or inaction, but in the sense "allowing something to come into being as it is."[5] As a disposition predicated upon an attunement to what is coming into being, *Gelassenheit* allows us to hearken to beings without imposing upon them outside forms, metrics, or identities. While his ethical philosophy challenges Heidegger's on the question of Being's precedence, Emmanuel Levinas, as we will see, offers a comparable sense of "letting-be" in his ethics of the face and how the encounter I have with the Other is already conditioned by the Other's alterity and his plea to "let me live": "To see a face is already to hear: You shall not kill,"

Levinas will say.[6] In Levinas's ethics, letting-be constitutes an attunement to the Other as well as a sense of responsibility we bear to the Other as such, the responsibility to let the Other be in his or her (or its) being.

While much of the work associated with the recent ethical turn in rhetoric and philosophy challenges longstanding distinctions between subject and object, it is not always clear whether the ethics of care and responsibility we find in these accounts extends to nonhumans as well. Levinas, for instance, denies ethical standing to nonhuman animals and at one point stops short of granting Palestinians the status of "Other" as understood in his philosophy.[7] Of course, we do not (indeed should not) have to take Levinas at his word, a point Diane Davis makes well in her postscript to *Inessential Solidarity* where she confronts the legacies of humanism in Levinas's thought. But the hesitancy Levinas feels toward extending ethical sensibility to nonhumans is telling, particularly for how it repeats a long tradition in the West of defining ethics exclusively in terms of human action. Most mainstream ethical theory, including many postmodern accounts, does not leave much room for the ethical dimension of material things. As Peter-Paul Verbeek observes, "in mainstream ethical theory 'objects' have no place apart from being mute and neutral instruments that facilitate human action."[8] If what rhetorical realisms suggests about things is true—that humans and things are and always have been entangled with one another in mutually constitutive and co-dependent ways—then we cannot accept an ethics that partitions humans from things in such neat and tidy ways. An ethics obtained from rhetorical realism needs to acknowledge the relations, responsibilities, and interdependencies that entangle humans and things and that subsequently bleed back into the questions at the heart of any ethical system: How should we live and how, by extension, can action be directed toward some notion of "the good life"? As I argue in this final chapter, things have as much of a role, and as much of a say, in what constitutes the good life as human beings. *Eudaimonia,* or the good life, is not the life lived alone in contemplation, as Aristotle sometimes suggests; nor is it the life lived apart from the things of the world. The good life instead is where humans and things come together to make a home—where they are at home with one another.

In this chapter, I want to build on the lessons learned over the course of this book about the epistemological and ontological approaches to rhetorical realism by finally taking up the question with which I began: Why should we care so much about things? While I reject the question's dismissive undertones, I think there is something valuable we can learn by taking this kind of question seriously, particularly when it is framed in the language of "care." As an idea, care suggests both *attention* and *tenderness*. Both of these meanings are significant when considering the question of ethics and ethical responsibility in the world of things. Taking cues from Heidegger, Levinas, and Silvia Benso, this chapter explores what a duel approach to care contributes to our understanding of public debates about ethical responsibility and whether or not *we* (itself a contested category) owe responsibility to *things*—whether *we* should learn to take better *interest* and *care* in the things we build and live with. Such questions may strike some readers as anthropomorphism of the worst kind; however, I hope to demonstrate that a rhetorical ethics rooted in a care for things not only makes sense theoretically (especially given the lessons learned from Jacques Derrida, Levinas, and others) but also opens the way to a renewed sense of responsibility that takes into equal account the agency, alterity, and temporality of things as well as human beings.

To explore what an ethics of care might contribute to our understanding of rhetorical realism, I turn to the case of the 2009 BP oil spill in the Gulf of Mexico. In the wake of the disaster, many on the United States Gulf Coast and around the world wanted to know, "How could this have happened?" Framing the question in these terms led many, including the U.S. Government, to conclude that BP's profit-seeking ethos and its willingness to cut regulatory corners were primarily responsible for the chain of events that led to the explosion on the Deep Water Horizon. While certainly true, the quick acceptance of this conclusion encourages us to ignore some of the larger ethical issues at stake in the event. As I argue in the latter portions of this chapter, reading the event in terms of rhetorical realism and a duel sense of care allows us to see BP's ethical failure as a failure to understand technological devices as things in their own rights and not just as instruments or resources for human workers and corporations. The ethical issue at the heart of the BP oil spill, then, is not unlike the one Aristotle describes in the *Nicomachean Ethics*: that of living the good life. However, as the disaster and its aftermath make clear, we can no longer continue to think of the good life as only what is good *for us*. We must also recognize that "the good life is not formed only on the basis of human intentions and ideas but also on the basis of material artifacts and arrangements."[9]

Ethics and Responsibility

Ethical concerns have long been central to rhetorical theory and practice. In his introduction to *The Ethos of Rhetoric*, Michael J. Hyde reminds us that for the ancient Greeks the word ethics (*ethos*; pl. *ethea*) referred to an abode or "dwelling place" where "people can deliberate about and 'know together' (*con-scientia*) some matter of interest,"[10] thus suggesting significant spatial and rhetorical inflections for ethics in the Greek tradition. For Aristotle, rhetoric and ethics were thought to share a similar subject matter: deliberation—specifically, deliberating on contingent matters of concern. In the *Rhetoric*, Aristotle singles out "ethical studies" as one of the offshoots of rhetoric,[11] a point he makes again in the *Ethics* when he discusses art and deliberation as branches of moral virtue. And in the Platonic tradition, where rhetoric is often associated with deceptive practices and manipulative speech, rhetoric and ethics have had a more contentious—although no less important—relationship insofar as ethical action in this tradition is usually determined by one's adherence to transcendental standards of truth and justice. In Plato's case, this means that any discourse that obscures or distracts us from understanding the truth of things is more than just corrupt or dangerous, it is ethically "wrong" as well. Plato and others' injunctions against the use of mere rhetoric have helped solidify a *normative* understanding of ethics in which static (and possibly divinely given) rules serve to guide and/or legislate moral action. In a normative sense, rhetorical action is guided by the "moral ought," an imperative that determines in advance what constitutes right and wrong, virtue and vice. Where exactly these moral imperatives come from is one of the key questions in normative ethics, and we find different answers in its three main theoretical traditions: virtue ethics, deontology, and consequentialism. However, regardless of whether we locate moral imperatives in the inherent character of the person, in some notion of rights, or in an action's possible outcomes or results, the overall goal for each of these normative traditions remains the same: to identify sources or sets of standards that can prescribe the most proper course of action in a given situation.

While normative ethics still retains a strong presence in philosophies of ethics—most notably in rights-based ethics and in recent versions of utilitarianism such as the one associated with Peter Singer—a growing body of literature in the postwar period argues for a shift in emphasis for ethics away from normative standards toward more ontological, intersubjective, and other-oriented notions of responsibility. In the continental tradition of philosophy, this turn toward other-oriented ethics was driven in part by the recognition that normative ethics not only failed to prevent atrocities such as the Holocaust, but may have been complicit in reinforcing the regimes of thought that allowed the annihilation of European Judaism (and otherness in general) to seem necessary and logical in the first place. As Silvia Benso recounts in her marvelous book *The Face of Things: A Different Side of Ethics*,

> The function and character of these [normative] ethics is necessarily limited, not only with respect to the domain in which they rule, but also in terms of credibility. The reality that "small" ethics tries to bridle by means of norms of behavior escapes their control. The rules they dictate are able neither to wonder over the infinite possibilities of good, nor to constitute a bulwark against the abyssal possibilities of evil reality manifests, as the factual event of Auschwitz suffices to prove beyond the disputability of any theoretical statement, since against its happening any kind of "small" ethics but also of traditional ethics collapses. An ethics that may still be viable must take such a failure into account.[12]

Other-oriented approaches to ethics see in normative ethics a fundamental failure to recognize the alterity and vulnerability of the other. If it is possible to have an ethics after Auschwitz, Benso and others argue, such an ethics cannot be rooted in universal understandings of right and wrong, as these categories have historically tended to privilege those with the power to define what is right and wrong and who, by extension, is worthy of respect and care. Thus, in the wake of such critiques of normative ethics following the second world war, many ethical theorists—particularly those in the continental tradition—began to argue for an/other ethics rooted not in normativity, but in the more primordial encounter I have with the other.

Because of its concern for the inherent vulnerability of the other, the idea of responsibility looms large in other-oriented ethics. This has also been the case in rhetoric and rhetorical theories of ethics where responsibility—albeit in forms different than what we find in Levinasian ethics—has come to matter a great deal due to the fact that rhetoric, in its most traditional formulations, involves the use of persuasion to change people's minds and their understandings of reality. As we saw in the previous chapter, rhetors have a responsibility to use the tools and techniques of rhetoric so that persuasion happens not through deception or manipulation but through assent won through careful deliberation about the issues at hand. At the same time, audiences have a responsibility as well to open themselves to the possibility of being persuaded: Persuasion is something we do, not something that is done to us, as Bryan Garsten has suggested.[13] In other words, in the traditional senses of both rhetoric and ethics, responsibility entails a kind of contract speakers and audiences agree to enter into with one another, thus suggesting that what makes rhetorical action ethical ultimately depends upon participants' willingness to *be responsible* to each other and to the rhetorical situation broadly understood. The obligation to respond—be responsible in the traditional sense—follows, then, from our understanding that actions have consequences, both for the present and for the future. We choose to be responsible, and to hold others responsible, because actions ripple out into the world and over time in ways we cannot always anticipate.

The Levinasian conception of responsibility differs somewhat from these causal understandings insofar as it emphasizes radical openness to the Other, and one's response-*ability* to the Other, rather than responsibility as something we consciously control or an action we choose willfully to do.[14] As we saw briefly in Chapter 1, Levinasian ethics places priority on exteriority and the encounter I have with the Other. For Levinas, the face to face encounter constitutes a relation that precedes and exceeds comprehension, identification, and symbolic action. It is the "face of the Other" (*le visage d'Autrui*) that comes first, Levinas argues, that comes before speaking (and thus the constitution of me as an "I" speaking to "you") to ground all forms of relation. And it is to the face of the Other, to the saying of the face, that I am responsible, to which I am called to respond in one way or another. Levinas's theory of the face is without question one of the most memorable pieces of his ethical philosophy, most likely because it seems to readers so specific and concrete. However, the language Levinas uses here can be misleading, especially if we take "face" to mean the literal face that is physically present when I converse with you. This is not what Levinas means by "face" (although the face may have to be a *human* face for Levinas, as we will see). For Levinas, the face can be "the whole body—a hand or curve of the shoulder,"[15] or occasionally the "saying" of a text.[16] In any case, the face is what *expresses*; prior to content or figuration (the said), it is the face of the Other that expresses, in its naked existence, the facticity of its existence which "resists possession, resists my powers. In its epiphany, in expression, the sensible, still graspable, turns into total resistance to the gasp."[17] The face is what summons the call that brings the I out of itself—indeed, calls me into question as an "I" by interrupting the singularity of my identity and bringing me out of selfishness—and toward "the responsibility and goodness of being-for others."[18]

To encounter a face, then, is already to be addressed, to be drawn into a relation where the obligation to respond precedes comprehension and symbolic action.[19] My being is not only a being-with others, but a being-*for*-the-other, with the Other understood not as a specific person but a "beyond being" (a Good Beyond Being, as Levinas suggests at the close of *Totality and Infinity*) to which I agree to be responsible, to play both host and hostage to its summons to respond. As Diane Davis explains, the saying of the face "comes through as a rhetorical imperative, an obligation to respond that holds the 'I' and the other in an extreme proximity, in a nearness so excruciatingly close that s/he touches me, affects me, overwhelms my powers of comprehension without absorbing me."[20] This imperative is rhetorical not in the sense of rhetoric as persuasion or identification—that is, it does not come through in formal acts of speaking or communicating—but in the sense that the saying of face, insofar as it precedes utterance, constitutes a kind of preoriginary persuade-ability or affect-ability that makes traditional enactments of rhetoric possible in the first place. To refuse the invitation of the face means, then, foreclosing upon persuade-ability as such, a move that, for Levinas, makes it possible for us to "murder" off the Other in order to avoid risking ourselves in the face to face encounter. To encounter a face, as Davis says, "is straightaway to be *faced* with the ethical dilemma: to speak or to kill?"[21] Death, for Levinas, is not a passage from being to nothingness or an annihilation, but, as Derrida explains, "the moment when the other no longer responds."[22] Nonresponse leads to the "death of the face of the other human being,"[23] thus violating Levinas's first commandment (revised from its sixth place in the Decalogue): "You shall not commit murder."

Levinas's ethics of alterity has been widely influential in rhetorical theory, informing a range of studies from memory and trauma studies[24] to the rhetorics of the euthanasia debates.[25] However, for all of the attention Levinas pays to otherness, there are some problems in how he conceives of responsibility and the obligation "I" have to "you" in the instance of address. In particular, the extent of Levinas's humanism, and his bias in favor of human beings, continues to raise questions about the coherence and efficacy of his ethical system. In her "P.S. on Humanism" in *Inessential Solidarity*, Davis concludes her study of Levinas and rhetoric by acknowledging the problem of Levinas's anthropocentrism and its tendency to define ideas such as the face exclusively in human terms. As Davis rightly notes, throughout his work, Levinas challenges the sanctity of the humanist subject—the one in control and mastery of his life and his agency. As Levinas does this, however, he also insists on some peculiar restrictions on who or what can actually participate in the face to face relation. In his essay "The Name of a Dog, or Natural Rights," for example, Levinas recounts his experience as a prisoner in a Jewish POW camp in Nazi Germany from 1940–1945. At one point, he describes how children and women would pass by the camp and gaze at the prisoners in such a way that their eyes "stripped us of our human skin. We were subhuman, a gang of apes [...] no longer part of the world."[26] About halfway through their long captivity, Levinas continues, a wandering dog the prisoners later would name "Bobby" arrived in the camp and began to greet the prisoners in the morning and welcome them home after each long day of work. "He would appear at morning assembly and was waiting for us as we returned," Levinas recalls, "jumping up and down and barking in delight. For him, there was no doubt that we were men."[27] The story is as touching as it is heartbreaking. However, for Davis the story also reveals something unfortunate about Levinas's view of things: "Despite his articulations of gratitude and affection, Levinas does not consider this canine refugee to be capable of an *ethical* relation in his particular sense of that term."[28] Rather than see Bobby as a fellow existent, Levinas appropriates Bobby's being in order to confirm some higher understanding of humanity, of what it means to be human (and subsequently *de*-humanized). In other words, Bobby matters for Levinas to the extent that his presence helps clarify or affirm something of his own identity. "It can witness to us only for us, being too other to be our brother or neighbor, not enough other to be wholly other, the nakedness of whose face dictates to us 'Thou shalt not kill.'"[29] This sentiment, of course, runs contrary to everything Levinas suggests about the saying of the face and the infinite obligation to respond that the face of the Other summons forth.

While questions about the exclusivity of the face are more pronounced today due to Derrida's commentaries on Levinas and the rise of animal studies, such questions also surfaced periodically during Levinas's lifetime. As Davis and Derrida each recount, in a 1986 interview Levinas was asked whether his ethical commandment, "Thou shalt not kill," could also be expressed in the face of an animal. Levinas's answer is telling: "The human face is completely different and only afterwards do we discover the face of an animal. I don't know if a snake has a face. I can't answer that question. A more specific analysis is needed."[30] Levinas certainly appears to want to say that the animal *cannot have a face*; however, Davis and Derrida note the ambiguity in his answer, which offers more of an equivocation than a direct response: "I *don't know* if a snake has a face." In spite of his uncertainty, however (his inability to offer a response, we could say), Levinas remains confident that, regardless of whether it has a face (or acquires a face after the fact), a snake does not have the ability to issue the same summons to respond as a human being. For their parts, neither Derrida nor Davis is convinced by Levinas's statements on the question of the animal or by his assumption that responsibility occurs only in the human face to face relation. For Derrida, Levinas's unwillingness to grant the animal a face may end up "calling into question the whole legitimacy of the discourse of ethics of the 'face' of the other."[31] Building on Derrida, Davis similarly wonders why nonhuman animals could not figure into Levinas's ethics of alterity and the face:

> No anthropomorphizing is required, I don't think, to suspect that this homeless creature's determination to show up for the prisoners—both to great them warmly in the morning and to welcome them back enthusiastically in the evening—may indicate that he is "capable of living for the Other and of *being* on the basis of the Other who is exterior to him" (*TI* 149) [...] Why is it necessary that the conscious assumption of this responsibility prior to freedom, of this obligation to "the life of the other," be absolutely unique to the so-called human animal?[32]

Levinas himself may not have been able to imagine obligation extending to nonhumans, but that does not mean that we cannot make this move for him. If the obligation to respond comes before identity, before "I" or "you" come into being as such, as Levinas repeatedly claims, then there is no reason why animals cannot also summon the imperative to respond. Animals can/do have a face, Derrida and Davis reason, and thus belong in our discussions of ethical responsibility despite Levinas's insistence that "the absolutely foreign can only be man."[33]

The Face of Things

Problems with Levinas's humanism notwithstanding, it is not terribly controversial today to claim that nonhuman animals have a place in ethics or that animals deserve our care and responsibility. As Bentham's utilitarian declaration on the rights of animals framed the issue over two centuries ago, "the question is not, Can they [animals] *reason*? nor, Can they *talk*? but, Can they *suffer*?"[34] For Bentham, the issue is not whether animals possess the same rational faculties as human beings, but whether animals, like human beings, have the ability to be *vulnerable* to and thus to *suffer* at the hands of the other. Of course, numerous questions remain regarding the ethical implications of human-animal relationships (Is it ethical to kill another animal simply because we like the taste of its flesh? Furthermore, is it morally permissible to experiment on animals if doing so can help produce cures for human diseases?). But among animal researchers and theorists, the question of whether to grant animals ethical standing has become, if not a mostly settled issue, then at least a great deal less contentious than it was for Bentham in the eighteenth century (or even Derrida a decade or more ago). The more confounding question for us today, then, is not whether animals warrant ethical consideration (I strongly believe that they do) but whether *things* also have a place in the sphere of ethical concern. To what extent can/should we talk about an *ethics of things*? Can a thing have a face? Do things summon an obligation to respond analogous to Levinas's Other or, perhaps even, Derrida's "real little cat"?[35]

To all of these questions, Levinas would say, no. But in a move similar to the one Derrida makes in *The Animal That Therefore I Am* and Davis makes in her postscript to *Inessential Solidarity*, Benso argues that it is possible to extend Levinasian ethics to things in such a way that we can claim that things do indeed have a face. "What if the human being were not the only Other?" Benso asks. "What if things, too, were Other? Or, perhaps, the other of the Other?"[36]

Benso realizes how difficult it is to make this claim, especially given Levinas's various statements about things and his humanist inclinations. She notes at the outset that Levinas himself was less than interested in developing an ethics of things—indeed, for him, the idea of such an ethics was barely even thinkable. "Things have no face," Levinas states unequivocally in *Totality and Infinity*.[37] Against Heidegger, Levinas argues that we do not encounter things of the world primarily as tools but instead as objects of enjoyment, as means to specific ends:

> Moreover furnishings, the home, food, clothing are not *Zeuge* [tools] in the proper tense of the term: clothing serves to protect the body or to adorn it, the home to shelter it, food to restore it, but we enjoy them or suffer from them, they are ends.[38]

As he elaborates later in *Difficult Freedom*, "things are those which never present themselves personally, and, in the end, they have no identity [...] Things offer themselves to be grasped, they do not offer a face. They are beings without a face."[39] The reason for the thing's facelessness, Benso explains, has to do with how Levinas understands things as distinct from human beings. Unlike the (human) face, things for Levinas "have a form, are seen *in* the light—silhouettes or profiles."[40] The presence of a distinct form giving meaning to things "deprives things of signifying with the same immediacy of the face."[41] What gives the face its drawing and disruptive power—its ability to summon the call to respond—lies in how the face puts into play, however provisionally and incompletely, an other-ness beyond Being. (This is why the face can never be a physical or even figural face for Levinas, as this would effectively localize the expressivity of the face in a particular form rather than in the dissolution of form.) However, because things already exist as completed forms expressing a content, it is impossible for them to have a face. For Levinas, my encounters with things, much like my relations with nonhuman animals, are secondary to the face to face encounter I have with you.

Benso's solution to this impasse is to supplement Levinas's ethics of the face with Heidegger's writings on things and the Fourfold. At first glance, this is a surprising pairing given Levinas's critique of Heidegger for his privileging of ontology over metaphysics. However, Benso argues convincingly that the two philosophers are more alike than we often give them credit. Indeed, she suggests that their individual differences may turn out to be exactly what the other needs to help realize a full-blown ethics of things: "What neither can achieve separately [...] might perhaps be obtained through an exposure of one to the other."[42] There is an ethics in Levinas, but not things, "since things are for the same, or for the Other, but not for themselves."[43] Conversely, there are things in Heidegger, even an alterity of things, but no ethics, at least according to the most common readings of Heidegger. Thus, "[a]t the intersection between ethics and things, Levinas and Heidegger meet," Benso argues. "The former offers the notion of a non-traditional ethics, the latter of nontraditional things."[44]

The key to this unusual union lies in Heidegger's late essays on the thing (*das Ding*) and the Fourfold (*das Geviert*), which Benso sees as potential bridges back to Levinas's account of ethics as the place of encounter of otherness. In "The Thing," Heidegger offers an important distinction between "thing" and "object." Etymologically, the word "object" signifies "that which stands before, over against, opposite us."[45] The word "thing," by contrast, comes from the Old High German word *Ding* which denotes a kind of "gathering."[46] It is this latter meaning that Heidegger is most eager to recover. A thing is a thing, rather than an object, because it *gathers* the Fourfold in such a way that, through gathering, "the thing things."[47] The unusual language Heidegger employs here reflects a view of things in which things act in accordance with their own being, as the beings they are, and not necessarily in the service of someone else's desires or intentions. *Thinging*, as he names this process, designates the process by which "the thing becomes an event, that is, a being whose nature is dynamic, vibrant, alive."[48] Heidegger offers several examples of the thinging of things in these late essays, including a bridge, a jug, a pair of peasant shoes, and a Greek temple. But for each of these things, what happens (and this needs to be understood as an active process) is a gathering, a bringing together and into presence of various forces, histories, and possibilities. And how a thing gathers is always distinct to that thing; it is what makes it *this thing* and not something else.

> The jug is a thing neither in the sense of the Roman *res*, nor in the sense of the medieval *ens*, let alone in the modern sense of object. The jug is a thing insofar as it things. The presence of something present such as the jug comes into its own, appropriatively manifests and determines itself, only from the thinging of the thing.[49]

But what exactly does a thing gather? Heidegger's answer is as perplexing as it is alluring: the thing gathers *das Geviert*, the Fourfold, the "simple oneness of the four:" earth and sky, divinities and mortals.[50] What exactly these four terms mean, or why there are four and not three or five for Heidegger, remains a source of contentious debate among Heidegger scholars. But for our purposes, the precise meaning of the terms (if they have precise meanings at all) matters less than the fact that, for Heidegger, a thing is not simply an inert lump of matter but an active process gathering in a singular way a multiplicity of forces and beings. In Heidegger's language, the thing "rings" the Fourfold—the thing is the "ringing of the Fourfold"—in such a way that "the four nestle into their unifying presence, in which each retains its own nature. So nestling, they join together, worlding, the world."[51] In setting up a world, the ringing of the Fourfold happens differently with each thing. The ringing of earth and sky, divinities and mortals occasioned by a jug, for instance, is different from the ringing set forth by a bridge. "To be sure, the bridge is a thing of its *own* kind; for its gathers the fourfold in *such* a way that it allows a *site* for it."[52] While we may dwell within the thing's particular way of gathering the Fourfold—with "dwelling" understood as a "sparing and preserving" that "safeguards each thing in its nature"[53]—this dwelling does not necessarily enable us to represent the appearance of the thing or the world opened up through the thing. When we try to represent the thing as a concept—as a knowable object standing against us—we run the risk of making that thing vanish, turning it into an object that we can use and control. The thing itself, as Heidegger says, "must be allowed to remain in its self-containment. It must be accepted in its own constancy."[54] For Heidegger, the thinging of the thing is what differentiates one thing from another (the jug from the bridge) as well as what withdraws from being and as such resists interpretation and objectification. "The unpretentious thing evades thought most stubbornly"[55] even as it grounds the earth and opens up a world.[56]

Heidegger's notion of the thing as a gathering has perhaps had the most lasting influence of the ideas explored in his late essays. Latour notably finds significant connections between Heidegger's reading of *das Ding* and his own version of actor-network theory which emphasizes the processes by which researchers go about tracing the relations between actants gathered together in an assemblage.[57] Less remarked upon, however, is how Heidegger's sense of the gathering power of things is actually achieved as a result of a fundamental character of *alterity*. This form of alterity, Benso suggests, is "comparable to, although not necessarily identical with, the otherness which Levinas retraces in persons, but is unwilling to recognize in things."[58] For Heidegger, the alterity of things lies in the "perennial difference and differing from themselves and from one another [...] which render their nature so evanescent, so frail, and so difficult to reach to any philosophical, even phenomenological, description."[59] Because things host the Fourfold in their own unique ways, and because their withdrawal exceeds

Care for Things 199

comprehension, we cannot simply approach things in a singular way. This is why Heidegger insists that in our dealings with the thing we relinquish the pretense of mastery (of turning the thing into an object) in order to hearken to what the thing's ringing of the Fourfold opens up. More than simply a passive response to the thinging of the thing, the hearkening Heidegger describes is a form of *Gelassenheit*, a letting-be or releasement of oneself to things, "to let things be in the alterity of their mirror-play which, expropriating the mortals, appropriates them to things."[60] To this end, "only one element is needful," Heidegger says: "to keep at a distance all the preconceptions and assaults of the above modes of thought, to leave the thing to rest in its own self, for instance, in its thing-being. What seems easier than to let a being be just the being that it is?"[61]

For Benso, the priority Heidegger places on *Gelassenheit*, on the letting-be of the thing to be the thing it is, suggests "the possibility that things too may be the source of an ethical encounter"[62] not unlike what we find in Levinas. "Silent, voiceless witnesses to our endeavors, things look at us and remind us, through the sheer expression of their pure presence, of another other, of another alterity—other than human, other than presence, other than being."[63] According to Heidegger, things offer mortals their most profound connection to the world in its worlding, that is, to the ways the world reveals and conceals itself from us. And in this process, we can add, we find a call to respond that sets into motion an ethical relation grounded in alterity and the obligation to "let the other" be/live. In reminding us of their alterity, things issue a call to respond similar to the one Levinas locates in the (human) face to face encounter. "We are called by things as things," Heidegger says.[64]

> When and in what way do things appear as things? They do not appear *be means of* human making. But neither do they appear without the vigilance of mortals. The first step toward such vigilance is the step back from the thinking that merely represents—that is, explains—to the thinking that responds and recalls.[65]

If we are called by things as things, then responsibility once again becomes key to our ethical encounters with things and beings other than ourselves. Things may appear through "the vigilance of mortals," as Heidegger suggests, but this does not mean that things are merely the projections or instruments of human beings. When the thing becomes an instrument for human manipulation, it does so at the expense of its thingness, of its ability to gather the Fourfold in its own unique ways. In these later essays, Heidegger's primary goal is to acknowledge and then safeguard the many ways beings disclose themselves—to cultivate an *ethics of care* that lets beings be in their being. The term care (*Sorge*) is not new to Heidegger's thinking, as we will see, but in these essays care acquires renewed emphasis and urgency. In Benso's terms, for Heidegger, "caring for the Fourfold can be accomplished only if mortals care for things, because things are the receptacle of the Fourfold. And things can be the receptacle only if they can be let be in their thinging."[66] Care and *Gelassenheit* come together in Heidegger's account of *das Ding* to suggest a variation on the face to face encounter we saw in Levinas: "Things thus impose an imperative which comes close to an ethical demand. They request an act of love—ethics—which lets things be as things, and which therefore opens up a space for the hosting of the Fourfold."[67] When we care for things, when we attune ourselves to the face of things that precedes and exceeds comprehension and signification, we open the way toward an ethics of things in which instrumentality—the "for the sake of which"—gives way to the active passivity of letting-be, of letting the other be/live while at the same time responding to the summons issued in the encounter "I" have with the Other ("you"/"it").

Responding to Things

In developing an other-oriented ethics of things grounded in *Gelassenheit* and response-ability—in our attunements to the vibrancy and alterity of things themselves—Benso offers a compelling alternative to ethical accounts of things based largely in normative assumptions about justice, agency, and responsibility. Such normative accounts tend to view things in an instrumentalist way: "They fulfill a function, and if they fail to do this in a morally acceptable way, the whistle should be blown."[68] As we have seen, the kind of responsibility we find in Levinasian ethics differs from those found in normative ethics insofar as it is a literal response-ability, an obligation to respond one way or another to the face of the Other, be that a person, animal, or thing. The face is "a demand not a question," Levinas says. "The face is a hand in search of recompense, an open hand."[69] Much like his account of the face, Levinas's language of hospitality and welcoming can be misleading (particularly in English translations) as it can suggest that the face of the Other demands only *one* kind of response. Again, this is not what Levinas means when he says that the Other issues an obligation to respond. As Dermot Moran explains, what is ethical for Levinas is simply "to provide the *appropriate* response, whatever that may be [...] Ethics for Levinas is the recognition that there must be a response not a specification of the kind of response."[70] While I may choose to ignore the face of the Other, Levinas insists that I am still defined by my response: "I can recognize the gaze of the stranger, the widow, and the orphan only in giving and refusing; I am free to give or refuse, but my recognition passes necessarily through the interposition of things."[71] What is clear for Levinas is that the call from the Other must be answered, that one must give their recognition to the Other in the instant of address. The content of the response matters less than that the fact that I allow myself to become responsible in the face of the Other, to, in Heidegger's terms, let the Other be in his/her/its being. This way of understanding responsibility differs considerably from our everyday ways of talking about responsibility. When we use the word "responsibility" we typically use it in one of two ways: to refer either to *causal* or *moral* responsibility. We say that someone is responsible in the causal sense when we say that he directly caused some event or state of affairs. Of course, being causally responsible does not necessarily make someone morally responsible as well; a state of affairs may come into being in the causal sense as a result of an accident or someone being under pressure. Thus, "only when somebody acts purposively and freely can he or she be held morally responsible for his or actions."[72]

Even if they are problematic from a Levinasian perspective, these ways of talking about responsibility continue to guide public understandings of responsibility. This is so, perhaps, because this way of thinking about responsibility allows us to apportion blame to individual actors with relative ease. Whereas Levinansian ethics places priority on the pre-symbolic dramas waged in the face to face encounter, causal and moral notions of responsibility claim to offer more stable ground upon which to draw conclusions not just about the nature of the good life but about what constitutes—or what constituted in the past—ethical action and responsibility. It is no wonder, then, that in the aftermath of environmental disasters such as the BP oil spill, we see a distinct public turn, not to the stances of *Gelassenheit* and responsibility, but to the discourses of blame and causality. For better or worse, these discourses offer readymade heuristics for making sense of complicated events like those that took place on the Deepwater Horizon in days leading up to the blowout of the Macondo well in April, 2010. But like other terministic screens, these discourses conceal as much as they reveal, and one of the things they conceal is what the other sense of responsibility we have been exploring might have to say about the ethical contours of this event, which if anything needs to be read not only as failure of moral responsibility on the part of BP but as a fundamental breakdown in its (and our) capacity to care for things.

On the evening of April 20, 2010, a burst of gas from deep within the Macondo well reached the top of a three-mile-long tube of cement and steel connecting the floor of the Gulf of Mexico to the Deepwater Horizon. In his meticulously researched account of BP and the business decisions that contributed to the destruction of the Deepwater Horizon, journalist Abrahm Lustgarten compares what happened next to a canon bursting: the gas and oil that originated 13,000 feet from under the sea floor blew bolts and valves apart on the rig's drill deck and sent drilling mud spewing into the room. A cloud of natural gas began to fill the rig. Workers on the drill floor quickly scrambled in response to the blowout. The drilling supervisor on duty on the drill floor immediately recognized the threat and activated the emergency valves on the rig's blowout preventer, "a three-hundred-ton piece of machinery lying on the gulf's floor meant to seal off the well in the case of a violent kick. But it was too late."[73] Unfortunately, gas was already building up inside the rig. Under normal circumstances, sensors on the rig would have detected the combustible gas and triggered a series of valves that would have kept it from burning up in the engines. All of these devices failed on the night of April 20, as did the blowout preventer on the sea floor. The first explosion came around 9:50 p.m., destroying the drilling floor and killing all of the men there. Another series of explosions quickly followed, and within minutes the Deepwater Horizon, a 33,000-ton structure towering over the Gulf of Mexico, erupted into flame. In all, eleven people died and seventeen people were seriously injured in the explosions and their aftermath. The rig continued to burn for eighteen hours as the surviving crew members were rescued by a nearby freighter. On April 22, the Deepwater Horizon listed and sank to the bottom of the Gulf of Mexico, in the process breaking the pipe connecting it to the Macondo wellhead on the sea floor. Mechanisms designed to sever the rig from the pipe and prevent a spill also failed, and so for the next eighty-six days, oil flowed continuously from the well, resulting in the greatest environmental disaster in United States history.

Figure 5.1 Coast Guard Responds to the Fire on the Deepwater Horizon, National Oceanic and Atmospheric Administration, public domain.

As television viewers around the world watched in horror as oil poured from the Macondo well at a rate of thirty-five thousand barrels per day, public attention quickly turned to the issue of responsibility: What went wrong with the gas sensors and the blowout preventer? Did the rig's workers and contractors make mistakes or cut corners in their attempts to seal the well? Or was BP's new leadership and corporate ethos to blame? In the immediate aftermath of the destruction of the Deepwater Horizon, most of the U.S. government and public's attention focused on BP, a corporation that even before the Gulf spill had acquired a reputation for cutting costs while at the same time expanding production whenever possible, even at the expense of the environment and worker safety. In 2005, an explosion at a BP refinery in Texas City, Texas killed fifteen workers and injured one hundred and seventy. As Lustgarten reports, BP executives in London had repeatedly denied requests from the refinery to replace outdated equipment at the plant, including a critical safety mechanism called a blowdown drum that could have been replaced for $150,000. In that same year, BP's flagship state-of-the-art offshore oil rig, Thunder Horse, sank in the Gulf of Mexico during Hurricane Dennis. Subsequent reports from BP and the U.S. government would show that the hurricane did not actually sink the Thunder Horse. Instead, the rig was the victim of several critical assembly errors in its pontoons that allowed water to rush in during the storm rather than being pumped out.[74] And in 2006, improperly inspected pipes at a BP oil field in northern Alaska ruptured, spilling 212,000 gallons of oil onto Alaska's North Slope. Subsequent investigations showed that, in an effort to cut costs, BP had reduced the number of corrosion inspections of the pipeline as well as a critical maintenance procedure called "pigging" that allows technicians to measure the pipes' metal thickness.

All of these incidents, including the 2010 blowout of the Macondo well, paint the picture of a company willing to take tremendous risks, including gambling with people's lives, in order to turn a profit. This, in fact, was the conclusion reached by the U.S. government in its investigation of the 2010 Gulf oil spill. President Obama's National Commission on the BP Deepwater Horizon Oil Spill and Offshore Drilling directly references "systemic failures" in corporate management as the primary causal factor in the events leading up to the explosion. As the report concludes:

> The blowout was not the product of a series of aberrational decisions made by rogue industry or government officials that could not have been anticipated or expected to occur again. Rather, the root causes are systemic and, absent significant reform in both industry and government policies, might well recur [...] Most of the mistakes and oversights at Macondo can be traced back to a single overarching failure—a failure of management.[75]

The report continues: "BP did not have adequate controls in place to ensure that key decisions in the months leading up to the blowout were safe or sound from an engineering perspective."[76] While the Commission report also names government regulations (or lack thereof) as another of the root causes of the disaster, most of the report focuses on BP and its failure to properly manage the risks it took in its various ventures and especially in the Gulf. For all intents and purposes, in the eyes of the U.S. government and the public BP was mostly (if not solely) responsible for the loss of life on the rig and the subsequent environmental disaster that continues to this day. Interestingly, under U.S. law BP assumed the status of "responsible party" just hours after the spill, thus entitling the government and affected citizens to leverage the company's substantial assets to fund the immediate disaster response and eventual reimbursements.[77] BP's responsibility was all but confirmed four years later when a U.S. district court judge in New Orleans ruled that BP was "most to blame" for the disaster. The judge went as far as to assign blame proportionately: BP was 67% at fault, compared to Transocean (the owner of the Deepwater Horizon) which was responsible for 30% of the disaster and Halliburton (the cement contractor) for 3%.[78]

It is undeniable that BP bears the brunt of the blame for what occurred on the Deepwater Horizon. At the same time, however, the degree of confidence the government and public showed in apportioning responsibility in this way should give us pause. For starters, it does not take a complex ecological theory to remind us that responsibility is rarely attributable to any single actor (or even mostly to one single actor). After all, BP was only drilling the Macondo well because the worldwide demand for fossil fuels continues to reward such risky "explorations." Perhaps you or I, as consumers of fossil fuels, are not as *directly* responsible as BP's corporate leaders, but our participation in the oil economy cannot be discounted when considering "responsibility" in this case. But why stop there? We could expand *ad infinitum* the network of responsible parties to include all scales and manners of actors, from the rig's blowout preventer to the Middle East where wars and conflicts have helped bolster the market for offshore oil drilling in the United States. But herein lies the problem: Responsibility in the moral and causal sense we are using it here ultimately requires an ethical accounting. In an effort to understand what took place in the Gulf in 2010, citizens, the U.S. government, and the media immediately took to the language of responsibility, demanding to know, "Who is responsible for this mess?" From an ethical standpoint, questions like this call for a response but not responsibility per se. "Who is responsible?" is a question that begs an answer, and a definitive one at that. In Judith Butler's terms, it a question that requires one to "give an account" where the account takes the form of a narrative that "must then establish that the self [or Other] was or was not the cause of that suffering, and so supply a persuasive medium through which to understand the causal agency of the self [or Other]."[79] Butler characterizes such demands as acts of "ethical violence." I would add that questions of this kind also run the risk of allowing us to believe that justice has been served simply because the "responsible parties" have been called to account.

But what if we asked the question another way? Not, "Who was responsible for the Gulf spill?" but, "What did responsibility mean in this case?" Rather than assume the existence of moral or causal agency up front, what if we instead begin where Levinas, Heidegger, and Benso ask us to begin: not in the said of the answer demanded of me but in the saying of the face that precedes and exceeds comprehension? Posing the question in this way invites us to consider the ways care and responsibility factored into the disaster and its aftermath. If the nonappropriative stance of *Gelassenheit* directs me to the let the other be—to be in its alterity the thing it is—then our assessment of BP's ethical failure must go further than questions of causal agency to address broader issues of care and responsibility and, specifically, the unwillingness to care for things, i.e., to stand face to face with things and heed the call to respond.

Rather than see things as gatherings of beings and forces that set forth a world, BP saw things in a more simplified way: as instruments or resources in the service of their human masters. Levinas and Heidegger each offer various critiques of this way of thinking, in their own ways situating the obligation to respond, to let the other be, as countermeasures to the logics of identity and instrumentalism. For Levinas, this is the logic of egoism, "which understands my relation to myself as the primary relation"[80] rather than as one rooted in the encounter I have with the Other. For Heidegger, it is the logic of modern science and technology that poses the greatest threat to *Gelassenheit* because it is modern technology that deflects our attention away from thingness—from the ringing of the Fourfold—to more instrumental understandings of nature and technology. In the modern epoch, Heidegger argues, technology is seen instrumentally as "a means to an end."[81] This stands in contrast to the root meaning of technology as *technē*, which "belongs to bringing-forth, to *poiēsis*,"[82] a mode of revealing we explored at length in Chapter 2. Modern technology assumes a "will to mastery" on the part of human beings capable of bringing technology and nature into closer accord with one another. This will to mastery "conditions every attempt to bring man into the right relation with technology,"[83] thus leading us to see things not in terms of their vibrancy or alterity but as instruments in the service of other goals and desires. Many of Heidegger's examples of modern technology highlight how the technological mindset encourages an instrumental relationship to nature in which nature is no longer understood in the Greek sense of *phusis* but as a resource or standing-reserve waiting to be appropriated. While modern technology may be a form of revealing, for Heidegger it is a revealing that is also a "challenging," one that "puts to nature the unreasonable demand that it supply energy that can be extracted and stored as such."[84] In contrast to an old windmill, which Heidegger says is left "entirely to the wind's blowing," in the age of modern technology

> a tract of land is challenged into the putting out of the coal and ore. The earth now reveals itself as a coal mining district, the soil as a mineral deposit. The field that the peasant formerly cultivated and set in order [*bestellte*] appears differently that it did when to set in order still meant to take care of and to maintain.[85]

Under this regime of thought, natural resources like coal and oil are seen as "stockpiles," on call resources waiting to be unlocked and exposed whenever we happen to need them. "Everywhere everything is ordered to stand by, to be immediately at hand, indeed to stand there just so that it may be on call for further ordering."[86] If it is possible to speak of an "essence" of modern technology, Heidegger maintains, this is only because technology at its core has little to do with actual machines or devices and everything to do with how we imagine our relationships with things and the world. The logic of modern technology "is the way in which the real reveals itself as standing-reserve."[87]

By only thinking of technologies as instruments and "the real" as standing-reserve, BP failed to appreciate the alterity of things—failed to be responsible to things as they issued the most basic of demands to recognize vulnerability as the essential condition of ethical life. In gripping and telling language, Lustgarten describes a crucial moment on the drilling deck of the Deepwater Horizon on the night of April 20 in which workers failed to heed warnings that the procedure underway to seal the Macondo well was not going as planned:

> From the drilling deck, the drill pipe was inserted into the wellbore and then opened to release the pressure in the well and reduce it to zero. It should have taken a few minutes, but the crew couldn't get the pressure to bleed all the way down. It dropped as far as 266 psi, meaning that the water in the wellbore still exerted that much outward pressure. But as soon as the drillers sealed off the drill pipe—the straw piercing down through the spacer to the well—the pressure jumped again, to 1,262 psi. It was as big a red flag as one could wave: a clear sign of a significant vulnerability in the well that was allowing gas to seep in from the outside.[88]

"BP could have stopped there," he adds. "The negative pressure test had done exactly what it was supposed to do: it unambiguously warned of a severe problem in the well. But they were so close."[89] No one could know for sure what exactly was going on one mile below on the sea floor, of course. Without the ability to directly access the wellbore, the crew had to rely on sensors and data to mediate what was happening as they worked to seal the well. Much like the I in Levinas's account of the encounter with the Other, the crew had no way of fully knowing what they were facing. The thing in this case exceeded knowledge and comprehension, withdrawing from the crew's understanding while at the same time demanding from them a response. Unfortunately, in this case the call went unresponded to in the rush of the will to mastery. The "Mayday, Mayday" that rang out less than an hour later "to whoever was listening"[90] might also have been heard as an admission that what happened on the Deepwater Horizon was not only the failure of technology and corporate responsibility. At the same time, it was a failure to accept a "clear sign of significant vulnerability" for what it is: the face of a thing calling oneself into question and into service.

Care for Things: Attention and Tenderness

If the face of things issues a demand, this demand is, in the broadest sense, to *take care*. In their own ways, Levinas's notion of responsibility and Heidegger's *Gelassenheit* call for some form of care-taking. For Levinas, care-taking comes when the commandment, "thou shalt not kill," takes precedence over the desire to know, name, or comprehend the Other. Coupled with Heidegger's notion of "letting-be," care constitutes an attunement to the Other that does not seek to define or foreclose upon alterity but to protect it, to "let it be" the being it is rather than what we want, need, or expect it to be. Care, then, is how we both attend and respond to things as things; in Heidegger's terminology, it is how we *hear* or *listen* to the Other in such a way that "we are already with him, in advance, alongside the entity."[91] As Heidegger says,

> Listening to [...] is Dasein's existential way of Being-open as Being-with for Others. Indeed, hearing constitutes the primary and authentic way in which Dasein is open for its ownmost potentiality-for-Being—as in hearing the voice of the friend whom every Dasein carries with it. Dasein hears, because it understands [...] Being-with develops in listening to one another [*Aufeinander-hören*], which can be done in several possible ways: following, going along with, and the privative modes of not-hearing, resisting, defying, and turning away.[92]

For Heidegger, listening (*hören auf*) is what makes possible Dasein's openness for Others. If being is fundamentally being-with Others, then listening is the way of such being, the way we care for the Other as well as for our ownmost potentiality for being. Listening, we could say, is a form of letting-be that is also a response issued in the face of the Other. And like *Gelassenheit* and responsibility, listening releases things from our designs by preserving "releasement to things" and "openness to the mystery"—"For man becomes truly free only insofar as he belongs to the realm of destining and so becomes one who listens and hears [*Hörender*], and not one who is simply constrained to obey [*Höriger*]."[93] If the Deepwater Horizon disaster teaches us anything, it is that failing to listen to things—to care for them as the things they are—allows the will to mastery to take even stronger hold over us, fostering a sentiment in which things and nature avail themselves but only as instruments or resources for the use and benefit of human beings.

As a mode of attunement, care orients us to how things participate in being and yet are never fully exhausted by it. Care is what attunes us to alterity and to the "beyond Being" of things; it is what allows us to hear the ringing of the Fourfold while at the same time honoring the obligation to respond that originates in the face of things. When I care for things, I take interest in—and therefore am attentive to—the things of the world. Care, as we are using it here, thus needs to be understood in an ontological-existential sense in which, following Heidegger, Dasein's thrownness in the world orients it toward the entities (things and human others) that exist—and matter—in the world with us. As one of the key concepts in *Being and Time*, care (*Sorge*) is what structures and defines Dasein's absorption in the world, its ownmost potentiality for being. In German, *Sorge* sometimes denotes "worry" or "grief." However, Heidegger is more interested is *Sorge*'s other meaning as a worldly and emplaced condition (as in the expression, "cares of the world"). In his classic study of the first division of *Being and Time*, Hubert Dreyfus recounts a conversation he had with Heidegger in which he reminds Heidegger of care's meanings in English as love and caring. According to Dreyfus, Heidegger responded by saying that was fortunate "since with the term 'care' he wanted to name the very fact that '*Sein geht mich an*,' roughly, that being gets to me."[94]

Being gets to Dasein because "Dasein is an entity for which, in its Being, that Being is an issue."[95] Being is something Dasein cares about because Dasein's being is always "Essentially ahead of itself, it has projected itself upon its ability to be before going on to any mere consideration of itself."[96] For Heidegger, to be is to understand that one's ownmost being is temporal and finite. As Dasein, here is what I can say for certain: Some time ago, I was born (thrown) into a world that preceded me and which I now share with other beings in the world, and at some point in the future I will face my own death, an event I have long anticipated but will never fully know or experience. All of these issues matter to me, all of them structure my involvements in the world, meaning that there is a strong temporal dimension to how care constitutes my being-in-the-world. As Heidegger says, "*Temporality reveals itself as the meaning of authentic care.*"[97] Care, he argues, has a threefold temporal structure that mirrors Dasein's thrownness in the world: Because being-in-the-world is essentially care, care reveals itself as being *already in, ahead of itself*, and *amidst itself*. "Dasein's totality of Being as care means: ahead-of-itself-already-being-in (a world) as Being-alongside (entities encountered within-the-world)."[98] As we have seen, the ahead-of-itself is grounded in the future, in my ownmost potentiality for being or my being-toward-death. Being-along-side, by contrast, takes place in the present, and being-already-in has the character of the past, of "having been." As its defining characteristic, care orients Dasein in time as a being attuned to its finitude, to its "thrownness into death."[99] As soon as we are born, we are old enough to die. For Heidegger, this means that death is not just something that awaits us in the future; it is something we live with every day, it is what grounds our condition of possibility as Dasein, and it is therefore the issue about which Dasein cares the most.

While the bulk of Heidegger's focus in *Being and Time* is on how the care-structure defines Dasein's being-in-the-world, he also makes clear that *Sorge* does not exclude other beings from care's purview or restrict care to human interests alone. Like anything, care takes place in the world—it is the fact that being *gets to me*. This means that care must also take place in and among things and other beings in the world: things and beings that, like

Dasein, are already in, ahead of themselves, and amidst themselves. "Because being-in-the-world is essentially care, being-alongside the ready-to-hand could be taken in our previous analysis as *concern (Besorgen)*, and being with the Dasein-with of Others as we encounter it within-the-world could be taken as *solicitude (Fürsorge)*."[100] Care is therefore not something solipsistic for Heidegger. Care cannot "stand for some special attitude toward the Self," Heidegger insists, because the Self is never anything so singular or autonomous, but always a Being-ahead-of-itself, a Being-already-in, and a Being-alongside.[101] Hence, care must be understood as a form of involvement in the world that, as Benso adds, "can explicate itself in activities as varied as 'having to do [...] producing [...] attending to [...] and looking after [...] making use [...] giving [...] up and letting [...] go, undertaking, accomplishing, evincing, interrogating, considering, determining [...]' but also 'leaving undone, neglecting, renouncing, taking a rest.'"[102] While Heidegger may himself not have understood such involvements as ethical, Benso argues that Dasein, as defined by *Sorge*, "is always ontologically involved and turns to entities within the world out of the (dis)interest and (dis)passion it has for them."[103] Manifested in concern (for what is handy or ready-to-hand) and solicitude (taking-care of others), care brings to the fore the fact that being is never lived alone but always with and amidst other beings/things in the world. These beings are what ultimately interest us, that call for our *attention*—not in the spirit of the will to mastery but, as Benso argues, in the spirit of humility and tenderness.

Attention thus assumes an important place in the care-structure and in our dealings with things. When we care for things, we attend to them; we are attentive to them. This sense of attention as attending can be found in the original prefix for the word "attention," *ad-*, which as Benso notes indicates "the movement of a tending toward."[104] Attention is an ad-tending to something,[105] a movement toward that which it tends. Thought in this way, attention is "an essential component of the human side of the ethics of things"[106] for it is in the ad-tending to things that we come face to face with the alterity of things.

> Attention waits for the other to make the first move, the first offer to which it will respond by being attentive. What is deferred in this movement of humility is, primarily, the power of a will that wants to modify, rather than being modified by, things.[107]

Not unlike the forms of epistemic humility we explored in the previous chapter, the movement of humility Benso associates with attention limits the pretensions of knowledge such that the Other may be hearkened to while at same time allowed to continue being the thing it is. At its core, then, attention, as Benso eloquently puts it, is "an act of love of the one who lets herself or himself be taken by hand and led by things. Not the erotic sensuality of passionality, but the more feeble and modest affection of tenderness is what constitutes such a love."[108] While attention is always directed toward something, it "does not know, yet, what will inspire its being attentive."[109] Thus attention is effectively a waiting-for, a patient and humble openness to things that, like the close of Milton's famous sonnet, rewards the service of those who only stand and wait.

This waiting-for should be not confused with passivity in the sense of apathy or disinterest. As Benso suggests, attention takes place somewhere between activity and passivity.[110] Like *Gelassenheit*, which for Heidegger describes an active-passivity in which letting-be is accompanied by listening and hearkening to the Other, attention draws us closer to things so that we become susceptible to what is other than ourselves. When we allow ourselves to be guided by things in this way, we experience the active-passivity of attention as a form of *tenderness* or "attentive touch,"[111] with tenderness understood not as subjective feeling but as an ontological horizon, "a way of being which, aroused by the appeal of things, enables the move to the ethical place of their encounter."[112] As a way of being enabling being-with Others, tenderness is an attunement in the Heideggerian sense; it is one of the moods or states-of-mind that "*disclose Dasein in its thrownness*"[113] and in so doing reveals Dasein's Being as being-in and openness to world. As a derivation of attention, tenderness discloses an *ethos* or dwelling place in which my being is opened up to a beyond Being: to the precariousness and fragility of things that are always on the verge of disappearing, of becoming instruments or objects standing against me rather than suspended in the face to face encounter from which the call to respond, to be responsible, originates. Tenderness thus orients my relations with things in terms of thrownness, meaning that I and things are all *already in*, *ahead of*, and *amidst ourselves*. "Not contour-less, but contour-free, tenderness continuously shifts into the different spaciousness described by the Fourfold in things, and lets itself be shaped by them."[114]

The trouble with care, attention, and tenderness, however, is that they are often belated; as was the case with the Deepwater Horizon, we oftentimes do not realize until after the fact that what occurred was a failure to care for things as things. As we all unfortunately know, care and tenderness sometimes come too late. This belatedness is so pronounced because care and tenderness are always tentative, bound to the manifestation of the face of things which comes and goes as frequently yet unpredictably as any other face to face encounter. But the belatedness of care and tenderness should not be enough to absolve us of ethical responsibility. In fact, belatedness may be exactly what is necessary to structure a different attunement to things and an/other ethics of things. If we accept Heidegger's claim that care is always already ahead-of-itself, projecting itself into something still to come, then perhaps there are ways we can better attune ourselves to things that anticipate the structures of care. "Since things are so frail and precarious, and hence precious, tenderness needs to be ever more tender," Benso concludes.[115] "In the end, all tenderness is an occasion for ever new tenderness.

For mortals, this implies an appeal to always be eccentered and excessive, beyond themselves, beyond their ontological being, altogether beyond being."[116] Being beyond ourselves, beyond Being, demands a vigilance in which the temporal structures of care occasion the continual renewal of tenderness as an ad-tending to things that is simultaneously grounded in the past, engaged in the present, and committed to the future to come. Ultimately, care for things means not imposing on things our own desires or intentions but responding to them as the things they are (then, now, and to come) and being willing, in the response, to have oneself changed.

Rhetorical Realism and the Good Life

In other-oriented theories of ethics, responsibility defines a relation that precedes and exceeds comprehension. Responsibility is our exposedness to the Other, the moment, prior to and beyond essence, when we acknowledge and accept the plea to let the Other be—to live and be the being it is. "Responsibility for the other, going against intentionality and the will," Levinas writes, "signifies not the disclosure of a given and its reception, but the exposure of me to the other, prior to every decision."[117] As we have seen, for Levinas the Other must be a human other, the face of a person that summons the rhetorical imperative that kick starts the ethical relation I have with you. While there is much to admire and much still to be learned from Levinas's (humanist) ethics of the (human) face, the exclusivity of the face we find in Levinas unfortunately reinforces the presumption that things (be they nonhuman animals or objects) do not belong within the realm of ethical concern. I believe this assumption is mistaken, not least because it unduly restricts the purview of ethics at a time when we need to be expanding ethics so that it can encompass a wider array of beings and relations whose effects increasingly reverberate beyond local actions and decisions. This is one of the lasting lessons we can learn from the Deepwater Horizon disaster. It is true that BP was mostly to blame for what happened on the Deepwater Horizon; however, BP's greatest failure extended well beyond its own factual culpability in the disaster to its willingness to ignore the obligations it (including its employees and contractors) had to things: to the pipes and the blowout preventer as well as to the earth, the environment, and the animals and people of the Gulf coast. Ultimately, theirs was a failure of responsibility, a failure to listen to things and care for them as the things they are. When we care for things, we do not simply embrace them; we agree as well to live and dwell with them, to make our homes with them as much with other people. As Rickert explains with respect to Heidegger, dwelling "is a way of being conditioned and permeated by things so that they are inseparable from what it means to live in the world."[118] In these terms, care and responsibility in the face of things constitutes a way of living in the world, one informed by an ethics of things attuned to all of the opportunities and challenges being-with others (in the broadest sense of the term) affords.

Writing in his unique phenomenological and ethnographic style, Alphonso Lingis offers one of most eloquent descriptions of ethics and alterity I can think of. In a chapter of *The Imperative* entitled "The Intimate and the Alien," Lingis describes arriving in an old colonial city and checking in to a hotel that was once the Palace of the Conquistador, built in 1502.[119] The strange experience of being welcomed as an Other into someone else's city leads Lingis to meditate upon the nature of "home" and "dwelling" and the roles these play in cultivating ethics of hospitality and responsibility. "To inhabit a home base is to feel ourselves anchored in reality and it in us," Lingis writes.[120] Blending Heidegger and Levinas (for whom Lingis served as an English translator), Lingis sees home and dwelling as two sides of the same coin. Similar to the gathering power Heidegger finds in *das Ding*, home, for Lingis, is what "summons us." It is the "warmth and tranquility that we keep sight of as we advance into the stretches of the alien and that our nomadic wanderings gravitate back to."[121] When we invite others into our homes, as in the Spanish expression *Mi casa es su casa*, we do so in order to share with them the summons that calls us here to dwell, to be at home. And this summons to dwell, to be hospitable to the Other, Lingis suggests, originates from many places and many beings, including human beings, nonhuman animals, plants, and even things themselves.

> The one who addresses to us the summons to come dwell here, with him, is the agency of a summons that is in the place itself: this is a good place to live. It invites human dwelling. This is what he knows who has discovered the wooded slope where a clearing welcomes the other animals in search of sun and opens forth upon the forested hills and the clouds where birds circle, and who sets out to build a cabin, saying, "Don't you see, someone should live here!"—not to displace what is there, but to dwell with the birds and other animals and skies. The agency of welcome and summons could well be other animals. The summons could come from plants.[122]

Whether it comes from our human neighbors or from the forest or the skies above, the agency of the summons to dwell arrives to us in the form of an invitation and an obligation: Gather here with us, the summons says, and with us help make this a good place to live.

With things—in the face of things—we make our home. "Things are not just patterns projected in space before us or streaming by; they take form in the place we inhabit. They await us in our home and along the paths extended from our door."[123] Before things ever become tools or instruments for human use, they are "furnishings," Lingis says. The language Lingis uses here borrows heavily from Levinas's account of things examined above. In contrast to Levinas, however, Lingis argues that when we learn to see things as "implements" (*Zeuge*) and "furnishings" (*meubles*) we come closer to appreciating how "attending to and dealing with things is not making of our outlying environment a workshop; it is furnishing our home."[124] Things do not just fill or occupy space in our homes; they "support us, sustain us, exalt us."[125] When we say "home," then, we mean that this is a place where things exist as things, where things depend on us and we depend on things. In the end, this is why care is so important for an ethics of things because it is only when we dwell with and care for things that we learn how to care for ourselves as well. Home is the place where care, attention, and tenderness affect new ways of being-in-the-world. To have a home, be it a house or the world at large, is "to actively care for the things appropriated."[126]

> We have to shelter things from the inclemencies of the weather and from our own and another's careless or reckless collisions with them. We have to be attentive to the needs of things that grow of themselves. We have to be attentive to, and supply for the needs of the land, the plants and the trees, the herds and the flocks.[127]

For Lingis, things are not just instruments or standing-reserves; they are "appearances" or "apparitions" that haunt and ensnare us through the "rhythm and musicality of their faces, shadows, reflections, and auras."[128] Even if we do not always understand things in themselves, we nonetheless heed the call of their summons to dwell, to attend to them in such a way that we "find ourselves among them and carried on by them into a time of fate."[129] For Lingis, this is what the good life means: sheltering things from carelessness while at the same time taking "refuge in the beat and melody of [thingly] apparitions."[130]

The idea that ethics should help us achieve something like the good life is not new to Lingis or an ethics of things. In the *Nicomachean Ethics*, Aristotle offers one of the first and still most widely influential theories of the good life. The word Aristotle uses here is *eudaimonia*, which usually translates as "happiness," thus suggesting that the goal of the *Ethics* is to outline an understanding of happiness and put forth a project for producing happiness in ourselves and our communities. This summary is an accurate enough description of the work; however, it also misses an important aspect of *eudaimonia* that Aristotle wants his students and readers to understand, which is that *eudaimonia* is a certain kind of activity and not the subjective feeling implied in modern meanings of "happiness." In Aristotle's account, *eudaimonia* means "flourishing" or "living well" in ways that are essential and unique to human beings; it is "the highest of all goods achievable by action."[131] Like his accounts of *technē* and *phusis*, Aristotle's conception of happiness follows from his understanding of means and ends. In contrast to *technē*, which as we saw in Chapter 2 has its cause and ends outside of itself, *eudaimonia* is always chosen "for itself and never for the sake of something else."[132] We choose happiness—choose to live the good life—not because doing so provides us some external reward or pleasure. Rather, we pursue happiness because happiness is an end in itself; it is, as Aristotle further suggests, self-sufficient, meaning that, as something final, happiness "makes life desirable and lacking in nothing."[133] Thus happiness cannot be improved upon by anything outside of itself. As the highest of all possible goods, it is both its own end and the defining characteristic of human being as such. The essential function of human beings, according to Aristotle, is to pursue happiness or the good life because, as Aristotle believes, "none of the other animals is happy, since they in no way share in contemplation."[134]

The good life, then, is nothing new for ethical theory. The challenge we face today is deciding whether an ethics of things such as the one offered in this chapter directs us (back) to something like the good life. I believe that it does because, in my view, learning how to flourish and live well with all kinds of others is (and always should be) at the heart of any ethical theory. Realizing this possibility, however, requires us to leave behind those systems that privilege universality, instrumentalism, and identity as the means and ends of ethical thought. It also requires us to expand what we commonly think of as happiness or the good life. For all of its nuances, *eudaimonia* for Aristotle is a mostly human affair guided by the belief that human being is an activity of the soul in accordance with virtue. While Aristotle's discussions of *technē* suggest that things have their roles to play in the production of happiness—as in the case of the builder who, by building, becomes just by doing just acts[135]—for the most part his account of the good life remains defined by human ways of being. This does not mean, however, that we cannot extend Aristotle's ethical insights to encompass a larger pageantry of things. As Verbeek suggests, an expanded notion of the good life that includes things may help us better understand our entanglements with modern technology so that we learn to cultivate different attunements through which things, much like human beings in Aristotle, hold sway and produce new possibilities for being-in-the-world. For Verbeek, one of the most valuable legacies of Aristotelian ethics is its emphasis on the good life as directed by *aretē* (virtue or excellence). In contrast to normative theories of ethics, Aristotelian ethics "was about excellence in living, or mastering the art of living."[136] Whereas normative theories of ethics force us to take sides in the human-technology relationship by asking us to focus on whether technologies are morally acceptable or not, an ethics of the good life "asks itself what a good way of living with such technology could be."[137] When we frame ethical questions about things in terms of the good life rather than morality, we find that it is increasingly difficult, if not impossible, to distinguish the "us" from the "them" because what qualifies as a good way of living inevitably includes the interests and agencies of both (and more) parties. While it may be possible to be happy while alone in leisurely contemplation, as Aristotle suggests,[138] for the most part the good life needs to be lived and perfected in the company of others because it is in the face of the Other that "I" am ultimately defined and called into question.

My suggestion throughout this book has been that rhetoricians have been trying in various ways to articulate what the good life means for rhetoric—what it means not just to speak well or honestly but to *live well* in the company of others. Even when things were not the direct subject matter of rhetorical inquiry, we saw how they occasioned rhetoric, how they provided a home for rhetoric to flourish for a time (however temporarily) as the thing it is. The challenge for rhetoric today, then, and to which this book serves as both a call and a response, is to try to see these engagements as evidence of particular attunements in rhetoric's history to the vibrancy and alterity of things. If things are nothing new for rhetoric, if indeed rhetoric has always been oriented to the limits of epistemology and the nature of being as I have argued, then one of the things we have left to learn is what the rhetorical tradition can still teach us about an ethics of things and what it meant—and could mean in the future—to care for things that occasion rhetoric's emergence and call for our responsibility as scholars and practitioners of rhetoric. At the very least, such an inquiry would serve as a reminder that attention to a thing is at the same time an ad-tending to that thing, a grasping that enacts a kind of ethical response. Students, animals, houses, children, classrooms, climates, computers: all of these and more have the power to pull us into their orbits with the simplest (but most essential) of commands: Care for me and together we shall live the good life. If we are prepared to consider this possibility, to share our rhetorical lives with things in the world, then we may find that this indeed is a good place to live.

Notes

1. Martin Heidegger, *Being and Time*, trans. John Macquarrie and Edward Robinson (New York: Harper and Row, 1962), 117.
2. Martin Heidegger, "On the Essence of Truth," in *Basic Writings*, ed. David Farrell Krell (New York: HarperCollins, 1993), 130.
3. Martin Heidegger, *Discourse on Thinking*, trans. John M. Anderson and E. Hans Freund (New York: Harper and Row, 1966), 54.
4. Ibid., 55.
5. Jennifer Bay and Thomas Rickert, "New Media and the Fourfold," *JAC* 28, no. 1–2 (2008): 222.
6. Emmanuel Levinas, *Difficult Freedom: Essays on Judaism*, trans. Sean Hand (Baltimore: Johns Hopkins University Press, 1990), 8–9.
7. In a 1982 interview following the massacres at the Sabra and Chatila camps in Lebanon, Levinas was asked whether the Other in his philosophy is not "above all the Palestinian." Levinas answers with the following: "My definition of the other is completely different. The other is the neighbour, who is not necessarily kin, but who can be. And in that sense, if you're for the other, you're for the neighbour. But if your neighbour attacks another neighbour or treats him unjustly, what can you do? Then alterity takes on another character, in alterity we can find an enemy, or at least then we are faced with the problem of knowing who is right and who is wrong, who is just and who is unjust. There are people who are wrong"; Emmanuel Levinas, "Ethics and Politics," trans. Jonathan Romney, in *The Levinas Reader*, ed. Seán Hand (Cambridge: Basil Blackwell, 1989), 296.

8. Peter-Paul Verbeek, *Moralizing Technology: Understanding and Designing the Morality of Things* (Chicago: University of Chicago Press, 2011), 54.
9. Ibid., 48.
10. Michael J. Hyde, introduction to *The Ethos of Rhetoric*, ed. Michael J. Hyde (Columbia: University of South Carolina Press, 2004), xiii.
11. Aristotle, *On Rhetoric: A Theory of Civic Discourse*, trans. George A. Kennedy (New York: Oxford University Press, 1991), 1356a21.
12. Silvia Benso, *The Face of Things: A Different Side of Ethics* (Albany: SUNY Press, 2000), 130.
13. Bryan Garsten, *Saving Persuasion: A Defense of Rhetoric and Judgment* (Cambridge: Harvard University Press, 2006), 7.
14. In his preface to *Totality and Infinity*, translator Alphonso Lingis explains how he received permission from Levinas to translate "*autrui*" (the personal Other, the you) as "Other." Following this convention, I use the word "Other" in this chapter when referring to specific persons and the word "other" (*l'autre* or *Autre*) when discussing the generic other or the idea of otherness as such.; Alphonso Lingis, preface to *Totality and Infinity: An Essay on Exteriority*, by Emmanuel Levinas (Pittsburgh: Duquesne University Press, 1969), 24.
15. Emmanuel Levinas, *Totality and Infinity: An Essay on Exteriority*, trans. Alphonso Lingis (Pittsburgh: Duquesne University Press, 1969), 262.
16. Diane Davis, *Inessential Solidarity: Rhetoric and Foreigner Relations* (Pittsburgh: University of Pittsburgh Press, 2010), 51.
17. Levinas, *Totality and Infinity*, 197.
18. Michael J. Hyde, *The Call of Conscience: Heidegger and Levinas, Rhetoric and the Euthanasia Debate* (Columbia: University of South Carolina Press, 2001), 99.
19. Davis, 57–58.
20. Davis, 56.
21. Ibid., 57–58.
22. Jacques Derrida, *The Animal That Therefore I Am*, trans. David Wills (New York: Fordham University Press, 2008), 111.
23. Ibid.
24. Michael Bernard-Donals, *Forgetful Memory: Representation and Remembrance in the Wake of the Holocaust* (Albany: SUNY Press, 2009).
25. Hyde, *The Call of Conscience*.
26. Levinas, *Difficult Freedom*, 153.
27. Ibid.
28. Davis, 147.
29. Derrida, 117.
30. Emmanuel Levinas, quoted in Davis, 157. See also, Derrida, 105–118.
31. Derrida, 109.
32. Davis, 154.
33. Levinas, *Totality and Infinity*, 73.
34. Jeremy Bentham, "Principles of Morals and Legislation," in *The Animals Reader: The Essential Classic and Contemporary Writings*, ed. Linda Kalof and Amy Fitzgerald (London: Bloomsbury, 2007), 9.
35. In his opening anecdote from *Animal that Therefore I Am*, Derrida describes feeling shame and embarrassment at being observed naked by a cat. "Who am I in the eyes of the cat?" Derrida wonders. Whatever the answer, Derrida makes clear that the cat in question is not simply a linguistic figure designed to get

his discussion started. "I must immediately make it clear, the cat I am talking about is a real cat, truly, believe me, *a little cat*. It isn't the *figure* of a cat. It doesn't silently enter the bedroom as an allegory for all the cats on the earth, the felines that traverse our myths and religions, literature and fables." While Derrida's analysis soon takes him farther afield from this point, his insistence on the reality of this particular cat reminds us that the question of the animal is, in many ways, also a question of rhetorical realism.; Derrida, 6.
36. Benso, 44.
37. Levinas, *Totality and Infinity*, 140.
38. Ibid., 133.
39. Levinas, *Difficult Freedom*, 20.
40. Levinas, *Totality and Infinity*, 140.
41. Benso, 46.
42. Ibid., 124.
43. Ibid., 127.
44. Ibid., 128.
45. Martin Heidegger, "The Thing," in *Poetry, Language, Thought*, trans. Albert Hofstadter (New York: Harper, 2001), 166.
46. Ibid., 171.
47. Ibid., 174.
48. Benso, 114.
49. Heidegger, "The Thing," 175.
50. Martin Heidegger, "Building, Dwelling, Thinking," in *Poetry, Language, Thought*, trans. Albert Hofstadter (New York, Harper, 2001), 150.
51. Heidegger, "The Thing," 178.
52. Heidegger, "Building, Dwelling, Thinking," 151.
53. Ibid., 147.
54. Martin Heidegger, "The Origin of the Work of Art," in *Poetry, Language, Thought*, trans. Albert Hofstadter (New York, Harper, 2001), 26.
55. Ibid., 31.
56. Ibid., 41.
57. Bruno Latour, "From *Realpolitik* to *Dingpolitik* or How to Make Things Public," in *Making Things Public: Atmospheres of Democracy*, 14–41, ed. Latour and Peter Weibel (Cambridge: Massachusetts Institute of Technology Press, 2005).
58. Benso, 114.
59. Ibid., 120.
60. Ibid., 123.
61. Heidegger, "The Origin of the Work of Art," 30–31.
62. Benso, 148.
63. Ibid., 149.
64. Heidegger, "The Thing," 181.
65. Ibid., 179.
66. Benso, 122.
67. Ibid., 123.
68. Verbeek, 4.
69. Emmanuel Levinas, "The Paradox of Morality: An Interview with Emmanuel Levinas," trans. Andrew Benjamin and Tamra Wright, in *The Provocation of Levinas: Rethinking the Other*, ed. Robert Bernasconi and David Wood (New York: Routledge, 1988), 169.

70. Dermot Moran, *Introduction to Phenomenology* (New York: Routledge, 2000), 349.
71. Levinas, *Totality and Infinity*, 77.
72. Verbeek, 108.
73. Abrahm Lustgarten, *Run to Failure: BP and the Making of the Deepwater Horizon Disaster* (New York: Norton, 2012), xi.
74. Ibid., 174.
75. National Commission on the BP Deepwater Horizon Spill and Offshore Drilling, *Deepwater: The Gulf Oil Disaster and the Future of Offshore Drilling (Report to the President)* (United States Government Printing Office, 2011), 122.
76. Ibid.
77. Ibid., 134–135.
78. Noah Rayman, "Judge Places Most Blame on BP for 2010 Oil Spill," *Time*, September 4, 2014, accessed June 15, 2026, http://time.com/3268978/bp-gulf-oil-spill-louisiana-court/.
79. Judith Butler, *Giving an Account of Oneself* (New York: Fordham University Press, 2005), 12.
80. Moran, 321.
81. Martin Heidegger, "The Question Concerning Technology," in *The Question Concerning Technology and Other Essays*, trans. William Lovitt (New York: Harper, 1977), 4.
82. Ibid., 13.
83. Ibid., 5.
84. Ibid., 14.
85. Ibid., 14–15.
86. Ibid., 17.
87. Ibid., 23.
88. Lustgarten, 318.
89. Ibid.
90. Ibid., 329.
91. Heidegger, *Being and Time*, 207.
92. Ibid., 206.
93. Heidegger, "The Question Concerning Technology," 25.
94. Hubert Dreyfus, *Being-in-the-World: A Commentary on Heidegger's* Being and Time, *Division I* (Cambridge: Massachusetts Institute of Technology Press, 1991), 239.
95. Heidegger, *Being and Time*, 236.
96. Ibid., 458.
97. Ibid., 374.
98. Ibid., 375.
99. Ibid., 378.
100. Ibid., 237.
101. Ibid.
102. Heidegger, *Being and Time*, 83, quoted in Benso, 77.
103. Benso, 77.
104. Ibid., n.7 226.
105. Ibid., 164.
106. Ibid.
107. Ibid., 165.

108. Ibid.
109. Ibid., 166.
110. Ibid., 164.
111. Ibid., 166.
112. Ibid., 167.
113. Heidegger, *Being and Time*, 175.
114. Benso, 170.
115. Ibid., 171.
116. Ibid., 172.
117. Emmanuel Levinas, *Otherwise than Being, or Beyond Essence*, trans. Alphonso Lingis (Pittsburgh: Duquesne University Press, 2006), 141.
118. Thomas Rickert, *Ambient Rhetoric: The Attunements of Rhetorical Being* (Pittsburgh: University of Pittsburgh Press, 2013), 223.
119. Alphonso Lingis, *The Imperative* (Bloomington: Indiana University Press, 1998), 41.
120. Ibid., 42.
121. Ibid.
122. Ibid., 43–44.
123. Ibid., 74.
124. Ibid., 75.
125. Ibid., 76.
126. Ibid., 78.
127. Ibid.
128. Ibid., 100.
129. Ibid., 101.
130. Ibid., 102.
131. Aristotle, *Nicomachean Ethics*, trans. David Ross (New York: Oxford University Press, 1998), 1095a15–17.
132. Ibid., 1097b1–3.
133. Ibid., 1097b19–21.
134. Ibid., 1178b23–26.
135. Ibid., 1103b2–5.
136. Verbeek, 156.
137. Ibid., 157.
138. Aristotle, 1177a27–30.

Bibliography

Aristotle. *Nicomachean Ethics*. Translated by David Ross. New York: Oxford University Press, 1998.

Bay, Jennifer and Thomas Rickert. "New Media and the Fourfold." *JAC* 28, no. 1–2 (2008): 209–244.

Benso, Silvia. *The Face of Things: A Different Side of Ethics*. Albany: SUNY Press, 2000.

Bentham, Jeremy. "Principles of Morals and Legislation." In *The Animals Reader: The Essential Classic and Contemporary Writings*, edited by Linda Kalof and Amy Fitzgerald, 8–9. London: Bloomsbury, 2007.

Bernard-Donals, Michael. *Forgetful Memory: Representation and Remembrance in the Wake of the Holocaust*. Albany: SUNY Press, 2009.

Butler, Judith. *Giving an Account of Oneself*. New York: Fordham University Press, 2005.
Davis, Diane. *Inessential Solidarity: Rhetoric and Foreigner Relations*. Pittsburgh: University of Pittsburgh Press, 2010.
Derrida, Jacques. *The Animal That Therefore I Am*. Translated by David Wills. New York: Fordham University Press, 2008.
Dreyfus, Hubert. *Being-in-the-World: A Commentary on Heidegger's* Being and Time, *Division I*. Cambridge: Massachusetts Institute of Technology Press, 1991.
Garsten, Bryan. *Saving Persuasion: A Defense of Rhetoric and Judgment*. ambridge: Harvard University Press, 2006.
Heidegger, Martin. *Being and Time*. Translated by John Macquarrie and Edward Robinson. New York: Harper and Row, 1962.
———. "Building, Dwelling, Thinking." In *Poetry, Language, Thought*. Translated by Albert Hofstadter, 141–160. New York, Harper, 2001.
———. *Discourse on Thinking*. Translated by John M. Anderson and E. Hans Freund. New York: Harper and Row, 1966.
———. "On the Essence of Truth." In *Basic Writings*, edited by David Farrell Krell, 111–138. New York: HarperCollins, 1993.
———. "The Origin of the Work of Art." In *Poetry, Language, Thought*. Translated by Albert Hofstadter, 15–86. New York, Harper, 2001.
———. "The Question Concerning Technology." In *The Question Concerning Technology and Other Essays*. Translated by William Lovitt, 3–35. New York: Harper, 1977.
———. "The Thing." In *Poetry, Language, Thought*. Translated by Albert Hofstadter, 163–184. New York: Harper, 2001.
Hyde, Michael J. *The Call of Conscience: Heidegger and Levinas, Rhetoric and the Euthanasia Debate*. Columbia: University of South Carolina Press, 2001.
———. Introduction to *The Ethos of Rhetoric*, edited by Michael J. Hyde. Columbia: University of South Carolina Press, 2004.
Latour, Bruno. "From *Realpolitik* to *Dingpolitik* or How to Make Things Public." In *Making Things Public: Atmospheres of Democracy*, 14–41, edited by Latour and Peter Weibel. Cambridge: Massachusetts Institute of Technology Press, 2005.
Levinas, Emmanuel. *Difficult Freedom: Essays on Judaism*. Translated by Sean Hand. Baltimore: Johns Hopkins University Press, 1990.
———. "Ethics and Politics." Translated by Jonathan Romney. In *The Levinas Reader*, edited by Seán Hand, 289–297. Cambridge: Basil Blackwell, 1989.
———. *Otherwise than Being, or Beyond Essence*. Translated by Alphonso Lingis. Pittsburgh: Duquesne University Press, 2006.
———. "The Paradox of Morality: An Interview with Emmanuel Levinas." Translated by Andrew Benjamin and Tamra Wright. In *The Provocation of Levinas: Rethinking the Other*, Edited by Robert Bernasconi and David Wood, 168–180. New York: Routledge, 1988.
———. *Totality and Infinity*. Translated by Alphonso Lingis. Pittsburgh: Duquesne University Press, 1969.
Lingis, Alphonso. *The Imperative*. Bloomington: Indiana University Press, 1998.
———. Preface to *Totality and Infinity: An Essay on Exteriority*, by Emmanuel Levinas. Pittsburgh: Duquesne University Press, 1969.
Lustgarten, Abraham. *Run to Failure: BP and the Making of the Deepwater Horizon Disaster*. New York: Norton, 2012.

Moran, Dermot. *Introduction to Phenomenology*. New York: Routledge, 2000.
National Commission on the BP Deepwater Horizon Spill and Offshore Drilling. *Deepwater: The Gulf Oil Disaster and the Future of Offshore Drilling (Report to the President)*. United States Government Printing Office, 2011.
Rayman, Noah. "Judge Places Most Blame on BP for 2010 Oil Spill." *Time*. September 4, 2014. Accessed June 15, 2016. http://time.com/3268978/bp-gulf-oil-spill-louisiana-court/.
Rickert, Thomas. *Ambient Rhetoric: The Attunements of Rhetorical Being*. Pittsburgh: University of Pittsburgh Press, 2013.
Verbeek, Peter-Paul. *Moralizing Technology: Understanding and Designing the Morality of Things*. Chicago: University of Chicago Press, 2011.

Index

Abbott, Don Paul 160
actor-network theory (ANT) 3, 11, 142, 198
Adorno, Theodor 16, 187
agency: of humans 10–11, 49–50, 66, 76, 133, 200, 204–5; of nonhumans 10, 17, 31, 212
Alexander of Aphordisias 71
Allison, Henry 163, 172
alterity 193, 198, 199, 206, 212
Ambient Rhetoric (Rickert) 9, 46
animal rhetorics 9, 13–14
animals. *See also* nonhumans: granting them ethical standing 195–6; as models of rhetoric behavior 5; rights of 195–6
anthropocentrism 19, 194, 195
Antiphon 81
anti-realism 12, 27–30, 32–41, 66, 147, 174; conflict with realism 27, 29
anti-realist epistemology 156–61
antistrophos 71
appearances and presentations of things 162, 169
a priori cognition of objects 33, 132, 157, 161–3, 166, 168
archaeological rhetoric 14
arche 76, 78, 81, 83
Aristotelian metaphysics 68, 70–4
Aristotle 19, 26–30, 45, 121, 190, 213–14; attitude towards rhetoric 17, 69–74, 103; conception of *logos* 102; inquiries into rhetoric 67; on justice with virtue 131; on language 102–3; rhetorical realism of 88–93; on *techne* 74–80
art. *See techne*
Aspasia of Miletus 54–5
attention 209–10
Atwill, Janet 75, 76, 79–80

Austin, John 148
average everydayness 91–2

Bacon, Francis 18, 104, 107, 108–9, 119
balance between abstract and the worldly 2
Barad, Karen 3–4
Bay, Jennifer 10
being: defined by Aristotle 81–3; interwined with knowing 103; and language 131–3; question of 187–8
Being and Time (Heidegger) 89
being of beings 17, 88, 89, 91, 93–6
being of objects 42
being-with-one-another 90–2, 96
Benso, Silvia 8, 19, 191, 196–7, 199–200, 209, 210
Bentham, Jeremy 195
Berlin, James 12, 36, 74, 146–7, 150, 156
Bernstein, Richard J. 153
bivalence thesis of realism 38
Bizzell, Patricia 104, 113, 133
Black, Edwin 67
Bormann, Ernest 151
Boyle, Robert 56, 106, 120
BP 201–6
2009 BP oil spill 19, 190, 201–6
Brassier, Ray 41
Braver, Lee 33–4, 36–7, 40, 130, 157, 161, 167, 169
bringing-forth 84
British Royal Society 18, 104–5, 106; view of rhetoric 106–11
British obsession with language in seventeenth century 103–6
Brock, Stuart 35
Brummett, Barry 19, 143–4, 146, 150, 152–3, 155, 156, 173–4, 176–7, 186

224   Index

Bryant, Levi 42, 128
Burke, Kenneth 5, 12, 48, 150, 172
Butler, Judith 204

care for things 207–11
Cassirer, Ernst 34
causal responsibility 201
characters' use in language 119–20
Cherwitz, Richard 47, 153, 173, 174–6
common sense realism 36
consciousness and reality 153–4
consensus theory 173
Coole, Diana 4
Copernican Revolution 18, 33, 57, 144, 146, 161–7
Corax 6
Corax fable 6–7
correlationism 41–2, 129–30
correlationist circle 129
correspondence theory of truth 104–5, 128, 130, 134, 152
correspondence thesis of realism 37, 48–9
Critique of Pure Reason (Kant) 33, 144, 162, 166
Croasmun, Earl 153, 173

Dalgarno, George 120
Dasein 89, 90, 94, 132, 188, 207–9
Davis, Diane 9, 46, 79, 145, 193, 194, 196
Deep Water Horizon explosion 19, 190, 201–6
Deleuze, Gilles 163
Derrida, Jacques 9, 33, 149, 151, 193, 194, 196
Descartes, René 120
dialetic 29; defined by Petrus Ramus 108; and rhetoric 71
Ding, das 197, 198, 200
discoveredness of average everydayness, 91
dispositio 107–8
doctrine of Forms (Plato) 27–8, 29
Dostal, Robert J. 159–60
doxa 30, 69, 89, 91, 154
Dreyfus, Hubert 39, 45, 208
Dummett, Michael 38
dunamis 85
Dunne, Joseph 69–70, 75, 85, 86, 87

Eagleton, Terry 147
Ecclesiastes, or, A Discourse Concerning the Gift of Preaching as it Fals Under the Rules of Art (Wilkins) 115–16
Eco, Umberto 117–18, 125, 127
egoism 205
elocutio 107–8
elocution 116
eloquence 110
empiricism 29
enlightenment 32, 45, 56–7, 104–5, 156–60
Ennius 1
Enos, Richard Leo 14
environmental rhetoric 10–11
Epicurus 26
episteme 76–8
epistemic humility 171, 172, 176
epistemic rhetoric 18–19, 30, 34–5, 145–6, 149–55, 164, 176, 186; critics of 153–4; originating from Sophists, 165
epistemological aspect of realism 40–2, 48, 103, 105, 106, 114, 128–34
epistemology 27; anti-realist 156–61; and rhetoric 149, 153, 154
Essay Towards a Real Character and a Philosophical Language, An (Wilkins) 106, 114–19, 122, 124, 126
ethical violence 204
ethics: and alterity 193, 212; approach to and responsibility 190–5; normative 191–2; other-oriented 191; and rhetoric 152–3, 176–7, 186–215; rights-based 191; of things 196–215
Eudaimonia 189, 213–14
existence as property of realism 28, 45, 47
exteriority 52–3
externalist perspective 37, 168

face of the Other 200
face to face relations 193–5
facticity of rhetoric 48
Fish, Stanley 112, 133, 147, 148
Fontaine, Jean de La 1
Fourfold 197–200, 205, 207
Frost, Samantha 4

Garsten, Bryan 157, 192
gathering power of things 197–8
Gelassenheit 187–8, 199, 200, 205, 207
Gerhrke, Pat J. 160
Geviert, das 198
Glanvill, Joseph 107, 111

Glenn, Cheryl 54–5
global realism 35
Gorgias 49, 50
grammar defined by Petrus Ramus 108
Grant, Iain Hamilton 41
Gross, Alan G. 88–9, 147
Gross, Daniel M. 91, 92
Grusin, Richard 3
Gulliver's Travels (Swift) 113–14

Hallenbeck, Sarah 20
happiness 213–14
Harman, Graham 41, 43–4, 129
Hartlib, Samuel 120
Hawhee, Debra 4, 9
Hawk, Byron 75
Hegel, Georg 33–4, 169, 171
Heidegger, Martin 14, 15, 17, 19, 43–4, 46, 47, 60, 69, 70, 73, 151, 172; on Aristotle 80–4, 87–96; concept of language 132–3; and *Gelassenheit* 187, 188, 208; on the thing and the Fourfold 197–200, 205–8
Heraclitus 26
Herzberg, Bruce 104, 113, 133
Hikins, James 45, 47–8, 49, 68, 153, 174–6
historiography 6, 10–17, 31, 53–8, 166, 187
history, Latour's conception of 32
History of the Royal Society of London, For the Improving of Natural Knowledge (Sprat) 109–10
Homo Mensura (Protagoras) 73
Howell, Wilbur Samuel 18, 108
humanism 51
Husserl, Edmund 43
Hyde, Michael J. 190

idealism 41, 47, 130; being blended with realism 144–6; Heidegger's viewpoint 94; objective 33–4; transcendental 27, 130, 145, 152, 154, 156–62
Ijsseling, Samuel 158
immanence *versus* transcendence 55–6
independence aspect of realism 28, 41, 49–51
independence of objects 37
insights and blindnesses 172
intelligible distinguished from the sensible 72
intersubjective theory of truth 152–3
inventio 107–8

Jarratt, Susan 67–8, 79
Jasinski, James 153–4
justice as universal virtue 131

kairos 49–51
Kant, Immanuel 18, 19, 27, 33–5, 38, 134; critique of rhetoric 105, 146, 157–8; theory of knowledge 144–5; and thing-in-itself 151, 167–76; transcendental idealism 156–2
Kantian Compromise 144, 145, 169, 173
Kellner, Hans 15, 54
Kennedy, George A. 9, 71, 79
kinesis 86
knowing intertwined with being 103
knowledge: defined by Kant 162; and epistemic rhetoric 34–5; limits of 174; objective *versus* cultural 41; of objects 33–4, 36; as property of realism 45, 47

Laclau, Ernesto 154
Langton, Rae 170–1
language: ability to capture truth and reality 103–4; to access reality 49; constructing universal language 18, 104, 106, 112–27, 156; emphasis on plainness of 104–11, 114; Heidegger's concept of 132–3; importance of 68; and interest in rhetoric 149; lesser importance assigned to it 3–4; material effects of 156; mathematical approach to its invention 119–20; obsession of in early modern Britain 103, 106–34; problems of natural language 103–4; relational dynamics of 121; representation conception of 102; revelatory conception of 102; as a terministic screen 147, 150, 156, 172
Latour, Bruno 11, 31, 32, 55, 57, 66, 103, 142–3, 187, 198
letting-be 187–9, 199, 207
Levinansian ethics 201
Levinas, Emmanuel 9, 19, 52, 188–9, 193–6, 205, 207, 211
Levinasian ethics 192, 200
Levinasian Other 145
Lingis, Alphonso 212–13
listening and openness to Others 207
living the good life 19, 189, 190, 211–15
local realism 35
Locke, John 18, 107

logos 70, 90–1, 93, 95, 102
Lustgarten, Abraham 201, 203, 206

Man, Paul de 172
Marback, Richard 10
Mares, Edwin 35
Margolis, Joseph 40
Markley, Robert 115, 125
materialism 3–4, 32, 46
McComiskey, Bruce 165
Meillassoux, Quentin 41–2, 129, 130
memoria 107–8
Mersenne, Marin 120
metaphysical realism 37, 39
Metaphysics (Aristotle) 72, 82, 85, 93
method, conception of by Francis Bacon 108
Miller, Alexander 28
Miller, Bernard 49
mind and dependency of knowledge 19, 33–5
mind-dependent objects 40–1
mind-independent reality 45, 53, 68, 154
mind reaching reality 38
Modern Constitution 55, 57
modernism 31–2
modern technology 205–6
moral responsibility 201
Moran, Dermot 200
Mouffe, Chantel 154
movedness and rest 83–4, 86, 93
Muckelbauer, John 13

naïve realism 12, 17, 36, 41, 154, 174
nature. *See also phusis*: in Aristotle's viewpoint 78–81, 85; and culture 11; separated from society 55–6; separation between humans and 51–2; viewed as a resource 205–6
Neel, Jasper 71, 72
Neo-Aristotelianism 67
new materialism 3
Nicomachean Ethics (Aristotle) 26, 27, 29, 75–6, 78, 79, 85, 190, 213
Nietzsche, Friedrich 148, 149, 161
nonhumans 11. *See also* animals; care and responsibility for 19; caring for 186; ethical dimension of 189; and rhetoric 2–5, 8–10, 13–16, 31, 57–8, 143
nonrhetorical style 108
normative ethics 191–2
noumenal reality 19, 33–4, 144, 145; as distinct from phenomena 168–70
nous poietikos 93

Objective Idealism 33–4
objectivism 35, 153
object-oriented ontology 3, 12, 32, 43
object-oriented rhetoric 4–5, 9–14
objects: beings in their own rights 43–4; as bundles of qualities 175; independence of 37; mind-dependent 40–1; withdrawn from us 44
Okrent, Arika 112, 119
Ong, Walter J. 66, 108
ontological realism 38, 42, 103, 105, 106, 114, 128–34
Other: encounter with 192; and exteriority 52; vulnerability of 192, 206
otherness 16, 193–4
other-oriented ethics 191–2
ousia 82

Pandora's Hope (Latour) 142
Parmenides 26, 81
passive knower thesis of realism 38, 161, 163
passive power thesis of realism 38
passivity of the subject 53
pathos 92–3
Pender, Kelly 75, 85
perspectivism 36, 175
persuasive speech 192; power and responsibility of 6
phenomena 144; as distinction from noumenon 168–70
phenomenal reality 34
philosophical realism 37–9
philosophy: of access 129; aversion to realism 157; beginnings of 1–2; being anti-realist 33; history of 6–8; materialist approach 2; and rhetoric 32; tension between divine Craftsman and methodological observations 27
phronesis 77
phusis 69, 70, 78–80, 93–4, 102, 213; difference with *techne* 80–88, 89
Physics (Aristotle) 73, 75, 82–4, 93
plain language movement in rhetorical theory 104–11, 114
Plato 1, 2, 8, 26–8, 29, 143, 158, 191
poetry and Kant's view of 158
poiesis 84
Politics (Aristotle) 90
Porphyrian Tree 121, 123
post-Kantian rhetorical realism 142–77
postmodernism 143

Poulakos, John 70, 79
pragmatism 39–40
preaching and use of rhetoric 115–17
presence-at-hand of objects 43–4
pronuntiatio 107–8
Prooemion 71
Protagoras 69, 73
Putnam, Hilary 37

Ramism 103, 107–8, 116
Ramus, Petrus 107–8
Raphael 26, 28
Ratcliffe, Krista 57
readiness-to-hand of objects 43–4
realism 12, 17; being blended with idealism 144–5; bivalence thesis of 38; common sense 36; conflict with anti-realisms 27, 29; definition 28; epistemological 40–2, 48, 103, 105, 106, 114, 128–34; forms of 35–40; global 35; independence aspect of 28, 41, 49–51; local 35; metaphysical 37, 39; multiple schools of 32; naïve 12, 17, 36, 41, 154, 174; ontological 42, 48, 103, 105, 106, 114, 128–34; philosophical theses of 37–9; as quasi-objects 103; range of perspectives 31, 32; in rheortical history 53–8, 66–7; rhetorical 30–1, 44–53, 145–6; speculative 3, 30, 40–6, 129–30; transcendental 163; uniqueness thesis of 37–8
realism of the subject thesis of realism 38–9
reality: being represented by language 103–4; connection to rhetoric 17; and consciousness 153–4; dual methods for understanding 26–7; fear of losing 142–3; Heidegger's viewpoint 94–5; human subjectivity of 150–1; independence of 174; placed under erasure 151–2; and rhetoric 149–55, 173; role in science and social inquiry 142
recalcitrance 102, 174, 176
referentiality in early modern period of rhetoric 104
relativism 18, 35, 153–4
releasement toward things 188
religious rhetoric 115–17
responsibility: to the Other 192; for things 211–12; in the world 186–215
rhetoric: in Aristotelian metaphysics 17, 70–4; and balance between the worldly and the abstract 2–3; epistemic 18–19, 30, 34–5, 145–6, 149–55; broadening the scope beyond language 4–5; connection to reality 17; creation of studies on 6; defined by Petrus Ramus 107–8; definition 6, 13; and dialetic 71; early British modern period of 103–34; emerges and responds to the world 46–7; environmental 10–11; and ethics 152–3, 176–7, 190–215; externality 7; facticity of 48; Francis Bacon's conception of 107–9; history of 16–17, 53–8, 187; and language 102–3; and nonhumans 3–5, 8–10, 13–16, 31, 57–8, 143; object-oriented 4–5, 9–14; in preaching 115–17; purported rejection of by the Royal Society of London 104, 107–13; and reality 149–55, 173; reduced to style and delivery 103–4, 108; religious 115–17; revival of modern rhetoric as a discipline 146–9; stake in realism 30–1; structuralist and poststructuralist influence on 147; understanding in 164–5; women's contributions in historical rhetoric 54–5; and women's rights 20
Rhetoric (Aristotle) 69, 71, 78, 88–92, 95, 190
rhetoric against rhetoric 157–60
rhetorical realism 14–16, 44–53, 145–6, 173; of Aristotle 88–93, 95–6; and British Royal Society 107; definition 13, 103; in early modern Britain 105–6; ethics and responsibility of 186–215; and the good life 19, 189, 190, 211–15; and historiography 53–8; post-Kantian 142–77; recent debates 29–30
Rickert, Thomas 9, 10, 46–52, 132, 152, 211
rights-based ethics 191
Rivers, Nathaniel 10
Rorty, Richard 39–40, 148
Rossi, Paolo 109
Royer, Daniel J. 34–5, 161, 165

Sayers, Sean 34
School of Athens, The (Scuola di Atene) 26–8
Scott, Robert L. 19, 145, 146, 149–50, 153, 156, 164, 165, 176–7, 186

Scuola di Atene (The School of Athens) 26–7
seeing world from the inside out 143
sensible distinguished from intelligible 72
Simons, Herbert W. 147
Singer, Peter 191
Skouen, Tina 18
Smith, Craig R. 2
social constructionism 3, 34, 66
social reality 151
society separated from nature 55–6
Socrates 1, 2, 26
sophia 77–8
Sophists 67–8, 73, 143, 165
Sorge 208, 209
sous rature (placing under erasure) 151
speaking-with-one-another 90
speculative realism 3, 30, 40–6, 129–30
Spivak, Gayatri 151
Sprat, Thomas 104, 107, 109–10
Stark, Ryan J. 111, 117
Stroud, Scott R. 160
subject: active or passive 38–9; passivity of 53
subject-object dichotomy 49–52, 175
Swift, Jonathan 113–14

Taylor, Charles 39, 45
techne 70, 74–80, 93–4, 102, 213, 214; being distinct 69; difference with *phusis* 80–9
technites 86–7
technological devices as material entities 19, 205–6
tenderness 210
terministic screen 147, 150, 156, 172
Thaetetus 1, 2
Thales of Miletus as founder of philosophy 1–2, 8
thinging of things 197
thing-in-itself 144–5, 151, 154, 163, 167–76
things: appearances and presentations of 162, 169; being variable and invariable 78; care for 207–11; ethics of 196–215; facelessness of 196–7; as a gathering 197–8; having rights 190; responding to 200–6; responsibility for 211–12
third sophistic 18
Tillery, Denise 113
Timaeus 26, 27
Tisias 6, 7
tools and readiness-to-hand verus presence-at-hand 43–4
Toulmin, Stephen 155
transcendence *versus* immanence 55–6
transcendental idealism 27, 130, 145, 154, 156–62
transcendental realism 163
transcendental subject 38–9, 166–8
truth: as an objective force 152; being communicated by rhetoric 148–9; being relative 164; dual traditions in search for 27–8; theory of 37
two-world problem 171

Ulman, H. Lewis 103
universal language 156; constructing 18, 104, 106, 112–27
Untersteiner, Mario 49
Usual Suspects, The (film) 50–1
utilitarianism 191

values 173–4
Verbeek, Peter-Paul 189, 214
Vickers, Brian 18, 111, 117
Vivian, Bradford 72
Vortestellugen 162, 169

Wallis, John 106
Warnick, Barbara 77
Western metaphysics 72
Wilkins, John 18, 105, 106, 111–17, 156; dream of a common language 117–27; view of rhetoric 128
willed by kairos 50
Wittgenstein, Ludwig 148
women's rights and rhetorics 20
words producing misunderstandings 109
world: balance with the abstract 2; influencing rhetoric 46–7
worldliness 46, 47
Worsham, Lynn 75